101 Successful Businesses
You Can Start on the Internet

101 SUCCESSFUL BUSINESSES YOU CAN START ON THE INTERNET

Daniel S. Janal

VAN NOSTRAND REINHOLD
I(T)P® A Division of International Thomson Publishing Inc.

New York • Albany • Bonn • Boston • Detroit • London • Madird • Melbourne
Mexico City • Paris • San Francisco • Singapore • Tokyo • Toronto

I⟨T⟩P® an International Thomson Publishing Company The ITP logo is a registered trademark used herein under license

Printed in the United States of America

For more information visit us on the Web, www.vnr.com or contact:

Van Nostrand Reinhold
115 Fifth Avenue
New York, NY 10003

Chapman & Hall Gimbil
Pappelallee 3
69469 Weinheim
Germany

Chapman & Hall
2-6 Boundary Row
London
SF,1 8HN
United Kingdom

International Thomson Publishing Asia
221 Henderson Road #05-10
Henderson Building
Singapore 0315

Thomas Nelson Australia
102 Dodds Street
South Melbourne, 3205
Victoria, Australia

International Thomson Publishing Japan
Hirakawacho Kyowa Building, 3F
2-Z-1 Hirakawacho
Chiyoda•ku, 102 Tokyo
Japan

Nelson Canada
1120 Birchmount Road
Scarborough, Ontario
Canada MIK 5C4

International Thomson Editores
Seneca 53
Col Polanco
115 60 Mexico D.F. Mexico

The ideas presented in this book are generic and strategic. Their specific application to a particular company must be the responsibility of the management of that company, based on management's understanding of their company's procedures, culture, resources, and competitive situation.

1 2 3 4 5 6 7 8 9 10 IPC 01 00 99 98 97

Library of Congress Cataloging-in-Publication Data Available

ISBN 0-442-02608-0

Dedicated to my wife, Susan.

Contents

Acknowledgments

This book is a collaboration of great minds who consented to share their wisdom and experience. In addition to the people interviewed for the book, I'd like to thank these people who have helped me over the years. We learn from our experiences and chance encounters. Sometimes it amazes me how much we really do learn from each other and how the most trivial of information gained one day can play an important role in our lives years later.

Leslie Laredo, Michael Kolowich, Jennifer Christensen, David DeJean at AT&T Interchange Online Network. Steve Case, Pam McCraw, and Doug Rekenthaler at America Online. Regina Brady, Keith Arnold, Michele Moran, and Kathy Gerber at CompuServe. Carol Wallace at Prodigy.

Pam Alexander, Christina Tavella, and Brian Johnson at Alexander Communications, Connie Connors and Lydia Trettis at Connnors Communications. Barbara Thomas, Ed Niehaus, Bill Ryan, Marcos Sanchez, and Skye Ketonen at Niehaus Ryan Haller. Kim Bayne of wolfeBayne Communications. Marty Winston of Winston & Winston. Ron Solberg and Bill Lutholtz of PRSIG.

Greg Jarboe, Charlie Cooper, Ryck Lent, Chris Shipley, Robin Raskin, and Bill Machrone. Tanya Mazarowski of Mecklermedia. Lorraine Sileo and Chris Elwell of Simba Information. Jeff Silverstein and Maureen Flemming of Digital Information Group. Kristin Zhivago at Zhivago Marketing Partners.

Launch Point Associates' Alan Crofut, Cliff Bernstein and Rory McDonough. The Internet Roundtable SocietyóBob Lash, Wendi Bernstein Lash, Michael Fremont and Scott Shanks. Ameet Zaveri, Terri Lonier and James McHugh for reviewing the manuscript.

Michael Krieger, Ken Skier, Maurice Hamoy, Brad Peppard, Tom Stitt, Gary Jose, Keith Hendrick, Jim Nichols, Jackie Clark, Eric Robichaud, Lynne Marcus, Mark Bruce, Bruce Freeman, Mark OíDeady, Peggy Watt, Sharyn Fitzpatrick, Pat Meier, Charlie Valeston, Frank Tzeng, Steve Hersee, Leigh Mariner, Ivan Levison, Larry Parks, Jonathan Parks, Howard Zack, Dave Arganbright, Joe Szczepaniak, Maryanne Piazza, Alan Penchansky, Tim Bajarin, Steve Hersee, Richard Goswick, David Toner, Irv Brechner, Marty Shenman, Jeff Tarter, Jane Farber, Allison Shapiro, Bob Kersey, Colleen Coletta, Jerry Duro, John Cole, Ken Wasch, Dave McClure, Greg Doench, John Kilcullen, Carol Rizzardi, Babbette Griffis, Mary Stanley. Thanks to Joel Strasser and Tom Richmond who gave me my start in PR.

Thanks to reporters who like a good story. Lance Elko, Selby Bateman, Pete Scicso, David English, Mike Hudnall, Bob Schwabach, Larry Shannon, Pete Lewis, Steve Manes, Keith Ferrell, Kathy Yakal, Ted Needleman, Bob Scott, Kerri Karvetski, Heather Clancy, Alan Bechtold, Dave Haskin, Jerry Olsen, Barry Brenesal, Gayle Ehrenmann, Ephraim Schwartz, John Blackford, Arlan Levitan, Matt Lake, Yael Li Ron, Jon Zilber, Scott Finnie, Adam Meyerson, Donna Meyerson, Michael Penwarden, Gina Smith, Leo Laporte, John Dvorak, Fred Fishkin, Mike Langberg, Michael Antonoff, Fred Abatemarco, Nancy Trespasz, Fred Langa, Jim Forbes, Paul Schindler, Phil Albinus, Donna Tapellini, Rich Malloy, Dan Rosenbaum, Dennis Allen, Rick Manning, Rich Santalesa, David Coursey, Tim Bajarin, and Scott Mace.

My trusted associates, Susan Morrow, Mark Bruce, and Bruce Freeman.

My mentor, Sandy Hartman. Great friends like Gordy Allen, Wally Bock, Roberta Morgan, and Dave Arnold.

Friends for life, Steven Kessler, Stuart Gruber, Barry Block, Alan Dauber, Alan Penchansky, and Len Zandrow.

The excellent staff at Van Nostrand Reinhold, Neil Levine, Mike Sherry, Lesley Rock, Judith Steinbaum, John Boyd, and Marianne Russell. Matt Wagner at Waterside Productions. Thanks to Paul and Sarah Edwards for their excellent foreword.

Thanks for feedback and encouragement from George Thibault and Steve Leon.

Special thanks to Susan Tracy. May all your fortune cookies come true.

Foreword

I was asked to write this foreword because of all the things I don't know about computers.

I use a Sharp notebook computer for work. I've seen people demonstrate incredible feats with it, but in my hands, it's been a kind of Pentium typewriter. It saves me having to scratch things out or make arrows to whole sentences I've written in the margins. I'm very grateful for this.

I'm Senior Editor at SUCCESS Magazine and Editor-in-Chief of a new magazine called Working at Home. Eight years ago, one of my tasks at SUCCESS was to edit what was then our only computer coverage, a column called "Technology Edge." When we surveyed readers back then, about 80 percent weren't interested in seeing anything on that subject at all. Like most people, they assumed that computers were boring machines developed by geeks who couldn't get dates. The purpose of the computers was to eliminate the jobs of the guys who were getting dates. (This is true, by the way.)

Then a columnist told us about a software program that helped you write a business plan by getting you past the difficult "staring-at-a-blank-sheet-of-paper" stage, which is where approximately 99.7 percent of all business plans fail (by never getting written). This program had you answer some questions and fill in some blanks in a business plan that was largely already written. I had the columnist review it and we offered it for sale to readers. A couple of months and several thousand copies of BizPlanBuilder later, we knew we'd found the only reason our readers would ever care about computers—not to balance their checkbooks or play solitaire, but to take a quantum leap in their lives, to go into business for themselves and start doing what they really want to be doing. And get dates.

That's what this fine book by Dan Janal is about.

When I first met Dan face-to-face at PC Expo, I'd read a book of his about starting Internet businesses. The book had astonished me. I could read it without putting on my computer-language decoder glasses. It was lively, made sense, and showed me how to sue what you have now to go into business, with the computer adding approximately 1 million pounds of leverage to your efforts When I talked to him, I was astonished again. He spoke English, wore a suit, and ran a whole consulting business helping normal people profit from computers, which I hadn't known was legal.

(I realize that a major motivation for reading a book like this is to figure out a way to make money that doesn't require you to change out of your pajamas, but really, I've met the biggest business honchos in the world, who can wear anything they want, and they all own suits. Sorry.)

When we mentioned Dan's earlier book in SUCCESS Magazine, readers bought a ton of them, because they hadn't known what he did was legal, either.

When I saw the manuscript of the book you are now holding, I arranged to get it excerpted in SUCCESS right away. You see, other books on using computers for business are written by computer specialists who don't know that much about business. Or they're written by people who aren't computer specialists—but who have small-time, non entrepreneurial minds. Dan has an entrepreneurial mind. He teaches you they "why" of things, so you can make the market work for you.

There is a story in this book about a guy who opened a bicycle shop on the Internet. The problem was that no one was buying his bargain-priced bicycles. He finally got sales cranking by offering hot-shot bicycles that carried a high price tag and big margins for him. You've got to love a story like that. The underlying reason for what happened is that the Internet is not a bargain basement in the usual sense. It's not a place to sell something you can buy cheaply in any small town in America—asn ordinary bicycle. It's a place to offer those same small-town residents the sleek, outer-space killing machines they don't stock at the local hardware store.

In other words, people use the Internet to get access they couldn't otherwise get.

You can, of course, pursue the customer by making access much easier. Some folks from Utah were selling American Indian silver and turquoise—a niche business for a teeny little tourist shop, right? But they noticed that they were getting a lot of orders from Germany and Japan. So they started publishing Web pages in German and Japanese. The customers from these pages spend twice as much per order as their American customers.

You can multiply the access channels that lead to your business. Amazon Books offers a commission of 8 percent on sales that come to them through your Web site. So there are, at last report, about 6,000 Web sites channeling customers to Amazon.

There there are the trillions of possible agency or middleman type businesses. The Internet can give you access to a marketplace that's to big, you can get the exact offering or price that you want. Bring together buyers and sellers of insurance, cars, travel, or anything else by posting offerings and collecting commissions on sales through your site.

Isn't your head charging with ideas now? There are the 101 ideas in the book, and then there are the 101-squared ideas you get from reading it. How many is that? I'm not sure. That's why we have computers. But the important thing is that Dan Janal has written a book for those of us who think Internet business is a neat idea—but who can't feed our families "neat." This book contains the stories of actual businesses that are making actual money on the Internet. And Dan generously invites you to swipe any of their ideas to create an Internet business of your own.

It's all perfectly legal. And you can work at home while you do it. You've got to love that. Andy you'll be needing some magazines to help you run your business. But first, read this book.

Duncan Maxwell Anderson
Senior Editor, SUCCESS
Editor-in-Chief, Working at Home.

Why You Should Open a Business on the Internet

OVERVIEW—OPENING YOUR INTERNET STORE

Who's making money on the Internet?

Lots of people.

People like you.

They operate businesses from their spare bedrooms at home, professional suites in office parks, and retail storefronts on Main Street. They sell products ranging from flowers to boats, from research reports to handmade jewelry. They are professionals, like lawyers and accountants. They are artists, like musicians, writers, and actors. They are software developers writing applications for needs that haven't been created. They are successful entrepreneurs and hopeful wannabes.

They represent virtually every age, from a seventeen-year-old cartoonist to a senior citizen selling a book about grandparenting. There's a father-and-son team that sells sport posters and people—not related—who work together and feel like a family. They live all over the world—a Canadian lobster company owner, an Australian software publisher, a tailor in Hong Kong.

Some people started businesses on the Internet because they are opportunity-driven entrepreneurs. Others were desperate victims of corporate downsizing. Some hold college degrees and others are still in high school.

Two things are for sure: The ones who majored in marketing don't make fun of computer geeks anymore, and the computer majors wish they had minored in business administration. They are a diverse lot with many different reasons for being online.

Some are making a ton of money, like CyberSource's software.net, which grossed $1 million a month selling computer software—after starting the business only a few months earlier. Quite a few companies have grabbed the brass ring and taken their companies public, pocketing millions for the founders and early investors.

Other companies are trying to break even or are waiting for their first sale. Some companies have invested tens of thousands of dollars, others have invested their beer money.

They are working hard. They are having a lot of fun. They want to be the first ones on the Internet's business areas to stake out their claims—even if the majority of Americans don't have Internet accounts yet.

These entrepreneurs expect a tidal wave of buyers and they want to be prepared when these consumers do come. They don't want to be left behind.

Some general-interest stores are swamped with ten thousand to a hundred thousand people visiting each day. Other sites are waiting for more people in their target audience to discover the benefits of online commerce.

Two years ago, when the first businesses went online, many waited patiently for their first customers as the Internet was not yet geared for mainstream shoppers. Today, many companies selling everything you can imagine are claiming that the Internet is a profitable place to conduct business. Chapter 4 presents more than twenty-five of the most successful plans for creating and operating a business on the Internet and shows examples of companies from every walk of life that are making money, not just wishing they were making money.

Online entrepreneurs are following the maxim: "While others wait for the rules of the game to be written, the window of opportunity is closing."

Which type of person are you? Are you waiting for the rules to be written, for the dust to settle, for the pioneers to show the way? Or are you ready to learn from others' experiences as well as your own, to take advantage of the gold mine that awaits the person offering the right products for the right prices to the right audiences that are flocking to the Internet?

Online sales are predicted to reach $7 billion by 2000, according to Jupiter Communications, *www.jup.com*.

Increasing numbers of people are actually spending money on the Web. According to a NetSmart survey, *www.netsmart.com*, in 1996, 54 percent of the people interviewed said they bought products on the Web, up from 37 percent a year earlier. Computer equipment tops the list of online purchase at 82 percent. Other key areas are travel (70 percent), financial services (46 percent), and automobiles (44 percent).

According to these numbers, people want to shop on the Internet. If your customers are there, shouldn't you be there as well?

ARE YOU THE RIGHT PERSON TO OPEN A STORE?

Let's take a quick quiz to measure your sales ability.

- Do you hate to sell?
- Would you rather not have to deal with the public face to face?
- Does the thought of making cold calls make you break into a sweat?
- Do you have good ideas?
- Are you capable of completing tasks?

- Can you write a decent letter, or adapt one from a book of sample letters?
- Can you learn from your mistakes?
- Are you stuck in a dead-end job, or about to become a victim of corporate downsizing?
- Do you have a good understanding of how to run a business, including marketing and financial operations?

If you answered "yes" to most of these questions, you have the potential to become a great success as an online entrepreneur.

That's because the key sales and marketing skills in the offline world—aggressiveness, persistence, and false friendliness—don't really matter on the Internet, where faceless transactions are the rule, not the exception, where consumers want information, not persuasion, and where customers hate to deal with salespeople.

The Internet is a world in which the cream rises to the top and merit counts more than flash. If you are the type of person who always says, "I have a great idea, but I need someone to sell it," then this book—and the Internet—is for you.

The way to sell on the Internet is through the soft sell, not the hard sell you see at consumer electronics stores and car dealerships. On the Internet you merely tell your story, present information, show pictures of the product, provide an order form or telephone numbers so people can call when they are ready to buy, and ask for the order. You might never see customers face to face or have any dialogue whatsoever with your prospects. You don't have to deal with the fear of rejection that is the number-one fear of would-be salespeople, myself included!

By the way, if you answered "no" to these questions, don't worry. You too can be a success on the Internet! Having good skills in sales, marketing, and social graces can only support your success as an online marketer. As long as you are committed to helping your customers be happy and successful, then you have a good chance of being successful as well.

So, whether you are a natural-born salesperson or tongue-tied; whether you know the five essential closes preached by every sales guru on the seminar circuit; or think that people will buy when they are good and ready, the Internet has a place for you!

HOW THIS BOOK WILL HELP YOU

This book is designed to help these kinds of people:

- *Wannabes*—You are stuck in a boring, mindless job, or one that has limited opportunities for advancement, earnings, or creativity; or you have been a victim of downsizing and corporate engineering and want to learn how to make money on the Internet. Welcome to the Internet, where you can test-drive an idea for less than $100 a month.

- *Household professionals*—You might be a household professional who takes care of the kids on a full-time basis and makes jewelry and crafts to sell at flea markets on the weekends. Welcome to the Internet, the ultimate flea market.

- *Current business owners*—You already run a business on Main Street or a professional service in an office park and want to reach new markets around the world.

- *Burnouts*—You're a jeweler who's been mugged at gunpoint in a dark alley and your insurance company won't take your phone calls. It's time for a new career—out of the view of the public.

- *Entrepreneurs*—You've read all the hype about the information superhighway and want the straight truth about what works and doesn't work in online marketing. You want good ideas on businesses to start, products to sell, and industry groups to invest in.

- *College students*—You've surfed the Internet for eight hours every day for the past year and want to see how you can build a business or a career.

HOW THIS BOOK IS ORGANIZED TO HELP YOU

This book is organized into two sections. Section 1 contains basic start-up information to help anyone who plans to put a business on the Internet.

Chapter 1, "Why You Should Open a Business on the Internet," shows you the opportunities for going online, demographics of who is online, what it takes to be a successful entrepreneur on the Internet, and business reasons to be online, as well as the pitfalls that you should be aware of and advice on how to overcome these negatives.

Chapter 2, "Internet Basics," helps you understand what makes the Internet tick. We'll explain the basic terms and technologies in a way that you can understand even if you've never sat in front of a computer.

Chapter 3, "Internet Business Practices," shows how sales and marketing are conducted on the Internet. You'll understand how online marketing differs from traditional advertising. You'll also know how construct your Internet business plan and go online in a successful, proven, step-by-step manner.

Chapter 4, "Thirty Killer Business Models," shows you the ways companies—regardless of industry—are making money online. You'll see how sharp entrepreneurs are creating profitable businesses on the Internet. You'll learn of successful examples and can check them out by going online at your convenience. You'll be encouraged to brainstorm and think of how each model could relate to your business. You'll be surprised at how many new ideas can come from reading this chapter and adding your own creativity!

In Section 2, you'll read chapters covering everything from selling consumer goods to professional services, from food and dining to travel and leisure, from real estate and mortgages to artists. You'll learn from overviews, case histories, in-depth interviews, and our own exclusive review of hot sites of more than 101 successful businesses on the Internet. You'll learn firsthand from experts what it takes to run a business. You'll see their failures as well as their triumphs—and learn from each.

If there's a business we haven't thought of, tell us about it and we'll probably include it in the next edition. Send e-mail to *dan@janal.com* with your suggestions! You can also get free online marketing help by subscribing to my free e-mail newsletter, *Dan Janal's Online Marketing Magazine*. To get your free subscription, send e-mail to *marketing@groupserver.remet.com* with the word "join" in the message box.

While you might be tempted to read only the chapter that relates to your specific industry, you will be well served to follow this reading plan: Read that chapter first; then read the rest of the book. You'll be amazed at how many good ideas can be gleaned from other industries. Some ideas can be applied immediately, some can be tweaked, and some won't apply at all. Imagine if one idea ignites a spark of creativity that launches you on a new path!

Each interview was conducted by e-mail, so the words you see are those of the entrepreneur. You'll catch each person's flavor and style. It's a good read!

Many of the people interviewed for this book participated in my previous book as well. We're hoping to conduct a study of these participants over a long period of time. We're also glad to report that all but a handful of companies are still in business! Also, while most were struggling when the first edition came out, now all of them are bona fide successes.

Companies that were just making their first sales two years ago now report that 25 percent of their income is from the Internet.

When you visit their sites, you'll be amazed at how simple and plain the designs are. That just goes to show that moneymaking sites don't have to be technological marvels. They have to have what people want to buy!

By learning from others' examples and experiences, you can increase your chances for success and decrease the time it takes to get there.

THE FOUR BASIC QUESTIONS

Let's cut to the chase. If you are flipping through this book there are four questions you want answered before reading anything else.

1. How Much Time Will This Take?

Running a business takes time. The people interviewed for this book spend between twenty and sixty hours a week running their Internet store. Most of their time online is spent marketing the site.

2. Do I Have to Quit My Day Job?

Entrepreneuring provides many opportunities to conduct a moonlight business while you continue your present employment or take care of the kids during the day. You can start a business on the Internet and handle the operations at night and on weekends. You might decide never to leave your day job and just operate the Internet business as a sideline, or you might find that business online is so good that you can devote your career to it.

3. How Much Money Do I Need to Get Started?

You'll see by the case studies that some people started with just a few hundred dollars, while others spent considerable sums. To use a ballpark figure, it takes about $2,500 in computer equipment to get started, as well as another $2,500 for someone to create your online store, register the site, and put it online. Then there's inventory, which varies store by store. An information business might not have any inventory costs at all, while a mail-order gardening tools catalog might have to invest tens of thousands of dollars. You also need to consider the costs of doing business, such as marketing, legal and accounting service, business permits, and taxes. The bottom line, then, is an average of $5,000 to start a minimal operation, with no upward limit.

Renting space with an Internet service provider (ISP) costs as little as $25–$50 a month. You can read about a full range of service options in chapter 2.

4. How Much Money Can I Make?

That question really can't be answered with a specific number, but you knew that anyway! The answer depends partially on how many people want your product or service, how many of those people are on the Internet, whether they can find you, and if you can offer them an attractive price. Fortunately, the indicators are very positive, as the number of people and stores, and sales figures, is growing rapidly.

It is important to point out that you will not get rich overnight on the Internet. That doesn't happen in real life, either. Businesses take a long time to develop and pay back their investors' time and money in the real world. It is no different on the Internet. It is important to set clear, identifiable, and attainable goals to improve your chances of success and lower your chances of burnout.

With those preliminaries out of the way, let's look at why you should sell your products or services on the Internet.

SEVENTEEN REASONS TO START A BUSINESS ON THE INTERNET

If you are thinking about making a commitment to running an online store, you should be aware of the advantages and disadvantages. Let's look first at the reasons in favor of opening a storefront on the Internet.

The Internet offers many advantages for companies that want to sell products, whether they are expanding a physical storefront or creating a company that exists only in cyberspace. Here are seventeen reasons for a company to have an online store.

1. Reach a worldwide audience.
2. Do business with an affluent market.
3. Be open twenty-four-hours a day—no time zone barrier.
4. Reach consumers when they are ready to buy.
5. Appeal to consumers who hate salespeople.
6. Open a new channel of distribution for your company.
7. ... or sell products only on the Internet.
8. Offer lower costs to consumers and beat competition.
9. Beat competitors to new markets because they aren't online.
10. Make additional sales more easily.
11. Create cost-effective catalogs that are long on details.
12. Exploit low cost of entry.
13. Enjoy no or low rent.
14. Reduce or eliminate inventory, warehouse, and money costs.
15. Reduce costs of salespeople because customers sell themselves.

16. Interact with customers.

17. Engage the senses by using audio, video, and multimedia to create relationships and sell products.

Let's look at each of these factors.

1. Reach a Worldwide Audience

People in virtually every country have access to the Internet and can place orders. I've received orders for my books from such far-flung and exotic destinations as Tel Aviv, Israel; Sydney, Australia; Calgary, Canada; and Seattle! People from all over the world can get access to your online store quickly and easily. Furthermore, you can reach these people for a mere fraction of what it would cost to reach them with traditional marketing tools like direct mail, television and print advertising, promotions, and even public relations.

2. Do Business with an Affluent Market

The profile of the average online consumer is very, very positive, as seen by figures listed earlier in this chapter.

3. Be Open Twenty-Four Hours a Day—No Time Zone Barrier

You have to feel sorry for my Uncle Bud. He had a hardware store on the main drag for thirty years. He had to close up shop for twelve to sixteen hours a day, even though he was paying rent twenty-four hours a day. He had to keep a person in the store on the slowest days and lose money so he'd have them around on Saturday, the busiest day. He closed the store on Sunday so he could get one day of rest. Then he lost all the business to the new superstores in the mall as customers shopped on Sunday.

That's not so on the Internet. Your storefront is open for business twenty-four hours a day. Whether people are looking for information at 5:05 P.M.

or 5:05 A.M., in their time zone or yours, they'll be able to find it because your online shop is always open for action. Someone in New Zealand could see your store, browse, and order in the space of a few minutes on Monday morning when you are fast asleep in your bed in your Sunday time zone. It is the neatest feeling to get an e-mail order from Europe late Monday night that is time-stamped Tuesday!

4. Reach Consumers When They Are Ready to Buy

Every store has its share of tire-kickers who just browse and leave. They are on the Internet as well. However, when they are ready to buy, your store is open for business. As Carol Wallace, a marketing ace at Prodigy, says, "You are never going to get more attention from any customer than when they are online. Both their hands are on the keyboard and both their eyes are on the monitor. You are interacting with them. They have preselected you. They want to see you. This is a very intimate selling situation."

Memorize those lines. They should form the basis of your business plan!

5. Appeal to Consumers Who Hate Salespeople

If you're in sales, you might find this hard to believe, but many people don't like to buy from salespeople! That's right. They hate the high pressure and power closes. Most people say "just looking" when salespeople ask them if they can merely "help." Because of that, the Internet is the perfect place for the consumer who likes to look around, size things up, draw her own conclusions—and then buy. These people don't like to be persuaded or manipulated. That's why they use online services, mail-order catalogs, and other sales situations that are not conducted face to face. Your Internet store taps this market.

6. Open a New Channel of Distribution for Your Company

Your company might be doing a great job now selling products through a physical storefront or by mail order. You'll also want to use the Internet to open a new channel of distribution for your products. As you'll see, for a very low cost of entry, you can reach millions of consumers all around the world for much less than the cost of opening a new store on the other side of town.

The Internet offers established businesses the opportunity to find new markets in their neighborhoods or around the world. For the company that is selling a product, like bikes or flowers, the entire world could be a potential market. You'll read many examples in the case study section of this book that show how companies on Main Street are selling products to people in faraway places.

7. ... Or Sell Products Only on the Internet

Some companies exist only on the Internet. These include information brokers who sell research information to other companies on hard-to-find data, and artists who sell pictures via the Internet but don't have their own gallery on Main Street. These companies exist because of the low barriers to entry in starting a business on the Internet.

8. Offer Lower Costs to Consumers and Beat Competition

Because online merchants have lower overhead—they don't pay for heating, air conditioning, water, security, janitorial services, and other fees imposed by landlords—they can pass the savings along to their customers in the form of lower prices. Companies can offer discounts to their online consumers. This tactic might attract them to the Internet in the first place as well as keep them coming back. See reasons 14 and 15 for two additional price-lowering factors.

9. Beat Competitors to New Markets Because They Aren't Online

If you operate a business on Main Street, you can't afford not to open a storefront on the Internet. Your competitors might already be there snagging business you didn't even know about.

You can put any business on the Internet and attract new clients by being listed in directories that show your name to prospects (and through other marketing tactics that we'll talk about later). Lawyers are getting referrals from other lawyers, authors are selling books, companies are selling flowers, gourmet foods, and even garlic to people all over the world just because they are on the Internet and their competitors are not! You can't afford not to be on the Internet if you operate a business.

10. Make Additional Sales More Easily

Research has shown that it is easier to sell to an existing customer than to develop a new one. The Internet can be very helpful with this. Once customers have bought from you, you can ask to send them e-mail that offers more information about the product, product upgrades, and related products. If they were happy with your pea pod seeds, then they just might buy rose plants from you next season.

11. Create Cost-Effective Catalogs That Are Long on Details

Print catalogs are great marketing tools, but they suffer from a lack of space and the expenses of mailing lists, postage, and printing. They can also become out of date quickly as suppliers raise prices. Online marketers have much greater flexibility with online catalogs. Because space is cheap, they can print descriptions and photos of their entire ten thousand–product line, not just the hundred items that the marketing department thinks will sell this year. The descriptions can be full and complete and go on for as much space as is needed. This is important for a company that sells to other businesses. For example, industrial-strength glue might require buyers to analyze complex chemical formulas to ensure the product meets their specifications. Printing and mailing outbound communications, such as price sheets, catalogs, and brochures, could strain a company's financial resources. However, the cost of publishing these materials on the Internet is minimal.

Companies are cutting their printing and mailing costs for catalogs and marketing materials by placing them online. Sun Microsystems announced it saved more than $1 million in one year by placing its marketing information online. It also saved a ton of money in related costs, such as manpower to mail the materials. Tandem Computers not only saved a great deal of money by placing its marketing materials on the Internet, it also reached five times as many customers!

Online catalogs can also include demonstrations, voice-overs, and other benefits of technology that print catalogs cannot begin to duplicate.

12. Exploit Low Cost of Entry

The cost of starting your online store can vary from a few dollars to tens of thousands, much less than the price of opening a store.

13. Enjoy No or Low Rent

Unlike a physical store, your cyberstore doesn't pay a fortune in rent. You might pay a monthly fee of $50 or less to store your site with an ISP, to connect your store to the Internet.

If you operate a sizable business, you might have the Internet hookup at your office. That will cost about $15,000—$150,000 to get started and recurring fees of about $1,000 a month—fees that are much less than remodeling an office.

14. Reduce or Eliminate Inventory, Warehouse, and Money Costs

Internet-based businesses can rely on drop-shipping their products to meet their customers' orders. They don't have to stock large supplies or products in expensive warehouses. Instead, they can offer the product for sale in their online catalog and order the products from their suppliers only when they receive payment from their online customers. Because the product is not bought until needed, the online merchant doesn't have to tie up money in goods or pay interest on that money. Instead, his money can be earning interest or invested in other profitable ventures.

15. Reduce Costs of Salespeople Because Customers Sell Themselves

You don't need salespeople online. Your prospects are their own salespeople. They sell themselves! That happens when you place your sales material online and prospects browse. They follow their own line of thinking, find answers to their own questions, and buy when they are ready. In order to construct this kind of sales plan, you must interview your top salespeople and ask them what questions people ask and how to best answer them. Many online consumers like the fact there aren't any pushy salespeople online to harass them into buying a product. Online selling is more immediate and less intrusive than dealing with salespeople.

16. Interact with Customers

Online communications offer merchants benefits of interacting with consumers that cannot exist in one-way print or television communications. Using e-mail, infobots (automated e-mail, similar to a fax-back system), and other online tools, merchants can create a dialog with consumers that leads to long-term relationships and sales.

17. Engage the Senses by Using Audio, Video, and Multimedia to Create Relationships and Sell Products

Vendors can showcase their products and services by using the Internet's multimedia capabilities. Using audio, video, or a combination thereof, merchants can make their products come alive on the Internet. Technology and tools are still immature, but the promise of interactive multimedia demonstrations is fast becoming a reality.

SIX CHALLENGES TO RUNNING AN INTERNET STORE

As you can clearly see, there are many compelling reasons to put your business on the Internet. Let's look at possible roadblocks.

The information highway is not paved with gold. You will have to invest time, money, and energy into making a success of your business. You can't just open your store and expect to make a million dollars overnight. It will take work. You will be able to do some of it yourself, but you will have to hire others to do parts for you, just as you would hire a plumber to install a bathroom in your storefront on Main Street. This section explores the potholes on the information highway—and how to overcome them. Here are six issues to be careful of in creating an Internet business.

1. Getting lost in the crowd.

2. Shifting prices for services.

3. Buyer reluctance.

4. Security.

5. Audience size.

6. Shopping as participant sport.

1.   Getting Lost in the Crowd

Imagine shopping at your local mall, except the mall has fifty thousand stores and not one directory that shows where they are located. Welcome to the Internet. Your first job, once you open your cyberstore, is to publicize and promote it so it stands out from the others. You'll learn many ways to do this in chapter 3.

2. Shifting Prices for Services

Prices for services are all across the board. Providers and suppliers are charging whatever they can get away with. That's the sign of an immature industry, not of price-gouging. Skills that are highly sought today, like HTML programming to turn your marketing material into a format the World Wide Web can read, are coming under price attack as more people learn the coding—and as automatic conversion programs hit the market and replace humans! As time passes, prices for all services will become very competitive.

3. Buyer Reluctance

People are wary about ordering products online. A report by Dataquest shows that only 25 percent of the people who bought products online paid with a credit card. This means 75 percent of the people ordered by phone or mail or visited a store after seeing an ad on the Internet. While this statistic shouldn't frighten you away, you should make alternative ordering methods available to all customers, like posting your phone number, fax number, mailing address, and store location (complete with annotated map and driving instructions!).

4. Security

Your data and customer records could be subject to attack by hackers who want to destroy things because they think it is fun or to show the world they are smarter than everyone else. Fortunately, security devices and business practices can protect your store most of the time. Remember, your store on Main Street can be robbed, too.

5. Audience Size

The online audience is only a fraction of the consumer audience. Many people are not online today. Your audience might not be online, or only a small part might be. However, as the Internet trend reaches fad and epidemic proportions, the audiences for each segment will grow. Experts expect that to happen in a very short time—months, not years.

6. Shopping as Participant Sport

Some people will never buy online because they want to see and touch the product. They might also like the stimulation of going to a store, interacting with live people, and fighting for a parking spot. Hard to believe, but it is true—and they are the majority! You might not ever be able to reach these people online. Or perhaps you will be able to create awareness online and arouse their willingness to purchase from your regular retail outlet.

Summary

Yes, there are risks to starting a business on the Internet, just as there are risks in starting any new business anywhere in the world. You need to study the facts so that you can make intelligent decisions. Not only do you need to study businesses and markets, you need to study yourself as well.

DISCLAIMER—THE SMALL PRINT

Here's the paragraph the lawyers want inserted. Not every business will succeed on the Internet or on Main Street. There are many reasons businesses fail, including lack of experience by the operator, lack of investment capital, bad marketing, intense competition, and improper product selection and pricing. Reading this book will not guarantee success. However, by studying it you can minimize the risks of failure and increase the chances for success.

The ideas and tips given in this book are not meant to be a comprehensive guide to starting and running a business. That would be the subject of 101 individual books. We direct you to your local library to read the loose-leaf materials published by *Entrepreneur* magazine on how to start a business in general, and for more than a dozen businesses in particular. Those books are comprehensive road maps for starting and running many traditional businesses. Their sound advice will be helpful in planning your Internet business as well.

Ask the reference librarian for other resources that the library has or can obtain for you. Of course, look for business resources on the Internet (start with the search indexes, like Yahoo!, at *www.yahoo.com*) or ask entrepreneurs for their advice, if they are willing to give it. Also, join mailing lists and newsgroups that cater to entrepreneurs and business owners in your field. For a list of newsgroups, go to Dejanews, *www.dejanews.com*. For a list of mailing lists, got to Neosoft, *www.neosoft.com/paml*.

You'll also notice that many of the businesses profiled in this book did *not* create business plans. I didn't either. However, this is not necessarily a good idea. Maybe we all would be more successful with clearer goals in mind at the beginning of the project and the realization that the plan can and will be adjusted along the way. You should have at least a modest idea of what you are doing, how much it will cost, and what you hope to gain from this venture. You definitely need some kind of plan or road map to help you get there!

If you start with this book and then read specialized books in the areas you want to pursue, you will be following a good plan.

DO YOU HAVE WHAT IT TAKES TO BE AN INTERNET ENTREPRENEUR?

I don't mean to present a picture taken through a rose-colored lens. Not every idea is destined for success. Some people really don't have what it takes to manage themselves, let alone a business.

As a first step, take a simple test to see if you have the raw materials to become a successful Internet entrepreneur.

Do You Have Discipline?

One of the keys to running a good business is to go to the store every day! Whether you are a corporate executive or a home-based entrepreneur, getting a few extra winks or getting up at the same time every day and going to the desk in the spare bedroom is the difference between failure and success.

Running an online store takes time. The business won't run itself. Your main activities will be to check the e-mail to answer questions from prospects and to take orders, ship merchandise, order new stock, keep the store looking attractive and fresh, and promote it. You'll see by the case studies in this book that some entrepreneurs spend only a few hours a week online while others live online. It's up to you. The more time you put in, the more results you will see.

Do You Have the Support of Your Family?

Running a business takes time, space, and money, all of which can be scarce resources. Will your family give you those resources and support you? Or will they guilt-trip you and sabotage your plans? It is important to get their buy-in and support up front. Perhaps the online store can be a family adventure, with everyone pitching in and making it a fun exercise. It seems that every teenager knows her way around the computer and that every teenager wants a job after school to make some spending money for clothes, dates, and cars. Perhaps the kids can handle simple e-mail requests for information, process credit card forms, and ship products. After all, isn't that task better than a job dishing out yogurt at the mall? Of course, younger children will want your time and won't be fascinated by the inner workings of big business, so you'll want to evaluate your relationships carefully before going online.

Have You Been on the Internet?

Trying to explain how sales work on the Internet is like trying to explain jazz to someone who's never heard it. You can describe the passion and excitement of music with words, but you'll understand it a whole lot more on a more personal level if you listen to a record. The same is true with the Internet. Get online, see what others are doing, and determine if it could work for you.

One of the best ways to learn about being a merchant on the Net is to be a customer on the Internet. Go to the Yahoo! search engine, an online directory of products and services, *www.yahoo.com,* and see what your competitors are doing online. Observe their layouts, see how they ask for the order, and take notes on what you like and don't like. Visit a few competitors' sites and see what seem to be the norms and standards in your industry. Then visit the sites of other industries and see if there are tips you can pick up. You can also get a quick survey of these sites by reading the chapters of case studies and interviews in this book.

Can You Cope with Change?

Everything changes quickly on the Internet. Today's standards for graphic design will seem antiquated in a few months. Limitations of technology today will be overcome tomorrow. There is a joke that time on the Internet is measured in dog years. Even that joke is old! You must have the ability to react to change quickly and to seize changing business models and mold them to your advantage.

SUMMARY

The questions in this section should get you started thinking about whether you should be an online merchant or not. This book will help separate the hype from reality. Running a business is work. It can be fun and financially rewarding, but there are no guarantees. This book will show you how many entrepreneurs are succeeding—but you'll also read about hard times and heartaches.

If you have a great product or great ideas, the Internet could be the place to help you sell it to an affluent, educated worldwide audience at a relatively low cost of entry. Good sales and marketing skills—the weak points of most start-up business—are nice but not required. You must determine if you have what it takes to succeed, like a good idea, the support of your family, and the time and finances to devote to the task. If so, the Internet could be for you.

2 Internet Basics

GETTING UP TO SPEED

Let's get your business online! You probably have some basic questions and fears about the Internet and how to make sense of the technology and how to run a business. This chapter explores these basic questions:

- Do I have to be a programming geek to run a business on the Internet?

- What *is* the Internet?

- What is the World Wide Web?

- What is a home page?

- What is a Web site?

- What equipment do I need?

- How do I connect my business to the Internet?

- How do I send files to an Internet service provider (ISP)?

- Who pays for the phone call?

- What is e-mail?

- What are infobots?

- How do customers find my home page?

We answer these questions from a decidedly nontechnical point of view and give you just the information you need. This chapter will help you understand what services you will need and the prices you can expect to pay.

DO I HAVE TO BE A PROGRAMMING GEEK TO RUN A BUSINESS ON THE INTERNET?

Take a deep breath of relief: You don't have to be a programming geek to get started on the Internet. Of course, it never hurts to learn about computers, but because there are consultants and agencies of every stripe to help you along every step of the way, this is not essential.

You can hire consultants to create your home page, connect it to the Internet, and fill orders. As with any business, your time is best spent providing the service and management needed to make sales and keep customers happy. Don't let a fear of programming or technology stop you from starting your business on the Internet.

This thought shouldn't surprise you. After all, if you opened a store on Main Street you could hire a plumber, carpenter, and painter to help you get up and running. The same holds true with the Internet. You can do as much or as little computer work as you like.

On the other hand, many people interviewed for this book performed many operations themselves, from creating their own home pages to sending the files to an ISP to promoting their site. It all depends on where you wish to place your talents.

WHAT IS THE INTERNET?

The Internet is the world's largest and least expensive marketing tool. By placing marketing material on the Internet, companies in Kansas can sell products to people in Saskatchewan.

Technically speaking, the Internet is a vast network of computers that gives consumers the ability to see and interact with information on those computers. The benefits for marketers is that consumers all around the world can browse through your store at any time of the day or night, whenever they are in the mood to shop, read your marketing material, and place orders via e-mail or the telephone.

WHAT IS THE WORLD WIDE WEB?

The area on which merchants can conduct business on the Internet is called the *World Wide Web* (also called *WWW* or *the Web*). If you imagine the Internet to be a city, then the World Wide Web is zoned for commercial activity. Advertising and commerce cannot be conducted on the areas of the Internet called *mailing lists* and *newsgroups*. There aren't any laws that prevent this; however, people go to those areas for unbiased and noncommercial information and react negatively to people who try to conduct business there. It is as if you go to the steam room in your health club to relax and someone sits next to you, strikes up a conversation, and then tries to sell you life insurance. Sure, there is no law to stop him, but you aren't going to buy from him either. In these cases, everyone wastes their time. So don't do it!

WHAT IS A HOME PAGE?

Merchants can post sales literature, product information, coupons, sales incentives, press releases, brochures, ads, and promotional materials and take orders in their own space on the Web, which is called a *home page*, Web site, site, online presence, or cyberstore. You can think of this mystical "place" as your storefront, billboard, convention center, shopping mall, brochure, newspaper, or magazine, in that it is where consumers can find out about your products and purchase them.

Your marketing information can be displayed with color graphics, lively text, and even sound and video files, although the last two are still a bit quirky at this stage of technological development.

Although the term *home page* is used, the space is really larger than a single page. In fact, as you look at your computer screen, the page actually can scroll down to allow merchants to post a great deal more material than can fit on a single printed page. To tap the full power of the Web, merchants can post an unlimited amount of information on *subpages*, which are linked to the home page through *hypertext links* that allow consumers to jump from one piece of information to the next immediately. These hypertext links embody the true power of the Internet because they enable consumers to find information anywhere in your cyberstore. Customers can pick the information that interests them and helps them make an intelligent purchase decision. Through the use of hyperlinks, consumers can transparently connect to computers of other companies and businesses in faraway places.

These tools give consumers the ability to comparison-shop in seconds without having to get into a car and drive to another mall. Shoppers can search for the information they need, check prices, warranties, and return policies, and then place orders—without leaving their homes.

The beauty of hypertext material is that customers themselves can create a personalized sales presentation. They don't have to read a boring set of facts that doesn't appeal to them. For example, if they enter a home page in which books, are sold, they can see options for reading about fiction, nonfiction, self-help, and mystery. They can use their mouse to select a category and see the titles in that section. In other words, they don't have to read a lot of information that doesn't appeal to them. They can read what they want and order when they are ready.

To put your material on the Web, it must be designed in a format that the computer can read. That format is called *HTML*, which stands for Hyper

Text Markup Language. The word processing programs Microsoft Word and Word Perfect can convert your text files to HTML automatically.

WHAT IS A WEB SITE?

The terms *home page* and *Web site* are almost interchangeable. Web site is becoming the favored term.

WHAT EQUIPMENT DO I NEED?

Merchants link up with the Internet using a computer, a modem, a phone line, and communications software called browsers. Let's look at each component.

Computer

Merchants can best operate their businesses with a Pentium-based computer, Windows 95 operating system, and a color monitor. These tools should provide the horsepower needed to operate the software that helps create home pages, load files to the ISP, correspond with customers via e-mail, accept orders online, and promote the site. Any Macintosh with 8 MB of memory and a modem is also capable of connecting to the Internet.

In the not-too-distant future, a CD-ROM drive will be part of the online advertising and shopping trip. That's because CD-ROMs can store and display graphics and sound faster than the Internet can deliver over phone lines. Internet merchants will want to use the CD-ROM as a delivery and display mechanism and the Internet as an order-taking system.

Modem

A modem is an electronic device that allows the computer to transmit and receive data from other computers via telephone lines. Modems are rated by the speed at which they transfer data; the higher the rating number, the faster the time to transfer data and the less waiting you and your customers have to endure. Most new computers sold today are equipped with modems in the 56 kbps class, which is adequate for use on the Internet.

Small businesses can comfortably use a 56 kbps modem if they create and post pages to an ISP or a commercial online service or rent space from a digital mall. Large businesses or those that attract a lot of customers and online orders might want to use their own heavy-duty computer system including a T-1 or T-3 telephone line leased from a local telephone company. This option costs a great deal of money and requires a tremendous amount of technical expertise.

Browser Software

A browser is a software program that lets consumers find your Web site and order your products. Browsers also have e-mail programs so consumers and merchants can exchange messages. They can also help create, update, and send new home pages to the ISP for automatic placement on the Internet. The two most popular browsers are Netscape Navigator and Microsoft Internet Explorer. Both are available at computer software stores, on the Web, and, in some cases, bundled with new computers. Both browsers work with PCs and Macintoshes.

The price of powerful computers is dropping every day. As of mid-1997 a name-brand 166 Mhz Pentium computer, 56 kbps modem, and monitor can be had for $1,200.

HOW DO I CONNECT MY BUSINESS TO THE INTERNET?

Merchants have several options for connecting to the Internet. Each carries a radically different price. Let's look at these options from easiest and least expensive to most intricate and costly.

- digital malls
- commercial online services
- Internet service providers
- direct connection

To find the best vendor, ask for recommendations from a computer user-group (lists of groups can be found in *Computer Shopper* magazine or in local computer newspapers and local papers or libraries) or someone who's already on the Internet. Let's explore the pros and cons of each option.

Digital Mall

A digital mall is the electronic version of a suburban strip mall. The digital mall hosts your site, provides the equipment and phone lines, and offers general maintenance and security. Good digital malls also offer business services such as marketing, advertising, and promotions to draw people to the mall, accept credit card transactions from consumers, and create the art and text for your home page.

Costs—Monthly rental prices vary around the country from several hundred dollars to several thousand dollars. Some digital malls also ask for a percentage of sales or charge a small fee each time a consumer visits your site. Marketing services are also an add-on fee. Some malls also charge a fee for processing credit card transactions.

Pros—A good digital mall can be a one-stop shopping solution for merchants hopping onto the Internet. You might benefit from the increased traffic created by associating with other companies hosted on the same mall. For example, when consumers visit the mall they see a directory listing of all merchants. A thematic mall, like travel services or financial products, might attract the perfect prospects for your travel agency or accounting services. Look for malls that group complementary companies in your industry, like assorted professionals (i.e., lawyers, podiatrists, and accountants), pastimes (i.e., sailing and travel), and tourist destinations (i.e., the Bahamas, Vail, and the Riviera).

Cons—If many popular commercial sites are on the digital mall, the entire system could slow down and annoy consumers. A digital mall site can become very expensive to operate if the landlord charges rent and takes a cut of your sales. Also, the shopper who is attracted to another store in the mall and stops by yours as he sees your store's listing on the directory, might not be a qualified prospect. For example, he might have come to visit the ski shop but doesn't have any kids, so he wouldn't be interested in your baby supplies.

Who should use it—Companies that believe they will benefit from associating with other businesses and those who want to pass off all labor relating to their home page, including programming, updating material, and marketing. Start-ups and people who are getting their feet wet with the Internet may also benefit; this is an easy and inexpensive way to test the waters to see if your company should be online.

Contacts—There are many digital malls. You find them by word of mouth, by reading messages on newsgroups and mailing lists, and from advertising sent by the digital malls themselves. Here is a short list—go ahead and browse, and see what they look like. These are not recommendations.

- Gigaplex   *www.gigaplex.com*

- Cybertown   *www.cybertown.com*

- Cybershop   *www.cybershop.com*

- London Mall   *www.londonmall.com.uk*

- Abbington Village   *www.abbington.com*

- Virtualynx   *www.virtualynx.com*

- Internet Mall   *www.internet-mall.com*

- Netmall   *www.netmall.com*
- Eshop Plaza   *www.eshop.com*

Commercial Online Services

America Online, CompuServe, and Prodigy are major commercial online services that connect to the Internet. They allow you to create your own home page for fees that vary by the services you need. For example, America Online's Prime Host service charges a $249 setup fee and $199 per month. They maintain all the hardware, software, and security for your home page. You need to design it, but that's easy with the software they have created. You basically answer a few questions and the computer lays out the material onto templates.

Costs—Variable.

Pros—You don't have to buy expensive hardware or learn about intricate technology to connect to the Internet. These companies are in business for the long term and have reliable hardware, support, and local phone access numbers in many cities.

Cons—Price could be expensive compared to local ISPs.

Who should use it—People who need a lot of hand-holding but nevertheless want to begin learning how to take control of their Web site. The online services have support staffs and help forums to educate merchants on how to maintain and promote Web sites.

Contacts—Here are phone numbers of popular commercial services that allow merchants to set up shop.

- America Online   888-AOL-1111
- CompuServe   800-848-8199
- Microsoft Network   206-882-8080
- Prodigy   800-776-3449

Internet Service Providers

An Internet service provider (ISP) is a company that stores your Web site on its computers, maintains those computers, provides other back-office operations, and connects your business to the Internet. There are thousands of small ISPs across the country that host businesses of every size. For a list of ISPs, go to The List, *www.thelist.com*.

Your ISP could be the most important ingredient to your success on the Internet. Its technical ability can make or break you. If it is thinly staffed or poorly trained, your cyberstore could suffer. If it charges too much, your profitability will be affected. If it nickels and dimes you for every service, you might hesitate before implementing needed changes, or surrender a substantial portion of your fees. You should call several providers, ask questions about these issues, and compare the answers.

Costs—Because this market is competitive, it makes sense to compare several ISPs to find the one that meets your needs and charges a reasonable price. Local ISPs charge small businesses $25–$100 a month for basic service. National ISPs charge much more but generally have more services, like round-the-clock technical support and maintenance.

Some ISPs charge additional fees for:

- Each time a person visits.

- The number of pages each person sees.

- A percentage of sales.

- Updating a Web site. This could cost $50–75 per hour. If you update your own Web site, there should not be a fee.

- Registering your business name with InterNIC provides you with a needed domain name. It costs $100 to register a domain name.

A domain name is your online business address. It is usually expressed as "company.com" where "company" stands for your company name.

Use this example from AT&T Easy World Wide Web Service, 800-746-7846, as a guiide for comparing rates.

Charge	Monthly	Nonrecurring
registration		$1,000
registration with one-year term plan		$500
service fee for AT&T customer	$295	
service fee for non-AT&T customer	$395	
data downloaded by end user		
0–200 MB	included	
201–500 MB	$155	
501–800 MB	$380	
801–1400 MB	$605	
1401–3500 MB	$1,055	
3501–7000 MB	$1,505	
7001–15000 MB	$2,005	
directory link	$50	
domain name registration		$100
training, first person		$895
training, second person		$395

U.S. West's !Interact Web Services begin at $65 a month for 5 MB of storage and 50,000 page hits.

Pros—You don't have to buy expensive hardware or learn about the intricate technology to connect to the Internet to run a business.

Cons—ISPs don't all offer the same services. Radically different pricing structures exist, so check several ISPs before signing up.

Who should use it—Businesses that don't want to invest money and manpower in large computer systems.

Contacts—The hundreds of ISPs throughout the country range from one- and two-person companies handling personal accounts in remote areas to multimillion-dollar corporations providing high-end access and programming for large companies. For smaller firms, check advertisements in local computer publications and daily newspapers, or in nationally distributed computer magazines. The larger services can be found in the yellow pages.

- BBN Planet   617-873-2000
- PSInet   800-827-7482
- Uunet Technologies   800-488-6384
- !Interact Web Services (U.S. West)   800-328-2879, ext. 121

How Do I Select an Internet Service Provider?

Most people who read this book will probably want to get onto the Internet via an ISP. To select a provider, ask these questions:

- *How long has the ISP been in business?* Because the Internet's commercial capabilities are relatively new, you won't find many older than two years.

- *What is the ISP's person-to-modem ratio?* When America Online experienced a system overload, its ratio of people to modems was 17:1. My local provider, Ccnet, has an 8:1 ratio. I usually get online every time I try, except, occasionally, around 9 A.M.

- *How fast is the ISP growing?* Many customers can be a bonus, as it shows stability and growth. They could be a minus in that the service might be overloaded with traffic and support needs.

- *How many people are on the support staff?* This is important, as you need to ensure that someone will be on hand to answer questions or to deal with problems in the computer system in the middle of the night.

- *Is technical support included?* If not, how much will it cost? Check to see how other vendors charge for support and see how each vendor stacks up.

CAN I UPDATE MY HOME PAGE MYSELF?

Yes. You can create and update your web site in your office and then send the files to the ISP through your modem. Your ISP can recommend file transfer software and teach you how to use it. Many people I talk to have been approached by companies that want to host their home pages and charge them a monthly rental fee and another charge to maintain or update the site. If you learn how to create your own pages, you shouldn't have to pay an additional fee. You can learn how to create pages with a course from your local community college or by reading *Creating Commercial Web Pages* by Laura Lemay and Brian K. Murphy, Sams.net.

HOW DO I SEND MY FILES TO THE ISP?

You create the files for your Web site with a special software program on your computer. When you are happy with the files, you send them to your ISP from your computer via the phone lines with a special software program like CUTE FTP, which can be previewed and downloaded from *www.cuteftp.com*. Once the ISP receives the files, they are immediately available on the Internet and can be seen by anyone who visits your site. Some of the newer versions of browsers and home page creation programs have the ability to send files to your ISP, so you don't need to buy additional software.

WHO PAYS FOR THE PHONE CALL?

If your ISP is local, you pay for a local phone call. If it is located far away, you pay for a long-distance phone call unless the ISP provides you with a toll-free number.

Can I Connect to the ISP from Anywhere in the Country for the Price of a Local Phone Call?

Most providers don't have local phone numbers all over the country, although Prodigy, CompuServe, America Online, Netcom, and a few others do. If you do a lot of traveling, this feature can be important as you'll save money if they have a local access number. If you don't travel, then this feature is not relevant.

Does My ISP Have to Be in My Hometown?

No. Any computer connected to the Internet can read any home page on the World Wide Web. If an ISP in your hometown does not have competitive prices, twenty-four-hour maintenance and support, or other features you need, you can find another ISP anywhere in the country. The only disadvantage to using an ISP in a distant location is that you might have to pay long-distance phone charges to access it to check your e-mail or update your home page files.

Direct Connection

A direct connection to the Internet means your computer hooks through your Internet service provider into the network of companies that provide the highest level of connect service, such as Sprint and MCI. If you go this route, you will have all the equipment and telephone connections to the Internet located at your office and operated by your employees. To compare this option to the previous one, think of renting versus buying. With the direct connection option you buy equipment, which could be less expensive in the long term or perhaps a viable option only for very large companies with experienced technical staffs.

Costs—A direct connection to the Internet is expensive, as you can see by the following chart. It also makes you responsible for creating the pages, maintaining the system, and providing security. For large companies with in-house computer departments, this is the way to go because you'll pay less in the long run and have more control over the contents of the home page. For mom-and-pop stores and start-ups, a direct connection is an expensive—and possibly unnecessary—alternative.

Building a Web site in-house includes the following expenses, which could easily run more than $100,000 a year:

- server hardware $3,000–$20,000
- Internet bandwidth (ISDN or T-1) $200/$2,000 per month
- ongoing support (system and $20,000–$100,000 per year
  site administration)

An in-house web site requires a substantial staff commitment. To ensure round-the-clock site availability, you need to staff twenty-four hours a day, seven days a week. Your staff will be required to troubleshoot complex hardware, telecommunications, and networking issues.

An in-house site can take a long time to set up.

- set up server   1–2 days
- install server software   1–7 days
- reconfiguring and testing 1–2 weeks

- install 1=1 line   1–4 weeks

- hire support staff   1 month

Pros—You own the shop and can depreciate equipment. This option offers the greatest amount of control and speed, as you are the only tenant on the line.

Cons—You must invest heavily in equipment and manpower to operate the system.

Who should use it—Large, established companies that want direct control over all aspects of Internet operations, including computer system maintenance and security, marketing, and materials creation.

WHAT IS E-MAIL?

E-mail is short for electronic mail. These are notes of any length you can send from one computer to another. Using e-mail a consumer can ask questions of merchants who can reply to their specific concerns. E-mail on the Internet is free and is provided as part of the normal service from most Internet service providers. E-mail is sent quickly to respondents, usually within a few seconds, although longer files can require more time.

E-mail knows where to go because you give it an address, just as you would a normal piece of mail. Each person who uses a commercial online service has a username, which could be a series of numbers and letters, such as *76004.1046@compuserve.com*, or a person's real name, or first letter and initials, such as *djanal@aol.com* and *dan.janal@mycompany.com*, or a nonhuman mailbox, such as *info@mycompany.com*. The addressing system is formatted like this: *username@service.ext*

What is a domain name?

A *domain name* is the name by which the Internet recognizes your company. Examples of domain names are *ibm.com*, *vnr.com*, and *janal.com*.

These domain names are part of your e-mail address, as in *dan@janal.com*. The Web site address can also be called a uniform resource locator (URL).

Domain names are assigned by a group called InterNIC. Names are assigned on a first-come, first-served basis unless the name is a registered trademark of another company (like Hertz, Avis, or McDonalds). If you want to protect your company name now—even before you are ready to go online—you can arrange to register a name with any Internet service provider, internet presence provider, or digital mall. It'll charge a one-time fee of $100 for two years. Renewal is $50. Any ISP can register your domain name.

What are those funny letters at the end of my domian name?

The extension tells you what kind of organization the name belongs to.

- .com—commercial

- .edu—educational

- .gov—government

- .mil—military

- .net—network

- .org—organization

There are proposals to add even more domains.

People in other countries, such as Germany, show an additional extension as part of their address: *Franz.Bruner@mycompany.com.de*

Other country codes are:

- au—Australia

- br—Brazil

- ca—Canada

- de—Germany

- ie—Ireland

- il—Israel

- jp—Japan

- kp—Republic of Korea

- se—Sweden

A Canadian company could register its name as mycompany.com.ca. However, this is not required.

WHAT ARE INFOBOTS?

An infobot is an e-mail version of a fax-back system. It is an automated way to reply to e-mail. When people send e-mail to an infobot's address, such as info@yourcompany.com, they receive a prewritten response immediately and automatically. This can be an effective marketing tool to tie in nicely to your print advertising campaign.

HOW DO CUSTOMERS FIND MY HOME PAGE?

Prospects find your home page by using their browser and typing your business's unique home page address (URL) or domain name.

Each store on the Web has its own address, just as in the real world. However, where your store address would be 123 Main Street, Anytown, Calif., the Web address looks like this: *www.mycompany.com*

You've seen these addresses throughout the book. Here's what the address parts mean.

- *http://* stands for hyper text transfer protocol. It tells the computer to begin looking for something.

- *www* stands for World Wide Web (but you knew that!).

- *mycompany.com* is the name of the company. Many companies choose to call their home page by their company name, like Wells Fargo, *www.wellsfargo.com*. Others do not, like Southwest Airlines, which uses its slogan, *www.iflyswa.com*. Your best bet is to use your company name as the domain name.

Companies that rent space from a digital mall, a type of Internet service provider, might have an address like:

www.digital-mall.com/vendors/ yourcompany.html.

This looks like a second-class address. You would want to ask your digital mall landlord to create an alias that would let users type *www.mycompany.com,* but the digital mall's computer would know it was really your address.

THE NEXT STEP

Now that you know the technical basics (or as much as you really need to know) and essential Internet terms, you are ready for the next chapter, which explores how to get started marketing and running a business on the Internet.

Internet Business Practices

3

ONLINE MARKETING IN A NUTSHELL

As we've seen, the Internet holds great promise for sales, but only if you know how to speak directly to the consumers in a manner consistent with their online culture. This chapter discusses:

- netiquette

- new paradigms for online marketing

- steps to opening your online store

- why isn't my site working?

- general business practices

Let's look at these important areas.

NETIQUETTE

Online consumers are a special breed. Unlike couch potatoes who don't mind the barrage of commercials hitting them when they watch TV, online consumers don't like hard-selling, image-building commercials devoid of information. They like to read and browse through information and content to make informed buying decisions. They are spending their time to be online—time that could be spent on other activities. They are also spending money to be online. With those two factors—time and money—they aren't in a mood to view junk mail.

A code of conduct called *netiquette* has developed on the Internet. This is the Golden Rule of the Internet and must be obeyed before commerce can be conducted. Some call it the etiquette of the network. I summarize it simply as "Information and advertising that is *unsolicited* is *unappreciated*." If you err on the side of politeness, you won't risk offending people. If you do offend them, you might find your e-mailbox full of nasty notes called flames that are filled with obscenities or threats to your life and your property. Yes, some people on the Internet can be nasty. They have a right to their privacy. Don't abuse it!

One reason for this code can be traced to the roots of the Internet. Scientists used it to share information. This sharing remains the overriding rule in the message boards known as mailing lists and newsgroups. People give their time and information freely, knowing they will learn from others along the way. They don't go to these areas for commercial information.

Some people have asked me whether they can post junk mail anyway because the practice isn't illegal and they have thick skins. I tell them not to and then I tell them this story:

Every night between 6 and 9 P.M. I get three to five phone calls. They are all from telemarketers selling newspapers, magazines, and insurance. They have the right to call. However, these calls interrupt my dinner and relaxation time. When I answer the phone only to hear some person mangle my last name, I am most definitely *not* in the mood to buy. I have gotten so disgusted by these calls that I either turn off the phone during those hours or don't answer it. Yes, I might miss a call from a friend, but that's the choice I make for peace and quiet. In the same manner, if junk mail floods the Internet, people won't go there anymore.

So don't muck up the environment! You'll only hurt yourself in the long run. It is perfectly fine to show your wares on your home page or Web site, or to buy advertising on another company's home page.

NEW PARADIGMS FOR ONLINE MARKETING

The Internet is a new medium, much like television was a new medium distinct from radio. When TV first came along, advertisers didn't realize they were dealing with a medium with a whole range of new capabilities. Instead, they did ads the old fashioned way—at first. They put a camera on an announcer who was seen reading a script and talking into a huge microphone, just as he would to make a radio ad. They didn't realize at that time that TV was a visual medium at its best showing pictures of people and products in action—a car cornering on a mountain road, a group of young people on the beach playing volleyball and drinking a soda, a little man standing in a little boat in a toilet bowl. Those are the images TV was meant for. The same principle is true of the Internet. We are dealing with a new medium that uses different tools to evoke different relationships with consumers.

This is especially true in regard to:

- space
- time
- image creation
- communication direction

Let's explore these concepts to gain a better understanding of how to create a message that will appeal to Internet consumers.

Space

Old advertising—Space is a commodity you buy. It is expensive and finite. No matter the standard size you buy (a thirty-second TV or radio commercial or a full-page ad in a newspaper or magazine), you have only begun to tell your story. You are forced to leave out information because of the limitations and constraints and costs of space.

New Advertising—Space is unlimited and cheap. You can post an encyclopedia's worth of information about your company and its products on the Internet for a modest amount of money. Because of this, you can tailor sales messages to different kinds of buyers: information seekers, the money-conscious, the value-oriented, and so on. If they are visual, you can post pictures and movies. If they are numbers-oriented, you can post reams of statistics. In fact, consumers can create their own sales script as they seek out information that interests them and avoid information that does not.

Time

Old Advertising—Time is a commodity you buy on TV and radio. It is expensive and limited. You have a short period of time to convey a message. Advertisers try to create an image about a company or a product through visual means because of these limitations.

New Advertising—Time is what consumers spend. It is a valuable commodity to them for two reasons: They are spending hard dollars to be online and they are spending real time away from other business or personal activities that constantly pull at them. In order to attract them to your store, hold them there, keep them coming back, and tell their friends to stop by, you must add value to their experience at your store.

 The first step is to have high-quality products and information that is displayed in an attractive manner. The second step is to add real value to the consumer's experience—value that might have only tangential reference to your product or sales or advertising as we know it today. For example:

- Wells Fargo Bank allows its customers to find their account balances online.

- Visa lets anyone read free information about how to get out of debt.

- Seattle Film Works lets people retrieve screen-saver software for free.

- Southwest Airlines has free travel information about vacation destinations it flies to.

These experiences help create goodwill with consumers that enriches the time they spend online.

Image Creation

Old Advertising—Images are created with static or motion pictures, music, lighting, and action, primarily. Information is secondary. For example:

- A cigarette manufacturer shows a film of a cowboy on a horse lighting up and creates the rugged image of the Marlboro Man.

- A sleek sports car door opens, a woman's bare leg emerges, and seductive music plays in the background as the announcer says, "The night belongs to Michelob."

- Teenagers are having fun playing volleyball at the beach and drinking Pepsi.

In each of these cases, image is created with words and pictures that trigger emotions. Information and data are not used at all.

New Advertising—Images are created with information. Because the tools for audio and video on the Internet are still fairly crude, the main way to get information across is through the printed word, of which the Internet takes full advantage. Sales scripts and product information can capitalize on hypertext, the feature that allows consumers to go from one piece of information to another at will instead of having to plow through an entire document in a linear format, from top to bottom. For example, let's say you are selling a product that can be understood on several levels, like food. You could have a picture of a piece of chocolate and a paragraph of seductive copy extolling the virtues of the dark, sensuous nature of the candy and its smooth, silky texture. However, a health-conscious person would want to know about the fat and calorie content of the product.

You can write that information as well. You can increase your sales opportunities by then showing gift box options and describing the flavors.

For a more technical product, like phone systems, you could begin by showing the phone and basic information about features, benefits, and price. That would probably be enough information for the owner of a small business. However, people buying large phone systems would have more detailed questions such as will it work with our current system? with our remote offices? The Internet allows you to create the right image right providing exactly as much information as the individual consumer needs to make a buying decision.

Communication Direction

Old Advertising—TV broadcasts images and messages to couch potatoes who sit by passively and either hear or ignore your message. If they have questions, they can't get answered immediately. For example, if a couch potato sees a picture of a car and wants to know how much it costs, he has to turn off the TV and drive to the dealer. If she sees an ad for beer and wants to know how many calories it contains, she has to turn off the TV and go to a store. Some commercials post a toll-free telephone number to call and begin a relationship in that manner, but that is the exception, rather than the rule (except, of course, for infomercials and shopping programs).

New Advertising—Consumers seek out your message. They choose to be at your cyberstore and read your information. Not only that, they expect communication to be interactive. This means the consumer can establish a line of communication with the company and find out answers to her questions quickly, if not immediately. Right now, the technology allows consumers to find information at your store and to send e-mail to your staff. You must respond as fast as possible to this message to build a relationship.

The first step is to create an email tool called an *infobot*, which is analogous to a fax-back system. In this case, the person hears or reads about your product, possibly from a print ad, and sends a message to an e-mail address. The infobot immediately and automatically sends a prewritten note to the consumer that answers most questions she would have. Of course, people will always think of a question your staff overlooked and send another note. At this point, human intervention is required. This is good, as the action begins to build a relationship between the company and consumer. From this, good marketers can create a customer for life.

Summary

The new medium requires that you understand the paradigms for creating relationships with consumers through current uses of time, space, image creation, and communication direction. Once you understand these concepts you can create your online marketing plan.

STEPS TO OPENING YOUR ONLINE STORE

Here are the essential steps to defining your marketing mission and developing a blueprint for success:

1. Decide your goals for going online.

2. Create content to achieve your goals.

3. Create art to give a nice display of information.

4. Convert content and art to HTML, a format the Web can read.

5. Connect to the Internet so people around the world can read your material.

6. Publicize and promote your Web site so customers will come to your cyberstore.

7. Make the sale.

8. Collect the money.

9. Send or deliver the product.

10. Stay connected with your customers on a regular basis.

1. Decide Your Goals for Going Online

One of the most frequent questions people ask about the Internet is "Is your home page a success?" This is a tricky question because most people don't have a definition for "success."

For some companies, the goal is clearly to make money by selling products directly. That goal can be measured. For example: We sold one hundred doodads last week and are rolling in dough. However, other home pages are designed to draw customers to retail outlets. Because store clerks don't usually ask how the customer found out about the store, Internet marketers might not know that their site is actually working! Some companies, like Kodak, don't sell products on the Web but use it to educate customers about product and show them where to buy from local leaders. Yet other vendors aren't even interested in selling products; they want to establish a brand image, like Ragu.

Your first step in determining whether your home page is a success is to define in advance what a success is. Is it money, market exposure, or something else? For example, specify the amount of money you think the site should generate and the time it should take to reach this goal.

Be realistic. Most traditional businesses say they will lose money the first two years and break even the third. Because of lowered costs of getting started and running a business on the Internet, these businesses find they can make money in a few weeks, break even in a few months, and really pull ahead in less than a year!

Use this space to write your top three goals. Be sure to use numbers so you can objectively see if you reach the goal. Then add a time frame. For example, "I want to sell $1,000 of proudcts by the end of the first six months online."

1. _____

2. _____

3. _____

Now circle the most important goal.

If you set your sights early and adjust them continuously, you'll be able to determine if your home page is a success.

2. Create Content to Achieve Your Goals

Once you know what you are trying to accomplish online, you'll need to create a home page, also called a Web site, that contains the materials that will support your marketing message. The home page describes your products or services and includes order forms so people can buy from you either via the Internet or by phone or mail. Your home page should display the material attractively so that your storefront looks inviting. A first step is to create an outline, flowchart, or storyboard that shows the content and its links.

The term "home page" is misleading. It can mean the entire Web site or the first page of the Web site. When referring to the home page as the first page or opening page it is really a table of contents or directory to your online store. The "page" is actually longer than a computer screen and can be quite lengthy. Small companies with one product can do a nice job of selling with only one long page (see Grip-It Strips, *www.grip-it.com*). Companies with more content will use additional pages—subpages—for information about products and ordering. This format gives you the ability to create chunks of information so customers can find what they need easily. The advantage is that customers can choose the information they want to read when they want to read it. They control the flow of information in a way that makes them comfortable buying from you.

The home page should contain the following lines, displayed as headlines or buttons, that link to corresponding subpages with more detailed information:

- *Name of company*

- *Mission statement*—explains what your business does and the market it serves. The statement itself should be printed in full on the opening page.

- *What you'll find here*—headlines of the information and products on your site. These headlines link to descriptions and pictures of products.

- *E-mail response form*—an interactive tool that helps people contact you directly and create a one-to-one relationship that can last for life.

- *Contact information*—your company's physical address and telephone and fax numbers.

- *Date of last update*—so people will know if anything has changed since their last visit.

- *Notice of special events*—entices people to visit your store and explore its contents.

- *Hot items*—tells people at a glance what the hot buys are this week. This information should be printed on the opening page and linked to subpages for each product.

- *What's new*—tells viewers what information has been added or changed. This information should be printed on the opening page as headlines and linked to related subpages.

- *Message from the president*—can show the true character and nature of the company in a way that gives it a personal, as opposed to impersonal, feel. The line on the opening page links to the actual message contained on a sub page.

- *Press releases*—give people a depth of understanding of the products and the company that might not be contained in sales materials. This line links to the press releases section, which can in turn include a menu page listing all the press releases.

- *Sales materials*—give broad and deep information about the products or services. This line links to the sales materials section.

- *Catalog*—shows the full range of products in your store, with descriptions, prices, and ordering information as well as transaction capabilities. This line links to the catalog section.

- *Registration form*—asks people to identify themselves so you can build relationships with them. Forms should ask only a few questions, such as name, physical address, e-mail address, and the scantiest of demographic material, as the more questions you ask, the fewer people will answer. Remember that people value their privacy and might not want to reveal their identities. If you require that people identify themselves before you allow them into your store, they might walk on by. This line links to the registration form.

- *Testimonials*—of your products and services by satisfied customers can help convince prospects to invest in your company. This line links to the testimonials section.

- *Employment notices*—show descriptions of jobs available at your company. This line links to the employment section.

- *Links to other sites*—are listings of information sources on the Internet your readers will find interesting. These links tie into other home pages.

- *Copyright notice*—protects your work.

You have the choice of creating this material yourself or hiring a marketing consultant to do some or all of the work. Fees range from $75 to $175 an hour. A modest site could take at least five to ten hours for a cost of $375 to $1,750. Pricing is very competitive and varies by region. The advertising agencies on Madison Avenue will build a dandy site for your company for $25,000 minimum. Marketers in San Francisco can build an even better one for you for about $5,000.

It is important to immerse yourself in the Internet and its culture to see what others are doing. You'll see what's working and what is lame, what was hot yesterday and cold today. You'll be able to integrate the best of what you see with your own materials. You won't waste time creating weak sites.

3. Create Art to Give a Nice Display of Information

This assemblage of content must be presented in a fashion attractive to your customers. Examples throughout the book show the character and personality of the business and creator. The best ones also show the marketing function in an enjoyable manner.

The home page is an extension of a company's marketing materials and therefore should incorporate the same colors, typefaces, themes, and messages found in the real world. Customers expect consistency from the companies they deal with. If they go online and see a radically different design, that will cause a conflict in their view of your company.

Some companies place *all* their print materials online, much to the dismay of self-appointed online experts. However, I disagree. If the material is well written, it can work online. But be careful to format the materials for the Web. That means adjusting margins, adding links, and moving pictures, if necessary. A print brochure can also be a starting point to which you add interactive elements like e-mail, registration forms, order forms, and multimedia elements.

It is important, however, to realize that large pictures and video can slow the time it takes the page to draw on the customer's computer screen. If the page takes a long time (more than forty-five seconds), customers will likely leave. You must balance the importance of art versus people's patience. If the art file is less than 10K, it will display quickly. Try reducing the number of colors in the original image to reduce the file size. Also, use the HTML command *alt=*, which will display text if the picture doesn't load. In other words, if you have a physical picture of a storefront to symbolize the online company store, use the *alt=* command to display the words "Visit our company store." Consumers will be able to find what they need quickly if you do this.

4. Convert Content and Art to HTML

After you or your marketing firm or department has created the content for your site, it must be converted into a file format the Internet can read. The format is called HTML, which stands for Hyper Text Markup Language. It is a fairly simple language to understand, as computer languages go. If you are comfortable formatting text with Microsoft Word or Word Perfect, then you can learn how to use HTML in just a few hours. A number of good books can guide you through this process, including: *Creating Commercial Web Pages*, by Laura Lemay and Brian K. Murphy, and *Creating Cool Web Pages with HTML*, by Dave Taylor.

The first HTML programs required a lot of hand-holding, but novices could create a series of attractive pages in a few hours. Fortunately, most major word processors today will let you save your original documents in HTML format by using the "save as HTML" or an equivalent. The Web will be able to read that file with all the formatting features (bold, italics, centering) and graphics you created. You can also add links to other subpages or to other Web sites. For a simple home page, this is the only program you will need! The popular Netscape browser also has an HTML editor to create and modify pages and to send the files directly to your ISP.

Several software companies produced more powerful HTML editors that give greater control over the finished work or provide attractive templates so people who can't draw a straight line can create pages that look professional. Here are several programs that I like:

- *HTML Assistant Pro*—a good editor that is easy to use. Brooklyn North Softworks, 902-493-6080, *http://brooklynnorth.com*.

- *SkiSoft's Web Publisher*—especially good at converting dozens of large files automatically and conforming to style sheets you create. This is very useful for companies with large manuals. SkiSoft Publishing, 617-863-1876, *www.skisoft.com*.

- *Hot Dog*—an all-purpose from Australia editor that is getting good reviews, *www.sausage.com*.

- *Asymetrix Web Publisher*—provides several attractive templates and a fill-in-the-blank format to create pages easily, *www.asymetrix.com*.

- *Icat*—helps put large catalogs online. The turnkey system lets you choose from hundreds of design templates that meet the needs of almost any business. Icat's software also will accept transactions. This type of software is called "shopping cart software," *www.icat.com*.

HTML is pretty easy to learn and you could do it yourself if you have the time and feel comfortable with computers. If not, you can hire an HTML artist to prepare your documents. The charge is about $75 an hour, but I expect the price to drop rapidly to about $35 an hour as every desktop publisher in the world learns how to perform this task. The costs for the conversion will depend on how many pages of material you have. For a rough estimate, plan on one hour per individual page.

5. Connect to the Internet

Now you are ready to let the world see your work! You need to connect your pages to the Internet. Please see the discussion in Chapter 2.

6. Publicize and Promote Your Web Site

Remember the saying "If you build it, they will come." If you believe this will happen to your home page, then you are living in a field of dreams. You must actively promote and publicize your home page so people can find it. If you are successful, people will tell their friends so that hundreds and thousands of potential prospects line up on your online doorstep. Fortunately, this step doesn't require a lot of money. However, it does require about five hours to get started and about an hour or two a week to prime the pump.

Here are the six essential steps to promoting your home page:

Register with search engine directories.

Link to complementary home pages.

Send press releases to reporters.

Hold contests.

Create a signature (electronic business card) that directs people to your home page and answer people's questions in newsgroups and mailing lists, the Internet's electronic bulletin boards.

Post messages to appropriate newsgroups and mailing lists.

Let's look at each of them.

REGISTER WITH SEARCH ENGINE DIRECTORIES

A search engine is a computerized index of businesses and organizations on the World Wide Web. It is an effective tool used by customers to find companies, much like the yellow pages of the telephone directory. Companies can place their listings on a search engine for free and get a direct hyperlink to their site. This is a free service because the search engine makes money selling advertising space to other companies.

Consumers can find companies by typing the name of the business, the industry or general category, or the product. For example, if you type "chocolates" the computer will show the URL for Godiva Chocolates and its competitors. You can then connect directly to Godiva's home page by clicking on the hyperlink.

The several competing directories on the Internet all will let you list your Web site for free. You should register your store on each directory. To register, do these basic steps:

1. Go to the search engine directory.

2. Go to the menu item that says *register a new site* or something similar.

3. Type in the name of your store, its Internet address, keywords that describe your products or services (e.g., a ski resort might use these keywords: ski, vacation, travel, entertainment, hobbies, sports, and romance), your email address, and a paragraph describing your products or services.

4. Click on the *submit* button.

Not only is this service free to merchants, it is also free to consumers, so there are no barriers to its use.

The most popular engines and their addresses are:

- Yahoo!   *www.yahoo.com*

- Web Crawler   *www.webcrawler.com*

- Lycos   *www.lycos.com*

- Hotbot   *www.hotbot.com*

- Excite   *www.excite.com*

- InfoSeek   *www.infoseek.com*

- AltaVista   *www.altavista.digital.com*

InfoSeek, Hotbot, AltaVista, and other search engines *automatically* search for new home pages and list them by keyword and company name. These services have tools that read opening pages and look for keywords and company descriptions. To ensure the best results, write a two-sentence company description that includes what people can find on your home page. Then place it near the top of your home page. For example:

> Dan Janal is a speaker, author, and Internet marketing consultant. You'll find lots of free articles and tips on how to market your products and services on the Internet.

Because some search engines pick up thse first two sentences automatically, the listing could look this:

> Janal Communications, *www.janal.com*. Dan Janal is a speaker, author, and Internet marketing consultant. You'll find lots of free articles and tips on how to market your products and services on the Internet.

Another way to ensure your page will be indexed properly in search engines is to use META tags, an HTML command. The syntax is:

> <META name="description" content="We specialize in grooming pink poodles.">

> <META name="keywords" content="pet grooming, Palo Alto, dog">

AltaVista will index both fields as words, so a search on either poodles or dog will match. It will also return the description with the URL. In other words, instead of showing the first couple of lines of the page, a match will look like the following:

Pink Poodles, Inc.
We specialize in grooming pink poodles.
pink.poodle.org/—size 3K—29 Feb 96

AltaVista will index the description and keywords up to a limit of 1,024 characters.

For a complete description of how to insert a META tag into your home page, read instructions in the advanced section of AltaVista, *www.altavista.digital.com.*

By listing your home page on a search engine directory, customers will be able to find you quickly and easily—and for free!

Two services will automatically register your Web site on hundreds of search engines for a fee, generally under $100. They are: Register-It, *www.register-it.com*, and Submit it! *www.submit-it.com.*

LINK TO COMPLEMENTARY HOME PAGES

You can attract new audiences to your home page if you create a link to a complementary home page. You can understand this concept easily if you've ever been to a pharmacy. My local pharmacy has a spot near the prescription counter where doctors, nurses, infant care providers, and other health professionals place their business cards. They assume that people who go to a pharmacy are concerned with their health and might be in the market for a caregiver. This tactic works well for the caregiving merchant, who spends the price of a few business cards, as well as for the pharmacy, which builds goodwill with merchants and customers by providing a service. Further, these merchants don't steal sales from the pharmacy because they don't provide the same products. Everyone wins.

The same can be true with your home page. You can expose your site to a new set of customers by creating links with other merchants' pages. For example, if you conduct eating tours of New York City, you can create a link to the home page of dozens of travel agencies. If their customers are going to New York and want to take a tour of the best ethnic restaurants in town, they'll know who to call. Good business sense requires you to create a link to those travel agencies. In this way, their customers can find out about your service while your customers learn about theirs.

To create a link, follow these steps:

1. Go to a search engine directory and find complementary sites. Our travel guide might type in the following keywords "travel, tourism, New York, restaurants, vacations, adventure, and guided tours." Be creative! Think of all possible people who would be interested in your service and where they would hang out on the Internet.

2. Send a note to the Webmaster (the person who oversees the home page) of each site asking for permission to link to her site and for her to link to your site. Common courtesy requires this step.

> Hi!
>
> I operate the Janal Communications Home Page, which contain important and interesting information for marketers Your readers would be interested in this page, and my readers would be interested in yours as well. If I put a link to your page, will you put a link to mine? The address is *www.janal.com.*
>
> Thanks!

3. When you get permission, add the link to your home page in a section with a catchy name, like "Related Sites," "Additional Information," "Related Reading," "Links to Other Home Pages," "Cool Web Sites," or "Our Favorite Home Pages." You can probably think of something more catchy than these, but they'll work!

Search for new sites every couple of weeks and send out new requests, as hundreds of new home pages go online each week.

SEND PRESS RELEASES TO REPORTERS

We live in an exciting time because the media considers the act of opening a home page news, just as a local newspaper considers the opening of a new store on Main Street news. Because cyberspace is national and international, major periodicals like the *Wall Street Journal*, *USA Today*, and *Advertising Age* list new home pages each week.

The best way to reach reporters is to send them a press release announcing the opening of your site. Here are the basic questions a press release should answer:

- What is the name of the store and its address (URL)?

- Who will the site appeal to?

- How will they benefit?

- What information, sales, and contests are at the site?

- What else makes the site special?

- What is the name, phone number, and e-mail address of the contact person so the reporter can ask for more information?

The finished press release could look like this:

For Immediate Release
Contact: Daniel Janal, 510-648-1961
dan@janal.com

Janal Communications Opens Cyberstore on World Wide Web

Danville, CA, August 1, 1997—Janal Communications, a leading provider of marketing services on the Internet, today announced it has opened its virtual storefront on the World Wide Web. The address (URL) is *www.janal.com*.

The home page contains free articles about how large and small companies can market their products and services on the Internet, such as *The Foolproof Positioning Statement.* A free copy of the *Online Marketing Update* newsletter is also available.

Readers can also participate in a monthly joke contest in which the best joke will receive a canvas tote bag from a computer show.

Viewers can also find information about Dan Janal's speaking and consulting services as well as his books and software, which include *The Online Marketing Handbook, How to Publicize High-Tech Products and Services*, and the *Publicity Builder* software program.

The site also includes links to other marketing home pages.

Founded in 1986, Janal Communications is a leading marketing and public relations agency that also provides speeches and training to corporations and associations.

Here's a template that you can use to write your own press release. Just fill in the blanks.

Your Company Opens Cyberstore on World Wide Web

Your City, State, Date—Your Company, short description, today announced it has opened its virtual storefront on the World Wide Web. The address (URL) is *www.youraddress.com*.

The Home Page contains _____. Readers can also participate in a _____ contest in which the winner receives _____ prize.

Viewers can also find information about _____. The site also includes links to _____. Founded in _____, long positioning statement.

One of the best ways to distribute press releases inexpensively is to use a press release distribution service. Two of the biggest are PR Newswire, *www.prnewswire.com*, and Business Wire, *www.businesswire.com*. For about $75, you can send a four hundred-word press release to all the reporters in a major metropolitan area, like Chicago or New York, as well as to reporters who write about a specific industry, such as computers or automobiles.

Better yet, consumers can read these press releases via the dozens of personalized news pages to which they subscribe for free (like PointCast, My Personal Yahoo!, Individual, etc.). Using this tactic, you can tell reporters and consumers about your new site.

HOLD CONTESTS

Contests are a great way to attract people to your Web site. By having a chance to win a cash prize or merchandise, people will want to come to your site. While they participate in the contest, they learn about your products and services. They just might buy something as well!

Contests serve a secondary function: You learn who is visiting your store. People who come to your store are anonymous. You don't know who they are or what their e-mail address is so you can't follow up with them. To participate in your contest, these faceless consumers MUST tell you who they are so you can send the prize to them if they win! There you have it! You've gotten their IDs!

What ideas make good contests? Lots. Here are a few: Name this site; design a logo; fill out a form that can only be completed by searching for clues on the home page (which means the consumer will learn about your company).

Prizes can be as small as $25, although some sites offer $1,000! You can also offer sample merchandise.

To promote your contest, you can send out press releases, as described above. You should also see what other companies are doing. For a list of current contests, go to the Yahoo! directory, *www.yahoo.com*, and search for contests.

CREATE A SIGNATURE (ELECTRONIC BUSINESS CARD)

A signature is a four- to eight-line message that appears at the end of an e-mail note. It can be thought of as an electronic business card. The signature is a marketing tool that directs people to your home page or retail location. It contains such basic information as your name, address, e-mail address, phone number, and mission statement. Here is an example of my signature.

Daniel Janal   *   Janal Communications   *   510-648-1961
Author, Speaker, Online Marketing Consultant
Online Marketing Handbook
101 Businesses You Can Start on the Internet
www.janal.com   dan@janal.com

For a FREE subscription to *Dan Janal's Online Marketing Magazine*,
send e-mail to Marketing@groupserver.revnet.com with the
word "join" in the text.

Your signature is automatically attached to the end of each message you send, whether it be to a newsgroup, mailing list, or private e-mail. This can be a valuable tool as you participate in discussions on the Internet's bulletin boards, which are called USENET newsgroups, and mailing lists. More than ten thousand groups exist to discuss everything under the sun from parenting to computers to travel. They can be good places to prospect for new customers. The next topic shows you how to use the groups effectively.

POST MESSAGES TO APPROPRIATE NEWSGROUPS AND MAILING LISTS

Netiquette, the etiquette of the Internet, dictates that you can't post ads in newsgroups and mailing lists. Instead, you can only answer people's questions, raise your own questions, and contribute free information to the discussion. This is a vital rule for publicizing your home page.

These restrictions are necessary because these message areas would be filled with commercials otherwise. Then no one would go there!

In this marketing strategy, you find appropriate newsgroups that would be interested in your home page and place a notice about it. Here's an example that a travel destination might place in a travel or sports recreation forum.

Check out my new home page. There's lots of information about windsurfing!

Awesome Windsurfing Trips, Inc. "California's Best Windsurfing Vacations"

www.windsurfers.com   info@windsurf.com

800-555-1212

The key word in the previous message is *information*. If you point people to information and not advertising, your message will be accepted as being positive.

Please avoid hype and overselling. Internet consumers have seen enough junk to last a lifetime. Using headlines like "Get Rich Quick" will evoke disdain rather than interest.

You can also promote free reports and white papers in the appropriate groups. Again, be sure to back up your message with information that is truly worthwhile.

You can find groups of people who could be potential clients by visiting newsgroups and mailing lists. You can get a directory of mailing lists by pointing your browser to *www.neosoft.com/Internet/paml*. You can find newgroups by searching the newsgroups listed with your ISP, or from Deja News, *www.deja.news.com*.

Because the names of some groups can be vague or misleading, remember to read messages for several days before posting a message. You might find that the group really doesn't meet your needs at all. For example, the multilevel marketing (MLM) list doesn't want to learn of new MLM programs; they want to learn how to sell more effectively. You don't want to run the risk of being flamed by the group members.

The next step is to contribute information to the people on the newsgroup. For example, if someone asks a question that you can answer intelligently, you should do so. So if you operate an herbal pharmacy and someone in the hiking newsgroup asks about treatment for poison ivy, you can offer your advice. People will see in your signature that your store sells herbal remedies. Your signature contains all the advertising that is allowed. Your message will stay visible for several days, so you could reach a large audience by contributing to the community.

If you use these tactics, you won't get stung, or worse—flamed. If you implement these publicity and marketing strategies, you'll help increase the traffic to your site. Many of these publicity and promotion methods are inexpensive. You can perform most tasks without the help of consultants. For a list of forty-five ways to build traffic to your Web site, complete with step-by-step instructions, read the *Online Marketing Handbook* by Daniel S. Janal, Van Nostrand Reinhold.

7. Make the Sale

The next step is to make the sale. You must ask for the order and make it easy for people to say "yes". Three options are:

DISPLAYING YOUR TRADITIONAL ORDERING NUMBERS

Some people want to order the old-fashioned way—on the telephone or by sending a check in the mail. To accommodate these conservative, safety-minded folks, place your address, phone number, and fax number on your home page and on ordering pages.

CREATING AN E-MAIL FORM

Customers more comfortable in cyberspace will want to ask you questions or send their credit card information via e-mail. Your HTML programmer can put a MAILTO command onto your page easily. When the customer clicks on the highlighted text, a mail window will open up, already addressed to you. He can type directly onto the page. You'll see his message appear in your mailbox. I received an order from Germany in this manner, complete with credit card information.

CREATING AN ONLINE ORDERING FORM

Your entire catalog of products can be on your home page. Place an order icon after each product description.

When customers click on the icon, they see a fill-in-the-blank order form, that they can complete and submit for processing. This form can be created and linked properly by any competent HTML artist or digital mall.

8. Collect the Money

Collecting money on the Internet can be a thorny issue today, but one which should be cleared up in a few months. A report by Dataquest, a leading computer industry research firm, shows that only 25 percent of people who have bought products online are comfortable sending their credit card information via the Internet. That means that 75 percent of consumers will not purchase products in this manner. This doesn't mean they won't order products; it just shows you have to provide customers with other means of ordering products. Here is the traditional way to collect money:

Print your address, and phone and fax numbers on your home page. People will contact you in the manner they feel most comfortable.

Here are several electronic commerce methods of taking orders:

Registration numbers—In this method, the customer gives you his credit card number over the phone line. You check out his information before he can order. If the information is correct, you supply him with a registration number, such as R1234. When he orders, he sends the registration number—not the credit card number—via e-mail or your order form.

As an added security feature, you could send e-mail to his account verifying his order. For example, "We are confirming your order for a yellow ski parka. To receive this product, please send an e-mail message. Thank you for helping us protect you from fraud."

If the person responds affirmatively, you can ship the order. If someone stole his registration number, the true owner, not the thief, would receive the confirmation note. If a fraudulent order was placed, the true owner would be able to cancel the order.

Deposits—You can ask people to send you a check that you would place in their account. As they order products, you deduct the transaction amount from the account.

Other methods for securing transactions are becoming available from such companies as Visa and Mastercard, Microsoft, and RSA. Be sure to check other home pages to see what other merchants are using, as well as visit the sites of the producers of this kind of software and service. As these security procedures are introduced and become more widely accepted, people will drop their reluctance to pay for their orders online. Other companies engaged in this business include:

- CyberCash   *www.cybercash.com*

- Digicash   *www.digicash.com*

- First Virtual Holdings   *www.fv.com*

- Mastercard   *www.mastercard.com*

- Visa   *www.visa.com*

9. Send or Deliver the Product

After you have verified the credit card information or waited for the check to clear, you can feel confident about delivering the product. To protect yourself, send the product via a carrier that requires a signature from the recipient. That way the customer cannot claim the product was never received and demand her money back. You can get a free account from Federal Express or Airborne. UPS actually charges people an annual fee in addition to the per-package charge, so I don't recommend using them. The U.S. Post Office's Express Mail Service will also get a signature from a customer. If you send a great deal of product, you can ask for discounts or lower prices from Federal Express, Airborne, and UPS.

This step can be cost-prohibitive for inexpensive items, so you might want to limit this action to costly products. In either case, you can pass along the costs of shipping and handling to the consumer.

If you have an information product (like a newsletter, report, or online research) or software program, you might want to deliver your product to the customer over the Internet to a person's e-mail box. That way you'll save the printing and postage costs, although you won't have a signature proving delivery. In a short while, several companies will have a digital notary service that provides proof that information was sent and received via e-mail.

10. Stay Connected with Your Customers

It is easier to sell products to existing customers than to hunt for new ones. Therefore, try to stay in regular contact with your customers. Consider offering them a newsletter or placing them on a mailing list so they can see your new products or learn about your sales. Be sure to ask their permission first, as netiquette dictates. If you do so, you'll be able to build a customer for life.

WHY ISN'T MY SITE WORKING?

This is one of the questions most frequently asked by frustrated merchants who ask me to review their sites. Because they are paying me good money, I spend a lot of time figuring out why they aren't making sales.

Here's a bottom ten list of the most frequent reasons.

Amateurish-looking site. A badly designed site will turn off many people. The Internet provides no innate credibility. You have to earn the trust. One way to win respect is to have a page that looks professional.

Too many links. Imagine a home page that links you to a page listing all the products, then to a page listing product categories, then to a page listing product names, then to a page listing the actual product description. All those requests would take three or four minutes to accomplish. No one would be willing to shop at your site. Yes, linking is important, but intelligent linking is the key.

Too little information. Just like the previous example, a page that has too many links and too little information will force the user to endure the slow redrawing of new pages. Prospects really have to want your product to stick around.

Too few ordering options. Many people are still afraid of sending credit card information online. You must provide for them to order in the way in which they are most comfortable: by phone, fax, and mail, as well as online ordering.

Bad products. Bad prices. Bad descriptions. If people can get the same products you sell at their local store for a better price, you'll lose the sale. If you can't compete against local merchants or premier mail-order catalogs, you'll die online. One client wondered why her canoes weren't selling—in the dead of winter.

Pictures that are too large. Large pictures take too long to display. People want to see a postage-stamp-sized picture first to whet their appetites. If they are interested, they might want to see a larger picture. Give them the *choice* of selecting the larger picture—don't force it down their screens at the first chance. One client plastered three large pictures that not only took forever to load, but were totally irrelevant to the sale process!

Distracting backgrounds. One client had a dark maroon and yellow striped motif in his logo, which he put on his site. The problem was that the maroon stripe covered the black type and made it unreadable. Other companies make similiar mistakes by using a busy background that distracts the eye.

No contact information on each page. Most sites list contact information on the opening page but don't on the product pages. This doesn't make any sense. Imagine if your prospect prints out a product page and puts it in her portfolio. When she is ready to make a buying decision, she won't know how to get in touch with you easily.

URLs that are hard to remember. Pick a URL that is memorable. The easiest is your company name. If that is already taken, add the word *company* to the end, or *this is* to the beginning, i.e., *thisiswidget.com* or *widgetcompany.com.* You might think people will bookmark your site if they are interested, but what if they saw your Mercedes Web site a few months ago when they were broke and were just window-shopping. Now they got a bonus and they are in the market but can't remember your name!

The site doesn't ask for the order! There's an old joke about a man who prays to win the lottery. Week after week he prays, and week after week he doesn't win. Finally, in frustration, he asks his Maker why he has been forsaken. Suddenly a voice from heaven shouts out, "Meet me halfway; buy a ticket." If you don't ask for the order, no one will buy. You can increase your chances of making the sale by offering incentives, like discounts, free shipping, limited time offers, and other techniques that work well in traditional marketing.

GENERAL BUSINESS PRACTICES

This section discusses the general business practices needed to operate a successful business. Because these topics are better covered in full-length books, it will also steer you to other resources to get a full understanding of operating a business.

Get Appropriate Permits

To start any business you need to get the appropriate business permits required by your state, county, and municipality. A good place to start is city hall or the county clerk's office. These offices usually have easy-to-follow information on what you need to do to comply with the law.

Consult a Lawyer

General business lawyers can save you a great deal of time, money, and hassle by advising you on how to start your business. They can alert you to local and state requirements that you might not be aware of. They can work to protect your assets. You'll want to use a general business attorney. Ask for references to find a good one.

All the advice in this book is presented openly and honestly. However, not every situation is the same. Before adopting any business strategy presented in this book, consult with an attorney specializing in business operations.

Consult an Accountant

Accountants can set up your financial records books and tell you how to operate your business efficiently. They can advise you on how to save money with financial planning and might be able to show you ways to shelter income from taxes.

Do Your Research

The best information for starting a business might be close at hand. Check out classes at the local universities and community colleges. The Small Business Administration (SBA) might be able to offer you a great deal of information for free. The local branch of SCORE (Service Corps of Retired Executives) might be able to provide you with a brain trust of experienced people willing to give advice to entrepreneurs for free.

WHAT YOU'VE LEARNED IN THIS CHAPTER

In this chapter you've gained an appreciation for netiquette, the etiquette of the Internet. You also learned how new advertising on the Internet differs from traditional advertising. We discussed the essential steps a marketer must take to create a plan for success on the Internet, important facts to list on a home page, and how to promote your store on the Internet. You also learned how to create relationships with consumers, make the sale, get the money, and deliver the product.

The next chapter shows you the business models that are making money for hundreds of companies. After that, you'll read dozens of case histories and examples of businesses that are proving the Internet is a great place to conduct business.

SOURCES OF ADDITIONAL INFORMATION

Getting Business to Come to You by Paul and Sarah Edwards and Laura Clampitt Douglas, Jeremy Tarcher.

Launching a Business on the Web, by David Cook and Deborah Sellers.

Making It On Your Own: Surviving and *Thriving on the Ups and Downs of Being Self-Employed*, by Paul and Sarah Edwards, Jeremy Tarcher.

Marketing on a Shoestring, by Jeff Davidson, John Wiley and Sons.

Online Marketing Handbook, by Daniel S. Janal, Van Nostrand Reinhold.

The Entrepreneur Magazine Small Business Advisor, John Wiley and Sons.

Working from Home: Everything You Need to Know about Living and Working Under the Same Roof, by Paul and Sarah Edwards, Jeremy Tarcher.

Working Solo, by Terri Lonier, Portico Press.

Working Solo Sourcebook, by Terri Lonier, Portico Press.

Thirty Killer Business Models

4

You don't need to reinvent the wheel to create a successful business on the Internet. You can save time and money by following in the paths of pioneers who have figured out what works.

This chapter shows you dozens of successful business models that are working today on the Internet. These aren't pipe dreams or the promise of the future but actual businesses that are profiting online. This book is designed to light the fire of your imagination and

- to spark you to think about how the Internet can help grow your current business using new business models.

- to design successful businesses in your field by adapting a successful business model from another industry.

- to dream of solutions to needs that are not being met.

The beauty of this research is that every business model can be adapted to fit businesses in many industries. The model of selling services online works, so it can help many different service professionals, from lawyers to accountants. The model of collecting leads and selling them to local merchants works for mortgage brokers as well as insurance salespeople.

My goal in writing this chapter was to uncover as many business models as possible and show examples of companies that have achieved success using them.

Your goal should be to think "How can this business model help my business? Could part of the model work? Can I clone this model exactly as it appears in the book and run with it to make my business grow? Should part of the model be tweaked?"

1. VIRTUAL STORE

A virtual store conducts business only on the Internet. It does not have an office on Main Street. Some of the most successful businesses online follow this model.

- **Amazon Books**, *www.amazon.com*, has $17 million in annual sales and grows at 34 percent a month. Forty-four percent of its business comes from repeat customers.

- **software.net,** *www.software.net*, sells more than $7 million of shrink-wrapped software a year, both in packaged form sent to customers via overnight mail and by electronic download. The company found it could also make significant income by selling advertising packages and taking advantage of manufacturers' co-op dollar campaigns. Read the case study in chapter 16.

- **Virtual Vineyards**, *www.virtualvin.com*, is another online success story, but the company doesn't reveal sales figures.

- **Internet Shopping Network**, *www.internet.net*, features 35,000 computer products from 700 manufacturers and does more than $1 million in sales per month.

Forrester Research estimates $518 million worth of online sales overall in 1996 and that the figure will grow to $6.6 billion by 2000.

This is a great business model to follow, especially if you are looking to start a part-time business on the Internet. The beauty of this kind of business is that start-up costs are very low. You basically create a Web site that advertises your product. Here's the key: You don't keep the product in stock. You wait until the sales come in; *then* you call your distributor (with whom you've created a relationship before going online) and have it send the product directly to your customer. You pay the distributor and keep the rest of what you charged. You don't have to pay for shipping, handling, inventory,warehousing or the cost of borrowing money!

Because your costs and overhead are lower than those experienced by retail stores in the real world, you can create a competitive advantage by offering lower prices than traditional stores.

You're probably wondering what products sell best on the Internet. Surveys show that the top sellers are travel and entertainment, books, CDs, computer hardware and software, and men's and women's clothing.

In my research I've found that the main reason people buy things on the Web is because they can't find the product in the real world. The Hot! Hot! Hot! Company in Pasadena, California, *www.hothothot.com*, sells hundreds of thousands of dollars' worth of salsas and hot sauces from its Web site (about 25 percent of its income). The sauces sell for less than $20, which makes them affordable. The reason people buy these condiments on the Web is because they can't find the variety they want in their local stores in Kansas. Price is not a factor—scarcity is.

When you think about what products to sell at your site, think of what is scarce or hard to find. That's why people in Arizona buy maple syrup from Vermont. Specialty products and regional items offer great potential for sales. Price is not a critical factor in sales if the product is hard to find.

I interviewed a bike shop owner who thought he'd make a killing by selling low-end bikes on the Internet because he could adopt the virtual store model—that is, not order the product until he had sold it so he could pass along savings to customers. He thought he'd sell millions of low-cost bikes.

That wasn't the case. No one ordered low-priced bikes because anyone in any small town in America can go to K-Mart or Sears and buy an inexpensive two-wheeler and ride it the same day. Instant gratification. The Web offered insufficient competitive advantages.

However, the story has a happy ending. The bike shop owner found that people bought the high-end, $3,000 super duper bicycles. Why? Because people in small towns don't have bike stores that service the high end. Not only did he make sales on the Web, he enjoyed a higher profit margin on the high-end bikes.

To operate a successful virtual business, you need to promote the business, stand out from the crowd, and offer unusual products.

As the Web becomes increasingly crowded, you will need to establish brand identity and credibility for your company. After all, if you were a consumer (and you are!), would you rather buy a book from a company you had not heard of or the Barnes and Noble Web site? Where do you think you'd get better customer service? As the Web grows, small companies will need to be on guard against the competition from established companies in the real world who set up Web sites. Right now there is a window of opportunity, as these four examples show.

2. REAL-WORLD STORE SELLING PRODUCTS ON THE WEB

Companies that sell products in the real world use the Internet to widen their sales territory. In this case, stores on Main Street are no longer dependent on the foot traffic in front of their store. They can sell products to anyone in the state, the country, or the world—pending tariffs and a certain amount of red tape! For companies that have direct mail or catalogs, the Web is a logical extension of their business.

- Egghead Software, *www.egghead.com*, sells software online and in dozens of stores in malls across America.

- Milne Jewelry Company, *www.xmission.com/~turq*, sells Southwestern jewelry in retail stores as well as on the Web. Someone noticed a significant volume of orders from Japan and Germany. In fact, those orders were for higher dollar amounts than orders from American customers! So the company did the next logical thing. It translated its pages into Japanese and German. When you go to its home page, you can click on a link to read the information in those languages. Talk about user-friendly pages! For more information, please read the case study in Chapter 5.

- Frederick's of Hollywood, *www.fredericks.com*, posted a two-hundred-page catolog on the Web and sold twenty times the dollar amount it cost to create and host the site in just one month. Surprisingly, half the buyers were male.

If you adopt this model, your store will never close. As with any Web-based business, people can read your materials and place orders twenty-four hours a day. You can make additional income as more people in more markets learn about and order products online.

A Web site is a test marketer's dream. Whereas a paper catalog is limited by expensive printing and postage costs, these limitations don't exist on the Web. You can highlight and promote a variety of products as well as describe your complete inventory, not just the few products that fit into your print catalog. You can create gift boxes for each holiday or special event. Using the latest technologies, your customer can create a customized catalog that shows only the products she's interested in.

You can also make money in this business model by selling co-op advertising space to the producers of the products you feature.

3. EXISTING STORE ADVERTISING ONLINE BUT SELLING PRODUCTS AT REAL-WORLD STORES ONLY

Some real-world businesses don't want to sell products online; they merely want to advertise their wares to build foot traffic to their stores on Main Street.

Nine Lives Clothing, *www.los-gatos.ca.us/nine.html*, sells used clothing from a store in Los Gatos, California, not on the Web. Why not? The company feels that the returns would be too high because people can't try on the clothes and the colors might have faded so that the customer's idea of "blue" and the product's advertised color don't match. The profit margin on these clothes is small, so the store can't afford to have a lot of returns. To read about this company's success, please turn to chapter 5.

4. PRODUCT AUCTION

Online auctions sell every kind of product under the sun, from computer products to travel vacations.

Onsale, *www.onsale.com*, was one of the first of this kind of company. People visit the site, look at products, and make bids. After a given time period, the auction is over and the product is sold. Many items are offered at any given time.

Auctions make money by charging the seller a fee of 25¢ to $2 to list a product. They make a 5 percent commission up to $25 and a 2.5 percent commission if the product is sold above that amount.

Some auction houses list two thousand new products a day, which could translate to about $3 million in fees and commissions a month.

One auction house reported an average sale of $30, but prices depend on the kind of products offered. One of the most expensive sales concerned the 1959 "Suburban Shopper Barbie" doll, which sold for $7,999 at Auction Web, *www.ebkayt.com*. The seller had been hoping to receive only $2,000.

Links:

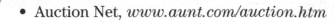

- Auction Net, *www.aunt.com/auction.htm*
- Hobby Market Online, *www.hobbymarkets.com*

5. PERFORMING ONLINE SERVICE

If your company provides a service that can be performed solely online, you can build a business around it.

- Secure Tax, *www.secure.tax.com*, lets customers prepare and file their IRS tax forms online. Ironically, service is advertised in daily newspapers that lead people to the Web site. Consumers can try the service for free. If they like it, they pay a fee.

- You First Health Assessment, *www.youfirst.com*, offers a personalized, confidential health risk assessment. Users answer questions about their family history, lifestyle, and health; these individual answers are compared to general population data to arrive at projectable health risks. You First reports are immediate and confidential, compare chronological age and risk age, and include a prioritized explanation of health factors. The service is provided by Greenstone Healthcare Solutions, a "disease management consulting company" and subsidiary of Pharmacia Upjohn, Inc.

- Submit It!, *www.submit-it.com*, registers Web sites with search engines for a fee. It claims to have processed more than one milion sites.

6. PROMOTING A SERVICE ONLINE BUT PERFORMING IT IN THE REAL WORLD

A good number of services can't be performed online. Dentists can't fill a cavity online no matter how good the technology is! And a plumber can't fix a leaky faucet via the Web. However, all service providers can go online to advertise and promote their businesses and lead people to make appointments.

- Steven L. Kessler, *www.janal/com.kessler.html*, is a New York City attorney who is one of the country's experts in civil forfeiture and racketeering law. His Web site includes his curriculum vitae (a very long and impressive résumé) and several articles he has written for the *New York State Bar Journal*, as well as information about law books he has written. He promoted his site only by registering it with the Yahoo search engine. As a result, he has received networking phone calls from dozens of attorneys, including two who presented cases at the U.S. Supreme Court, the editor of a legal trade publication who asked him to write an article, and from numerous prospects who had questions about the law.

- The Plumber, *www.theplumber.com*, has a unique Web site in which questions about plumbing are addressed. The site even has a FAQ file. This technique can help build the trust and credibility that is essential when hiring a tradesperson.

7. SERVICE HYBRID

Service providers can conduct business both online and in the real world. For example, you could provide some part of the business service online and the rest offline. You might get leads from new business online and perform the service in the real world.

For example, I review Web sites and suggest ways to improve the marketing components so companies can make more money. I promote the service on my home page. People contact me via e-mail or the phone. I review their site using the Internet. Then I send them a report via e-mail and discuss the findings over the phone. For information on having your site critiqued, go to *www.janal.com/webreview.html*.

8. SERVICE AUCTION

One of the most innovative business models in the online world is that of conducting an auction for services.

TravelBids, *www.travelbids.com*, is a travel discount auction composed of the Airfare Auction, Resort Auction, and Cruise Auction. It provides a legal and ethical way to save 6–12 percent (and sometimes more) on your next trip. Simply make a reservation yourself directly with any airline, resort, or cruise company, but don't pay or give them your credit card. Then list your trip here. Many travel agents from around the United States then bid on your business, and the winning agent will take over your existing reservation and issue the ticket to you. You'll receive the largest possible discount as a result!

The company makes money by charging travelers $5 per listing. Travel agents pay $15 per bid.

Travel agents want this business because they don't have to advertise or spend time holding your hand to create the trip. They save time and make money.

Large travel companies also use this model. Look at The Savvier Traveler, *www.savtraveler.com* for discounts on cruises. American Express, *www.americanexpress.com/travel* offers cruise discounts not available at their retail outlets.

9. REFERRAL NETWORK

One of the truly great online business models is the referral network model. Its initiator was Amazon Books, *www.amazon.com*, whose "Associates Program" allows people who have Web sites to make money by selling books. Each salesperson or "associate" places book reviews and notices on his Web site. Each review has a hyperlink to Amazon. This link includes the ISBN number of the book and the associate's identification number.

If a person reads a review on the associate's home page and clicks through to Amazon and buys the book, the associate gets an 8 percent commission. Amazon handles all paperwork and shipping. It costs nothing to become an associate, although one must comply with marketing and licensing requirements, which include putting some sales information and an Amazon logo on their pages. Amazon provides all the HTML coding and artwork. Because this information is sent via e-mail, Amazon doesn't have to pay printing or postage fees.

As of February 1, 1997, Amazon had six thousand associates. In essence, the company has salespeople all over the world who are selling its books, yet it cost Amazon next to nothing to create this sales force (except programming time and management skills). Certainly this is a small price to pay compared to hiring a six-thousand-person sales force and supplying it with hard copy literature and sales aids!

People learn of the Associates Program when they visit the Amazon home page.

Think of the possibilities. As a marketer, I can review or list books about marketing, advertising and public relations at my Web site. A teenager can review her favorite novels. A person with a hobby like cooking, gardening, or fishing can review his favorite niche books. We all can make money for our efforts. Meanwhile, Amazon gets free advertising on thousands of sites marketing to targeted niches.

Now take this business model and adapt it to your business. My publisher, Van Nostrand Reinhold, learned of this technique and now operates its own associates program. For information on getting commissions for sales of books from Van Nostrand Reinhold, go to *www.vnr.com*.

10. GENERIC MALL

In the real world, malls serve as magnets to attract people to a variety of shops catering to many needs and wants. Online entrepreneurs are adapting this paradigm to the Web. There are two types of malls: generic and thematic (which could include a hobby, profession or geographic location).

Generic malls take any business as a client. This might be a great idea if you believe a greater number of stores attracts more customers. However, both companies that might want to rent space from a mall owner and the mall owners themselves should consider a number of factors. For a case study on The Internet Mall, please see chapter 17. For links, check out *www.halcyon.com*.

Malls can attract a great number of people if the mall operator does a good job of promoting the site. That's a big if. Before signing up with a mall, find out its plan for advertising your site as well as the mall itself.

Look at the design of the mall interface. Is it easy to find each store? Are stores listed by category or by company name? If the former is true, you could benefit from the synergy of someone looking for the same kind of product. You could win the sale by offering the right product or price. If the latter, your listing could be next to two hundred other companies with absolutely no synergy. Believe me, no one has time to look at two hundred companies. The companies beginning with the letter *A* will get a lot of visits, but the *P*s probably won't.

If you investigate malls, make sure there aren't charges for number of visitors, amount of data moved or advertising services, or a percentage of sales going to the mall operator. After all, what are you getting for your money? If a mall charges for any of these features you should seriously think of putting up your own site, because the mall isn't bringing any benefits to the table.

If you are thinking about creating a mall and selling space to vendors, make sure to provide value-added services to your clients, or there is no reason for them to sign up with you instead of going it alone. You can make money by creating Web pages, adding additional services, like audio and video, charging for links from the mall to an existing home page, selling advertising, and selling promotional programs.

Yet another way to make money is to grow a substantial business and sell out. HitCom Corp. has signed a letter of intent to purchase Virtual Cape Cod, a Cape Cod, Massachusetts–based city information guide, *www. virtualcapecod.com*, from Azotus Technologies, Inc. Terms were not announced, but Anthony Hitt, chairman of HitCom, said it was a combination of cash and stock. HitCom anticipates adding $240,000 to its 1997 sales as a result of the acquisition.

11. THEME MALL: GEOGRAPHIC, PROFESSIONAL AND HOBBY

A *geographic mall* is one in which an entrepreneur creates a Web site around the theme of a specific location. The mall owner makes money by selling space on the site to merchants in the geographical area. Additional fee-based services could include Web page creation and updating and links to existing pages. The mall operator is responsible for marketing the site as well, although individual merchants will benefit if they do additional promotional work. This idea works because tourists going to a particular destination are interested in a variety of services, like lodging, restaurants, and sight-seeing. It is a great idea to link all these service providers together.

Good examples of geographic malls are:

- Eureka Springs   *www.virtualeureka.com*

- Santa Fe Food/art   *www.interart.net/default.html*

- Maui Net   *www.maui.net*

A variation on this theme is to create a mall featuring service professionals in a specific industry, like law, The Seamless Website, *www.seamless.com*, or speakers, Expertise Center, *www.expertcenter.com*. These malls can be effective because a customer can choose among a variety of professionals. In the case of speakers, a meeting planner might search for a keynote speaker and then find additional speakers to teach assorted seminars. The mall can be a one-stop shopping center for the meeting planner.

Another model that works is the mall based on a hobby, like sailing. Such a site can feature Web pages and ads that cater to the boating enthusiast. For a case study, read about MarineMart, *www.marinemart.com*, in Chapter 5.

In all these cases, owners of online malls can make money by:

- Creating a complete home page for the client who doesn't have one and charging for the service as well as updates.

- Adding a link to a client's current home page and charging for it. Clients who have their own sites might want to pay for a link from the mall site to attract more prospects.

- Selling advertising to sponsors who want to reach the target audience.

12. VIRTUAL TRADE SHOW, CONFERENCE, AND EXPOSITION

Virtual trade shows are online extensions of conferences in the real world. They can also exist only online. In this model, you create a trade show around a theme and sell advertising, home pages, and links to existing home pages to vendors. You must convince them you can attract a large audience of qualified customers. In many ways this model is the same as a thematic mall, but calling it a "virtual trade show" might sound more interesting and hipper than competing malls.

This model offers benefits to exhibitors:

- It reaches consumers who couldn't attend the actual event.

- Attendees of the real show can view sales material beforehand so they can map out their agendas, plan to visit booths, and make appointments to talk to salespeople.

- If the site stays up after the show, the same attendees can retrieve sales and marketing data they are truly interested in.

- It accommodates companies that couldn't afford to exhibit at the real trade show. These companies benefit by gaining exposure to the targeted audience. After all, prospects don't care if you actually exhibit at the show; they are interested in seeing the product in action and talking to a salesperson. These two activities can take place anywhere at any time.

For an example, see Promotional Products Association, *www.trdeshow. ppa.org*.

Online trade shows can make money by selling portions of the educational seminars via the online medium. Jupiter Communications and Audionet presented the seminar portion of the Consumer Online Services IV Conference in New York City live on the Internet. The fee was $99, half the price of a hotel room in the Big Apple, a bargain by anyone's standards. Online attendees could see the Virtual Exhibit Hall, chat with other online participants, and submit questions to panelists via e-mail.

To promote the online portion of the conference, Jupiter and Audionet sent e-mail to targeted lists. The announcement told of the offer, its benefits, and listed the speakers and their companies. Additional information and registration material could be found on the Web site, which appeared as a live link.

13. SUBSCRIPTION

Most general-interest print publications have not succeeded in charging a subscription price for online editions. That's because consumers can find similar information (headlines, stock quotes, company financial information) free on the Web. Companies that tried to charge for subscriptions but dropped the idea after failing to get enough subscribers include the

New York Times, *USA Today*, and *Utne Reader* (which went off the Web entirely). ESPNET Sportszone offers free articles *and* a subscription service.

One of the few examples of a company selling subscriptions is the *Wall Street Journal Interactive*, *www.wsj.com*, which counts more than seventy thousand subscribers. However, the fee is very low. Subscribers to the print edition pay $29.95 a year for the online editions. Subscribers to the online edition only pay $49.95. That really says something about pricing if one of the great names in journalism can't charge more than $50 a year for its material!

Jupiter Research predicts that online subscriptions will grow from $120 million in 1997 to $966 million in 2000.

A Newspaper Association of America (NAA) survey of newspapers with Web sites finds 36 percent reporting they made money in 1996 or will do so in 1997. Another 24 percent said they will be profitable within four years. Companies that are profitable generate revenue from multiple sources: subscriptions, advertising, Internet access and Web hosting, and premium-priced products, according to the NAA.

Despite the warning, it *is* possible to make money with the subscription model. Information must:

- be highly valued
- be hard to find
- meet the needs of an audience that has funds to spend
- be reasonably priced

Let's look at the Knight Ridder Information Company's ScienceBase product, *www.krinfo.com/dialog/krinfo/scibase.html*.

KR ScienceBase is designed to help research scientists and managers in the pharmaceutical, chemical, and biotechnology industries gain a competitive edge by easily and economically conducting detailed searches across a broad range of databases that currently access over 1.5 million titles from some of the world's most prestigious libraries and research institutions, including scientific and related collections from such renowned sources as the Royal Society of Chemistry, the U.S. National Library of Medicine, and the U.S. Patent and Trademark Office.

Scientists use keywords to search thousands of periodicals to find articles that match their interests. They can search for all articles written about asthma research printed in Germany and France in the last six months and find the citations; the process takes mere seconds. They can read the titles and citations for free. To read the entire article requires an additional charge, usually a nominal fee—from a nickel to three dollars. Knight Ridder shares these proceeds with the original publisher of the work. The fee for this service is a monthly subscription charge of $50, which includes an unlimited number of searches. The service works because it follows the four basic rules: targeted material, hard-to-find information, targeted audience, and reasonable fee.

This model works for adult sites as well. These generally charge a monthly fee against a credit card. Discounts are given for longer-term subscriptions, (e.g., a monthly fee is $9.95, the annual fee might be $99 instead of $120.)

14. PAY-PER-VIEW

Companies that can't get people to pay for subscriptions for a lengthy time period can make money by selling access to their Web sites on a pay-per-view basis.

Real Voices, *www.realvoices.com*, allows customers to listen to motivational and inspirational tapes via the Internet. People pay a one-time fee to listen one time.

Adult sites also use this business model. Customers can access their services on the spur of the moment and not make a long-term commitment to a subscription.

Game sites use this model as well. The Arena, a Web-based multiplayer gaming environment available on Earthlink, *www.earthlink.com*, charges $2.75 per hour.

15. CREATING EDITORIAL CONTENT AND SELLING ADVERTISING

Companies are garning profits by selling advertising space on their Web site. While only a handful of companies are making serious money at this today, as the Web audience grows ad sales can become a significant source of revenues for companies that can deliver targeted prospects. Advertising revenue on the Web will grow from $312 million in 1997 to $5 billion in 2000, according to Jupiter Research.

Two Web sites that offer outstanding content and interactivity to gain repeat audiences are:

- Smart Business Supersite, *www.smartbiz.com*. For a case history on this company, please see Chapter 8.

- Parent Soup, *www.parentsoup.com*.

The biggest winners in the advertising game seem to be search engines and content sites. According to *Netscape World* (May 1997), the largest companies receiving advertising revenue in the second quarter of 1996 were:

- Netscape $27.7 million   default page for most users

- Infoseek $18.1 million   search engine

- Yahoo $20.6 million   search engine

- Excite $12.2 million   search engine

- Lycos $12.8 million   original content

- Cnet $11.4 million   original content

- Zdnet $10.2 million   original content
- Web Crawler $7.3 million   search engine
- ESPNET Sportszone $6.3 million   original content

16. AGGREGATOR

An aggregator is a company that attracts an audience by providing them with links to targeted services, like games, news, information, or software. Happy Puppy, *www.happypuppy.com*, is one of the most active sites on the Web. It has links to dozens of online games. Shareware.com, www.shareware.com, has links to thousands of shareware programs. The Public Relations Society of America's Technology Section, *www.prsa.org*, has links to dozens of daily newspapers, phone books, maps, PR agencies, and advertising agencies.

Aggregators make money by selling advertising on their pages. Some might charge for links to additional sites, but most provide them for free because the more information and sites an aggregator's site has, the more valuable it is to the audience.

It is important to respect the copyright and intellectual property rights of the linked site. Aggregators do not reprint material on their sites and represent it as their own. Be aware that a controversy is brewing in this area. Unscrupulous businesses *are* displaying copyrighted content on their sites and selling advertising. The original copyright holder is deprived of this income. She also misses the opportunity to interact with the reader and is thus deprived of the chance to add his name to her database and initiate a long-lasting relationship. This is a serious threat to the copyright holder, who loses both current and future income. Expect this area to be fraught with controversy in the near term.

17. CREATING SERVICE CONTENT AND SELLING ADVERTISING

Providing a worthwhile service online that attracts great numbers of people allows you to create a business that makes money by selling advertisements to companies that want to reach your audience. Examples of online services include those that provide road maps and routing directions (Mapquest, *www.mapquest.com*) or phone numbers and e-mail addresses (Four 11, *www.four11.com*). Several companies offer free e-mail services to ensure people come to their site regularly. While users view and compose mail, they are exposed to advertisements. Two companies that follow this model are Juno *www.junomail.com*, and Rocket Mail, *www.rocketmail.com*.

18. CREATING AN E-MAIL NEWSLETTER AND SELLING SPONSORSHIPS

Making money online is not limited to Web sites. You can create a newsletter for a targeted audience and distribute it via e-mail. Because eighty-nine million people have e-mail and about twenty-five million have access to the Web, according to *Business Week* (May 5th, 1997), you can reach a substantial number of people in this manner.

This business model can work for any company trying to drum up new leads and increase traffic to its Web site. Here's the plan:

1. Create a five-hundred-word newsletter that offers real content, not fluff or advertisements.

2. Add a fifty-word advertisement promoting your services; include links to your Web site and e-mail address (as well as a phone number for people who won't order via the Web). Example: This newsletter is sponsored by Smart Computer Systems, the leading provider of quality computers for small offices. Visit us at

www.smartcomputersystemsxx.com, send e-mail to smart@ x.com, or call 800-555-1212. Mention this ad and receive a free pocket protector.

3. Create a mailing list of people who have asked you for information in the past. It is vitally important that these people *opt in* (the hot new term of the day, which really means ask to subscribe) so you don't violate netiquette.

4. Be sure to include subscribing and unsubscribing options. I prefer the short and sweet "to subscribe, send a note to you@yourcompany.com and type *subscribe newsletter name* in the subject box." To test various marketing messages, change the message to read "subscribe marketing" or "subscribe marketing 2."

5. Critically important: Encourage people to forward the newsletter to their friends. This message helps you take advantage of the goodwill of your readers.

6. Emphasize that the newsletter is free.

There's no telling how many people will eventually subscribe to your newsletter, but if previous history is any example, it could be huge. Industry analyst Robert Seidman's newsletter reached so many people (and the right ones) that *NetGuide* magazine offered him a column!

(Author's Note: You can subscribe to *Dan Janal's Online Marketing Magazine* by sending e-mail to *marketing@groupserver.revnet.com* and typing "join" in the message.)

Once you have built a substantial subscriber base, you can sell sponsorships or advertisements to companies that want to reach that marketplace.

In the immature phase of pricing on the Internet, publishers are charging a wide range of prices, ranging from $ 25–50 per thousand readers on the low end to hundreds of dollars on the high side. Publishers can claim larger fees if they can show they have highly targeted audiences.

19. SELLING LEADS FOR TANGIBLE PRODUCTS *MIDDLE MAN*

A new crop of virtual businesses is making a ton of money by performing the services of middlemen. They attract customers who are interested in buying a product, like a car, airline tickets or a mortgage, and then find companies that want to do business with them. The online company attracts customers by offering fast access to information and the ability to compare rival services. The formal marketing term for this trend is *disintermediation*.

 Auto-by-Tel, *www.autobytel.com*, arranges for the purchase of cars. Consumers go to the Web site and fill out a form that lists the kind of car they want to buy as well as the options. Auto-by-Tel finds a local auto dealer, negotiates the best possible price, and notifies the consumer. If the consumer wants to buy the car, she can go to the dealer and complete the financing. There is no haggling over price.

Auto-by-Tel makes its money by charging dealers $500–$1,500 a month for leads in addition to an initial subscription fee ranging between $2,500 and $4,500. Dealers benefit because the cost of a sale drops to $25 from $425 and because the number of salespeople required to close the deal is reduced, according to the National Automotive Dealers Association.

The company has 1,945 dealers in its network. It processed forty thousand vehicle purchase requests in December 1996.

Companies that adopt this model can make money by charging the merchants and/or the customer.

A rival firm, AutoVantage, *www.cuc.com/ctg/cgi-bin/Auto/home*, operated by CUC International, a very large membership club that also sells products and travel services online and in the real world, posts testimonials from users who say they have saved $2,500–$4,000 by using the service.

Middlemen across the country live in fear of this Internet business model. They are afraid the Internet can replace their services by taking leads from the Internet and giving them directly to the competing online company. Parts of their fear might be real, but there is nothing from stopping THEM from creating this type of service!

20. SELLING LEADS FOR INTANGIBLE PRODUCTS

Companies in the service industries, such as insurance, are gathering qualified leads online and selling those names (with permission of the prospect) to local agents. Quotesmith, *www.quotesmith.com*, provides instant term life quotes from 130 leading companies. Consumers can find the lowest quotes when buying or renewing policies. They can even apply online to the company of their choice without having to deal with a salesperson. The service is free to the consumer. In this model, the companies that get the leads and make the sales pay a fee to the site promoter.

Other industries that can use this model include mutual funds and stocks and any other business that needs to bring buyer and seller together.

21. SELLING CLASSIFIED ADVERTISING

Companies can make money by creating classified ads that reach a target market. Entrepreneurs charge the buyer, seller, or both. If the site attracts a good number of visitors, the owner can sell advertising to companies that want to reach these markets. For example, Career Mosaic, www.careermosaic.com, charges companies to list new job postings. People looking for jobs can search for free. Numerous dating services charge both the placer of the ad and persons looking for dates.

22. TRANSACTION SERVICE

Companies that make money from transactions, like stockbrokers, can offer their services online. Because technology reduces the cost of placing orders and handling paperwork as well as decreases the need for stockbrokers who offer information, online stock trading firms can offer much lower commission rates on trades. They can eat the other guys' lunch. E-trade, *www.etrade.com*, is a discount brokerage that exists only online and offers trades for about $29.95, a figure that pales in comparison to what a full broker or even a discount broker charges. There's always room for competition, as Datek, *www.datek.com*, charges only $9.95 for a trade!

23. ADVERTORIAL SERVICE

Advertorials are ads masquerading as editorial copy. If a reader were to visit such a Web site, she would think impartial reporters and reviewers wrote the articles. In reality, staff members of the promotion firm that created the site write the product reviews. Companies employing this business model appear to be editorially independent but are actually funded by the advertisers. In other words, if you don't advertise, your product won't be listed. There is nothing illegal about this business model, but careful marketers should state that the site features clients' products and should not be confused with an unbiased magazine. Advertorials exist in the real world as well. You see them as inserts in the best publications, including *Business Week* and *USA Today*. The layouts are similar to the regular part of the magazine but the word *advertisement* is usually printed somewhere on the page. On the Web there are no such restrictions.

24. CREATING STANDARDS

Software and technology vendors seek to create long-term equity by creating standards on the Web based on their products. Companies like Real Audio and Netscape have given away millions of copies of their products for free so that consumers and businesses standardize on them. As the large base is set, expensive tools are sold to companies to create content that can be accessed only with the free software.

Ex.

For example, Real Audio created a standard in the way sound files are transmitted over the Internet. Companies that want to broadcast news reports, music, sports programming, or religious services pay a fee to Real Audio to create and distribute their content programs. (These companies make money by selling advertising.)

Expect to see this business model used by companies trying to set standards in teleconferencing, video, and other applications. PointCast, Real Audio, VocalTel, HotDog (an HTML editor), and Netscape all used this model so successfully that they were able to sell products in retail stores—even though free versions were available online! PointCast sold seventy thousand units at retail from November 1996 to February 1997 and had downloaded more than one million copies online.

25. GIVING AWAY FREE SAMPLES

People love getting something for free in real life as well as on the Internet. Many software companies give away free demo or trial versions of their products in the hopes that prospects will turn into buyers.

Hard goods companies also benefit from this model. Seattle Film Works gives away free rolls of film. FREEZ-IT, *www.freezit.com*, gave away more than ten thousand samples of its face cream. Another benefit of this marketing approach is that you'll create a valuable database of prospects that can be used for other marketing purposes (provided you have asked them for permission to rent out their names and e-mail addresses, as is proper netiquette).

26. THINKING OUTSIDE THE BOX ON NEW TECHNOLOGIES

Take advantage of the new technology of the Internet and create new businesses. Alternatively, look for new markets for the technology.

For example, E-Snail from Stak International Corporation, *www. infoc@www.stack.com*, puts an electronic twist on traditional paper mail. The company offers a service that sends e-mail messages to a printer in Colorado who forwards the hard copies via the United States Postal Service. The service helps people in foreign countries send mail to the United States faster and less expensively than using their own government's mail services.

Faxaway, *www.faxaway.com* lets users send e-mail, which is converted to faxes, anywhere in the world for savings of up to 90 percent off phone rates.

Safeguard's Net Tape, *www.sgii.com/products.html*, lets users back up their computer files onto the Internet. If their computer crashes, there's a copy stored off site.

27. EXPLORING A NICHE

One easy way to create a successful business plan on the Internet or in real life is to find a model that works in one market (professional, geographic, or otherwise) and refine it for your market. For example, a mall that specializes in products for Kwanza, could lead you to think of creating a mall that sells products for Cinco de Mayo. A travel service on the Web catering to one target group, like gays, could lead to a similar business that targets single mothers. The list is endless. So look back at all these wonderful business models and find the ones that are compatible with your special interests and talents. Then think, "Which one can I customize to meet the needs of an audience I love to serve?"

A friend of mine told me his wife wanted to start a gift basket business online I told him there were twelve hundred similar businesses online and she wouldn't stand a chance. However, she had an angle—she was diabetic. Not one of the other businesses catered to diabetics, who can't eat sugar! She can sell gift baskets filled with healthy foods suitable for diabetics.

The moral here is to find a successful business, then target it to meet a significantly sized audience. If the audience is large, you will have a lot of imitators trying to carve up the market. But if you select a subset of that market, the big guys might not want to compete with you, as the rewards are too small for them to care.

28. FRANCHISE

If you develop a good business model on the Internet, you might be able to sell franchises to other entrepreneurs.

U.S. Web, *www.usweb.com*, is a franchise that sells Internet service provider, and Web development services. Backed by the huge Ziff-Davis company and others, U.S. Web is competing with local ISPs and design shops by offering customers a standard of quality for service and a trusted name.

29. SELLING OUT!

Building a successful business on the web could lead to an offer of a buyout by a larger company.

- Modem Media, an advertising agency, sold out to a larger advertising agency for an undisclosed amount, rumored to be twenty million dollars.

- CCNET, my local ISP, created a business with about seven thousand subscribers. It sold out to a larger company, Verío, which also bought other local ISPs. ISPs generally are valued at $20 per subscriber, so the deal might have been worth $140,000.

Entrepreneurial companies with hot technologies could also be takeover candidates.

30. GOING PUBLIC

Two Stanford University graduate students created Yahoo!, the ubiquitous search engine, as a hobby. As the Web grew, they accepted venture capital to grow the business. In 1996 the company went public, which made the founders millionaires. On Valentine's Day 1997, founders David Filo and Jerry Yang held stock worth $140 million.

SUMMARY

Is it too late to start a business? Not at all. For every opportunity listed here, there are probably ten more that haven't even been dreamed up yet. As more people go online, as more technologies mature, the opportunities for building and growing businesses will explode.

Yet there are practical considerations to account for. Every business plan can be copied. The advantages that Amazon created in the bookselling field can be easily cloned by large, well-known booksellers like Barnes and Noble or Borders. The unique service of Auto-by-Tel was copied quickly by AutoVantage.

But all these companies seem to be prospering. As the tide of consumers coming online rises, it seems to raise all boats. But remember: You can never expect to coast and grow. There'll always be someone trying to do what you do—only better.

Case Studies

OVERVIEW

Now that you have an overview of reasons you should open a business on the Internet, ways to think like an online marketer, have the basic tools to promote your business, and exposure to numerous examples of successful business models, it is time to explore the large number of enterprises you can create on the Internet.

The chapters that follow present the highlights of 101 businesses you can start on the Internet. These businesses include:

- businesses that exist only on the Internet, like software.net, an online software retailer

- offshoots of existing businesses, like Lobster Direct, which sells crustaceans and lox by mail and Internet

- companies that use the Internet to draw customers to their offline store, such as Nine Lives Clothing

- professions and careers that serve the Internet community, like HTML programmers and Webmasters

Each business profile contains:

- *overview*—what the business entails and the background you need to get started

- *rewards*—pros of starting this kind of business

- *risks*—cons of starting this kind of business

- *special marketing considerations for the home page*—insightful tips that can make the cyberstore a success

- *hot sites*—examples of great sites

More than forty businesses are profiled at length, with illustrations from their home pages. Another twenty businesses and professions are described in short interviews presented in a question-and-answer format. These episodes will give you a clear impression of the joys and sorrows of starting a business on the Internet.

ABOUT THE INTERVIEWS

The businesses profiled in this book were found through online searches and recommendations from online surfers. No one was paid to be in this book and no one received compensation of any sort.

I wrote the questionnaire and sent it to the business people, who answered via e-mail. This is truly a virtual book that happens to be printed on paper. All the online addresses appear on my home page, *www.janal.com/links.htm/* so you can review the interview subjects' home pages easily.

The veracity of the answers is the responsibility of the business owners. I've trusted them to be honest and open. All respondents gave their permission to have information included in the book.

I asked all the business owners how much money they made on the Internet. Some people were, naturally, hesitant to reveal this information for a variety of reasons: They don't want their competitors to know how much money they are making, thus encouraging competition; they don't want their spouses to know how much money they are losing; they just plain aren't comfortable talking about their finances in a world full of kidnappers and weirdos.

In order for the personality, enthusiasm, and emotions of the entrepreneurs to come alive, we did not edit the interviews, except for light changes to protect them from their own typos.

The voices that come through are those of the writers, so you'll experience a dynamic, earthy, conversational tone. This could be the new media version of Studs Terkel's book *Working*—an oral history of working in cyberspace.

I've included respondents' own smileys and emoticons, those funny keyboard characters that convey emotion in an otherwise silent and faceless world. Here's the short course on smileys. Tilt your head to the left and you'll see the expression displayed in text in the left-hand column and as a smiley in the right-hand column.

- smile   :-)

- wink   ;-)

- sad, frown   :(

Another key emoticon is the grin, which appears as <g>. Additionally, several online abbreviations are used:

- TIA—Thanks in advance

- IMHO—In my humble opinion

People gave freely of their time and information, knowing that someone could come out of the woodwork and compete with them. These are true Internet entrepreneurs who believe in the code of contributing to the community.

This book is not meant to be read from cover to cover. You will probably want to read the first section on how to do business on the Internet and then skim the chapters about businesses that interest you. If that's your modus operandi, fine. However, browse through the other interviews, as they contain a wealth of information about how to start, run, and market a business on the Internet, and how to integrate work with your personal life. All these stories are fascinating! They offer you practical tips, even if you don't plan to start that particular business.

Updates

The first edition of this book included many in-depth interviews with companies that were just starting up. Of course, back then, the Internet was so new that the only companies online were new to the experience. Some had made significant sales, some had limited success, and others were literally waiting for their first order.

Now that the Internet is a bit more mature (but by no means fully developed) we've raised the barrier. To be considered for this book, the business had to be making money through its online activities.

Again, many compies didn't want to tell us exact dollar amounts for various legitimate reasons. However, you can see by their enthusiasm for their business, acumen with marketing strategies, and sheer willingness to be online after all this time that they must be doing something right.

The biggest change that I've noticed is that page design has improved dramatically. The first edition boasted that you could go online with a page you created yourself—art included. I don't think that's the case any more. Pages need to look professionally designed and have attractive (but small) graphics. While some off-the-shelf software can turn out attractive, artistic templates that meet the needs of many small businesses, other companies might prefer to attain an original look by hiring a professional designer.

WHERE ARE ALL THE MILLIONAIRES?

As you read the case studies and interviews, you might notice that not everyone is making a million dollars. The fact is that no one I spoke with has gotten rich quick. The media might have portrayed several flower, wine, and T-shirt Web enterprises as leading the way, but the vast majority of businesses seem to be getting by and waiting for the rest of the world to realize that they should be online and buy from online merchants.

In this way, the Web seems to be a place where people can make a business, but not a killing, at this time. Many people interviewed are looking to make a modest sum or to increase business in their traditional stores and offices. I've decided to include these stories because they can inspire you to continue working away on your online store for the big payoff when more and more consumers use the Internet as a preferred shopping vehicle.

If we take off our blinders, we might also begin to realize that running a business on the Internet is no different than operating a business in the real world—it takes time, money, and patience. If the average retail store in the real world takes three years to turn a profit, then why should we think that online businesses can become instant winners? While businesses on the Internet have lower start-up costs than traditional companies, they still have expenses. Hardly any company—online or off—has been profitable from day one.

5

Consumer Products

The sale of products via the Internet will grow to $6.6 billion by the year 2000, up from $518 million in 1996, according to Forrester Research. As more consumers, rather than nerds, go online, growth will be explosive for many product areas and companies. Indeed, we found many companies that are building strong businesses on the Internet alone, or are adding to the sales of their stores on Main Street. Sales are poised to grow exponentially as the Web becomes easier to use, easier to find products with, and more comfortable with accepting advertising to promote products, and become more comfortable ordering online.

Relatively few categories comprise 52 percent of the sales, according to Forrester: PC hardware and software, adult entertainment, CDs, and gift items (especially flowers).

The study shows these categories garnering the following percentages of sales and dollar amounts in 1996:

- computer products   32 percent $323 million
- travel   24 percent $276 million
- entertainment   19 percent $194 million
- gifts, flowers   10 percent $103 million

- apparel   5 percent $89 million

- food and drink   5 percent $78 million

- other   5 percent $75 million

This chapter looks at entrepreneurs who use the Internet to create new customers for the products they sell in stores on Main Street or through mail-order catalogs. Through case studies and interviews, you'll see how companies sell products including jewelry, clothing, teddy bears, boats, collectibles, and flowers to a variety of markets.

SELLING PRODUCTS ON THE INTERNET

Overview

Literally hundreds of companies sell products in every conceivable category on the Internet. Yet there are still opportunites for entrepreneurs to enter the field by selling different kinds of products to specific segments of the market. For example, although there are jewelry stores on the Internet, an entrepreneur working from her house might find an eager market by specializing in modern designs, while others sell more traditional wares.

Don't be scared by big companies that are online. Consumers know you by the quality of your products and the advantages and skills you bring to their design, creation, and marketing. You probably wouldn't want to sell chocolates head-to-head against Godiva, but you could outflank it by selling chocolates in the shape of company logos or toys, which Godiva doesn't do.

If you create earrings, bracelets, belt buckles, and the like, you can find a ready market on the Internet, which is home to dozens of companies selling these kinds of products. You can differentiate your products by specializing in regional tastes, such as Southwestern, Appalachian, Western, modern, traditional, and avant garde, to name a few.

Rewards

Selling products could be the perfect entry point for the wanna-be Internet entrepreneur, the part-time worker or the full-time corporate executive who creates products as a hobby—for example, jewelry, knit goods, candles, or calligraphy. Such a person can keep his day job and ship products as the orders come in.

For companies on Main Street, the Internet provides an additional channel of distribution to reach new customers around the world. You'll read about Milne Jewelry of Salt Lake City, Utah, selling its fine products to people in Germany, as well as the Virginia Diner selling peanuts and gift baskets to people around the world.

Risks

Selling products online involves certain risks that can be minimized with proper planning. For example, hustlers and frauds in the offline world prey on companies that are on the Internet. Therefore, it is a good idea to verify credit card orders and check the address against the clearing-house's records. When you send products you should use a service that requires a signature showing receipt of the product, such as Federal Express, Airborne, UPS, and U.S. Post Office Express Mail. In the near future you'll be able to charge people by debiting their digital bank accounts. You can also join a digital mall using a registration number system, which asks customers for a credit card number and provides them with a registration number with which they can order products. These steps can thwart criminals.

Special Marketing Considerations for the Home Page

Web sites should make browsing for products fun and easy.

Browsing should be done by categories that lead to more and more detailed levels of information. For example, a store that sell books, music, and videos should have those three options listed first. A consumer selecting music would see another menu offering a search by title, artist, or type of music. In this manner, she can easily find the products she seeks.

The less desirable alternative is to present a laundry list of all products, which could frustrate and confuse consumers; they will run to another site if you make their shopping experience less than desirable. This is an important consideration on the Internet, which delivers graphics slowly. Merchants should design pages that have thumbnail pictures of products rather than full-screen views because of the time needed to display art.

Merchants can use traditional tools such as coupons, sales, and promotions to attract customers to their cyberstores and traditional outlets.

All product cyberstores should be listed on as many directories as possible. See chapter 3 for a list of directories and instructions for using them. Owners should also try to link their store to as many digital malls and complementary sites as possible.

Figure 5–1. Coupons on the Web site help drive traffic to stores on Main Street. This tactic also helps companies track the effectiveness of their sites. Copyright 1997, Nine Lives Quality Consignment Clothing.

Case Study: Milne Jewelry Company

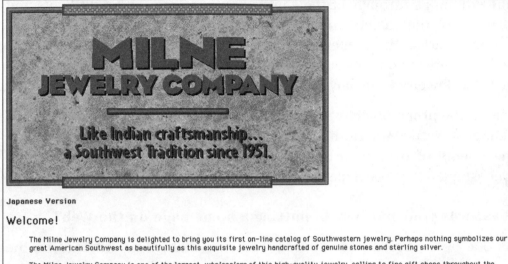

Japanese Version

Welcome!

The Milne Jewelry Company is delighted to bring you its first on-line catalog of Southwestern jewelry. Perhaps nothing symbolizes our great American Southwest as beautifully as this exquisite jewelry handcrafted of genuine stones and sterling silver.

The Milne Jewelry Company is one of the largest *wholesalers* of this high-quality jewelry, selling to fine gift shops throughout the United States. Over the years, we have assembled an unparalleled team of artists and craftspeople. Customers familiar with their work have written us with requests for additional pieces and more information. This offering is our response to those requests.

Made of the earth, wind, sea, and blessed by the spirits of the Gods, the jewelry shown on the following pages are the *ultimate gift*, a gift that will be cherished forever.

Figure 5–2. Because the Internet reaches a worldwide audience, merchants should offer their home pages in several languages. Copyright 1997, Milne Jewelry Company.

Milne Jewelry Company

PO Box 58958

Salt Lake City, UT 84158-0958

(original interview 1995)

turq@xmission.com

www.xmission.com/~turq

What is your company's background?

Milne Jewelry Company was established in Saint George, Utah, in January 1951 and has maintained an exceptional reputation for high-quality merchandise and service to clients for over forty years. As a family business, Milne Jewelry Company is founded on the principles of honesty and integrity that are the trademark of founder Wes Milne.

As a wholesaler of Native American Indian silver and turquoise jewelry and jewelry of the American Southwest, our product lines are featured in fine gift shops throughout the United States—from the bright lights and glamour of the casino cities to the rustic Western grandeur of several national parks. Many international airport, hotel, and resort gift shops delight tourists and collectors alike with the authentic quality and beauty of Milne Jewelry Company designs.

One of the prime objectives of Milne Jewelry Company is to promote the talents of Native American Indian artists and craftsmen; we currently use the talents of over three hundred silversmiths—representatives of the highest quality artisans making jewelry today.

What was your purpose in putting a home page on the Web?

As one of the first three hundred Web sites making an entrance on the Internet, and not knowing what to expect, we mainly just wanted to test the waters and get our feet wet. We wanted to see what kind of opportunities might be available with this new medium of advertising and selling. The first Web site we saw was Grants Floral on the Branch Mall. Our assumption was "If they can sell flowers, we can sell turquoise!" [You may be aware that as of spring 1994 there was no information available on commercialism on the Internet and the World Wide Web.] Our main goals were to reach new markets and build name identification. Customer support and product knowledge is of high priority to Milne Jewelry Company. Including the Internet in our communication systems seemed to be an effective and low-cost way to meet a wider variety of needs of our domestic and international customers through Web sites, and e-mail. We have been extremely pleased with the results so far.

How has the home page helped your business?

A good example might be our entrance into the Japanese market. For years, Japanese visitors to the United States have been delighted with the quality and beauty of our truly authentic American product. We get many requests from these customers asking how they can get additional pieces of jewelry once they get home to Japan. (The Japanese like to buy our products in the United States—not Japan.) We are now able to make our products readily available to our retail friends in Japan with a Japanese version of our catalog—and they can still say they purchased their jewelry in the United States.

Some stats you may be interested in:

Distribution of all sales from Web site

United States—56 percent

Japan—18 percent

All other countries—26 percent

Distribution of international sales only:

Japan—40 percent

All other countries—60 percent (average 4 percent per country)

Average orders:

United States—$54.25

Japan—$122.00

All other countries—$69.50

The strong sales to Japan are not accidental. Years of watching our retailers and tracking their sales showed us the Japanese were our best customers. This market was specifically targeted.

What advice would you offer a business on the Web?

To have no great expectations. Building a business on the Internet takes time and effort.

Case Study: Nine Lives Quality Consignment Clothing

NINE LIVES

Quality

Consignment

Clothing

Welcome to Nine Lives!

⬤ **Special Promotion:** For a limited time you can obtain a free coupon good for 10% off your (over $50) purchases at Nine Lives. Have your printer ready!

Enjoy yourself...

Nine Lives is a consignment clothing store which carries only the **highest quality** pre-owned women's and men's clothing and accessories. Nine Lives is located in beautiful **Los Gatos**, facing the Town Plaza.

Nine Lives is on the Internet to provide a way for you to shop through the inventory, verify hours of operation and store policies, and to keep you informed of new information related to the store.

The most popular items in the store inventory are presented here in the form of an Electronic Storefront for you to shop at your convenience.

Shop the Nine Lives Inventory:
⬤ Women's Clothing ⬤ Menswear

Personal Shopping Assistants are a **FREE** service of Nine Lives. **Select** an action from the choices below and then **Contact** your assistant.
⬤ Hire An Assistant

Figure 5–3. Nine Lives uses its cyberstore to lead people to its actual store in Los Gatos, California. Copyright 1997, Nine Lives Quality Consignment Clothing.

Nine Lives Quality Consignment Clothing

M.J. Nesbitt   *ninelives@chezhal.slip.netcom.com*

9 Montebello Way   *www.los-gatos.ca.us/nine.html*

Los Gatos, CA 95030   408-354-9169

(original interview 1995; update February 1997)

What do you do and who is your primary audience?

Professional women and men who are looking for top quality clothing and accessories in like-new condition at one third of retail price (or less!!).

How will they benefit from your product?

Customers will be able to dress up to a level they could not otherwise afford, or save money on the items they would ordinarily buy at full retail prices. The Internet (Web) page is "out there" to make it easy to see what is inventory, what the consignment policies of the store are, and to provide business and contact information.

Does your product differ from others?

No, but making the inventory of the store available on the Internet through the World Wide Web is unique. The Personal Shopping Assistants, which store profiles and e-mail against them, are also extremely rare on the Web. They are unheard of in stores the size of Nine Lives.

Is this business an offshoot of your existing business or does it exist only on the Internet?

The Web is definitely an offshoot of the real business. We cannot sell our products through the Web. People demand a chance to try the clothes on before they buy, and the margins are too slim to offer a return policy through the mail.

Was the Internet store meant to generate income on its own or to steer people to your other outlets?

The Internet storefront is 100 percent designed to steer people to the real store. Every aspect of the pages is focused on getting the customers to visit the physical store.

Where is your workplace?

The server is at home (converted dining room) but the inventory is maintained from the store (through the Internet) by dialing the server.

What is your background and training?

I have a master's in management. No retail or computer experience to speak of, except as a user (word processing). My husband, the Webmaster, has worked as a UNIX instructor for the past ten years, and has an MBA.

Getting Started

When did you start your business?

Nine Lives (the real store) opened in February 1993. The virtual storefront opened in January 1994.

Did you create a business plan before going online?

No. It was done incrementally in spare time, with no real plan. Each feature was added as the Web evolved.

How much time did it take to get up and running?

The initial pages and inventory search took about a week. Personal Shopping Assistants took a weekend to create and have taken months to fine-tune.

Did you create the pages yourself or did you get help?

We did it all.

How much did it cost to get started?

The computer was already part of the family and my husband was online quite a bit with Prodigy, so we had modems and a second phone line. No software was needed (UNIX has everything we need) so the only initial cost was the Internet account ($100 start-up) and then monthly fees.

Did you need to go to an outside source for start-up capital?

No.

How did you promote your site?

We listed it on every index in the world.:-O We also put the URL on our flyers, our store signs, and Nine Lives business cards.

How much did it cost to promote your site?

No $$. Just time to look for new indexes and get it listed.

How long did it take until you got your first sale?

Visitors appeared immediately through the Web. Five to ten from the very first day.

How much has your company made?

$100/week of new business, savings of $100/week from advertising we do not have to do, costs of $50 a week for the site, net $150/week. It's a small site.

How much money do you expect to make?

Another $200–$300/week.

What mistakes did you make that you wish you hadn't made?

We are happy with things as they have progressed.

What advice would you give someone starting a business?

Concentrate on providing service. Save people time, trouble, or $$$. There is no other long-term reason to be there, unless you count entertainment.

What skills would a person need to be a success?

Infinite patience, the ability to redesign Web pages based solely on log file audit trails, an *extremely* organized approach to managing a business.

What special qualities are needed to run your site?

Programming, business organization, and communication.

My Day

What does your average day look like?

I work in the store five days a week, where I do all the inventory maintenance through normal POS [point of sale, the displays you see at the checkout counter] activities.

My husband works a normal job, then comes home and works on the Web site in the evenings.

What does your job entail?

Entering and selling eight hundred items every three months. The rest is completely automated. The whole inventory presentation and query system on the Web site is automated.

How many hours a week do you spend working on your site?

Myself, none to one hour a week. My husband, one to twenty hours a week depending on whether we are stable or adding/debugging a new feature. My delightful husband usually spends about ten hours a week on the site, answering mail, checking the inventory system, and adding little touches here and there. I do not have to do anything except enter all the inventory. Lucky for me this is not extra work. The POS terminal in the store is connected to the Web server, so entering the intake items for the purpose of printing labels and entering sales serves to keep the inventory up to date.

What was the hardest aspect of the work in the beginning?

Learning the correct answers to technical questions asked by customers and reporters. My husband says writing the Personal Shopping Assistant part of the software was a challenge.

What do you like most about your work?

The feeling we are doing something new, exciting, and truly valuable with this new technology.

What do you like the least?

Major changes to the software right before the end of the month. (Are you listening, dear??)

How did the start-up phase affect your personal life?

Ha! For both of us, the start-up phase nearly replaced our personal lives.

Are you glad your store is on the Web?

Yes. We have tremendous exposure through the Web. There is no way Nine Lives could afford that much publicity using traditional marketing. In addition, my husband landed his most recent job partly due to the strength of the site.

Given what you know now, would you do it again?

Yes. The publicity from the Web page has been tremendous. Nine Lives has been on CNN, written up in *Women's Day* and *Smart Money*, and has appeared in numerous other publications.

The Future

What is your next venture?

The menswear section just opened, after being in the planning phase for months. Next: Who knows?

1997 Update

What is the most important thing you learned in the past year about marketing on the Internet?

For us, located in Silicon Valley, the Internet is a more effective marketing tool than traditional print advertising. Our response from a wide range of print advertising over the last year typically was low; only a few visitors ever mentioned that the advertisements were what made them come to the store. The Web page is responsible for several real visitors a day on average, in addition to the hundreds of virtual shoppers we see daily on the Web site. We have also seen, since 1994, when the site was created, that the trend toward using the Internet as a vehicle for shopping is climbing steeply. Three years ago it was an oddity, but today it is as accepted as flipping through a magazine. We have also learned that the site does not have to provide entertainment, stock quotes, weather reports, or a virtual world to be useful. It simply has to provide value.

What is the most effective way to get people to come to your site?

Our site receives half of its traffic as a result of searches on major Web search engines, and another 40 percent from topical pages listing our store as a shopping destination. The remaining 10 percent is occasional traffic resulting from browsing. We have taken time to ensure that the titles of our pages are interesting and we check for listings of our pages on other sites presenting shopping information. The titles ensure that searches will present our pages as interesting destinations, and we never hesitate to ask for listing on other appropriate sites. These activities keep our site visible and attractive.

What is the most effective way to get people to return to your site?

Visitors return to Nine Lives because they have a specific need, and within a few clicks they can determine whether a trip to the real Nine Lives store can meet that need. Shopping on the Web at Nine Lives works. It saves people time and effort, and they return because the information they received is accurate and the quality of the experience is predictable. The Web site is the fastest, cheapest, simplest way to shop effectively. We hear repeatedly from shoppers who visited the Web site first that our site saved them hours of aimless wandering in huge, crowded malls.

What is the most effective way to get people to buy products or services?

While we do not sell direct because our products do not lend themselves to mail-order sales, we have been asked numerous times to consider direct sales. This proves that a Web site with quality information and true value will result in sales. The level of direct sales on the Web is nowhere near what some of the predictions of the past few years have suggested, but it is still increasing. This does not worry us, as the Nine Lives Web site is already successful as an information source. It is the value of the goods, services, or information offered by the Web site that causes repeat traffic.

How much money have you made?

Nine Lives is not directly generating sales through the Web site, but we are directly avoiding costs. The Web site allows Nine Lives to reduce advertising expenses to a quarter of what similar businesses spend, while enjoying greater reach. The Web site puts Nine Lives's entire inventory listing on the screen of the visitor, which would not be possible by any other advertising method regardless of cost. We also believe the Web site reduces the number of phone calls that would have to be answered during business hours. The nature of the Nine Lives inventory (every item unique) means that shoppers would not have any idea whether Nine Lives carried an item they would buy unless they could communicate with someone at the store. The Web site deflects the inventory check calls that would otherwise require staff to answer. Finally, the coupon on the Web site has resulted in a small number of sales directly traceable to the Web site. When a customer arrives with coupon in hand, it is evidence that the Web is working. Every day the Nine Lives Web site contributes to the success of Nine Lives. The Web has absolutely lived up to its promised potential for this small business.

Case Study: Flower Stop Marketing Corp.

Flower Stop Marketing Corp.   *www.flowerstop.com*

Chuck Haley   800-L-D-Roses (800-537-6737)

PO Box 7070

Colorado Springs, CO 80933

(original interview 1995; update June 1997)

Who is your primary audience?

We're still trying to figure that out. Outside of the normal demographics of the Internet, which are changing all the time, we don't have specific demos on our customers. The Internet demos of the net seem to parallel those of the traditional flower-buying public. Consequently there appear to be more florists online than any other industry.

How will they benefit from your product?

It can be easier to order flowers online than from a local florist or an 800 number. Often customers don't have all the information needed by the florist in order to process the order and when it comes time to verbalize to an operator what they would like to say on the enclosure card, they become tongue-tied. When they place their order on the Internet, they can take their time to complete all the information needed and compose the appropriate card for the occasion. Another benefit is that the accuracy is not dependent on the operators' spelling skills or ability to understand unique voices on the phone or decipher handwriting. The order comes through exactly how the customer wishes in typed format.

How does your product differ from others?

Along with being in the top 300 FTD florists in the country, Flower Stop also features a product line unique in the flower industry. Flower Stop's parent company is Pike's Peak Greenhouses and we ship our famous Long

Distance Roses AE, and Long Distance Flowers AE direct from our own greenhouses by FedEx AE to the lucky recipient.

Is this business an offshoot of your existing business or does it exist only on the Internet?

Flower Stop and Long Distance Roses started in 1983. They have been marketing through 800-L-D-ROSES (Long Distance Roses) and 800-GIVE-FTD since their opening. Long Distance Roses has been marketing on CompuServe, GEnie, and Delphi for six to eight years.

If it is an offshoot, was it meant to generate income on its own or to steer people to your other outlets?

Flower Stop on the Internet was designed from the beginning to take orders. By providing customers full graphics and description of the products and having a complete order entry form Flower Stop has one of the easiest ordering systems on the Net. We prefer to get orders online because the accuracy of spelling makes it easier for us to enter the order into our system.

Where is your office?

All our Internet operations are run from our Long Distance Roses headquarters.

What is your background and training?

Born and raised in the flower business, I have spent years in all facets of the industry from growing, wholesaling, retailing, and direct marketing. I started working on the Internet a year ago.

When did you start your business?

This is a family business that my brother and I purchased ten years ago.

How much has your company made?

In the past five months Flower Stop has received 400 orders for $18,000.

Getting Started

Did you create a business plan before going online?

Not really. Our experience with online shopping from CompuServe etc., was a good indicator of what we could expect. We looked at it as being able to open another location for the cost of a good ad campaign.

How much time did it take to get up and running?

We made the decision to go online in July 1994 and were up and running by the first of October 1994.

Did you create the pages yourself or did you get help?

We hired two outside firms to put our site together. First, we hired a programmer to write all the HTML and set up the order entry form. We also hired a commercial artist to design the home page graphics and scan in the transparencies of the products.

How much did it cost to get started?

It cost about $20,000 to get the site up. From then on it has cost another $20,000 for things like upgrades to the site, fees to get listed in electronic malls throughout the Internet, fees for our access provider, and advertising to get exposure.

Did you need to go to an outside source for start-up capital?

We used funds from inside the company and redirected some of our ad budget to the Internet store.

What mistakes did you make that you wish you hadn't made?

Since this is largely experimental still, I'm not sure what of the things we have done will turn out to be mistakes. The cost of getting online is so reasonable, it's hard to believe that any mistake can cost enough to worry about.

What advice would you give someone starting a business?

Getting online at this point is so easy I can't imagine why a company wouldn't do it just for the exposure. [Down the road someone is going to have to foot the bill and it will be the commercial element. Afterall, they stand to gain the most.] The next decision is to determine your purpose and level of involvement. If it's more for advertising [like Zima] then you will approach the Internet with that objective and go for the information and exposure to build product and/or company recognition. If you're going for online sales, then you need to build your store for taking orders and providing the information that the customer needs to make an informed buying decision.

What skills would a person need to conduct business?

My advice is to determine the aspect of online marketing that interests you and spend your efforts in that area. Then you can hire people to fill in the gaps. There is no shortage of displaced programmers who would be anxious to serve you.

What education is necessary to run your site?

It's more important to have someone in charge of the content of the site. In this case, marketing is still the key. If you want to be a do-it-yourselfer, you will need to start by learning how to get all the latest versions of software needed to get online and learning how all of them interact. Since there are programs to do just about anything you need done, the real challenge is finding them and installing them. Once they are installed, any bozo can operate them. This is where good programmers will earn their pay.

How did you promote your site?

The first decision we made was to develop a home page that was graphically superior to anything on the Internet at the time. By doing that, we were able to get exposure in the likes of *PC Magazine* (2/7/95), *Computerworld*, and several local newspapers throughout the country. We were featured by IBM in their introduction of Warp/2 at the Comdex show last year. We were featured in another book and we have received a lot of attention from the Internet community itself. Our next decision was to get listed in all the search engines, which is an ongoing project. And, finally, we have a link in more malls than any other florist on the net.

How much did it cost to promote your site?

Some listings are free, especially in the search engines. But the price for exposure ranges from $50/year to $2,700/week. We lean toward the lower cost options.

How long did it take until you got your first sale?

We got our first sale on the third day. It was a birthday arrangement from a customer in Hong Kong to a recipient in Manchester, England. Another lesson is to be prepared for international interaction.

How did the start-up phase affect your personal life?

The whole computer experience was new to me. Since my children had all left home, the time was right for a new adventure. I now have parallel systems at home and at work.

My Day

What does your average day look like?

There is no average day when your own your own business.

What does your job entail?

Just about everything. Mostly I'm involved in the retail divisions.

How many hours a week do you spend working on your site?

Not much, really—ten to twenty hours. A lot of it is spent answering questionnaires like this.

What percentages of time are spent on each task?

Conducting business—60 percent; Marketing—10 percent; Selling—10 percent; Upgrading site—10 percent

What was the hardest aspect of the work in the beginning?

Getting a comfortable workstation. Hours at the computer can cause a lot of back pain if your station doesn't fit.

How long did it take to get established?

N/A

What do you like most about your work?

It's a new adventure and I'm learning new skills.

Are there any hazards to running your site?

I haven't found any yet.

How much money do you expect to make?

Lots!

General

Are customers concerned about security for their credit cards?

We installed PGP (Pretty Good Protection, an encryption program) and less than 1 percent use it. Their other choice is "call me for credit card information." Less that 1 percent use that. Judging from the orders we get with their credit card information, I would say that there is no concern. After all, everyone knows that the merchant takes all the risks of the transaction.

How do you process orders via credit cards?

We transmit the credit card number electronically to our bank from our computer and get an approval number. Any order not approved is canceled.

Are you glad your store is on the Web?

Definitely. I believe that although home computers will not take over our lives, they will become a communications tool as common as the telephone.

Given what you know now, would you do it again?

We are so far away from where we will be in the next five years, the question is premature.

Where can people find advice about running a site like yours?

Books like yours are being written and published on a regular basis. Due to the changing nature of the Internet, more books will be written just to keep up with these changes. Also, there is a lot of information on the Internet itself.

What was your goal for going online?

Flower Stop's first experience with electronic sales started as a vendor with CompuServe and AOL in 1988! At that time we were promoting Long

Distance Roses (flowers shipped direct from the grower overnight via FedEx) which was a rather new concept to the market. In October 1994, Flower Stop opened its Website. Our very first order was a birthday arrangement from Hong Kong to Manchester, England. Our goal has always been to make ordering fresh flowers easy and accessible.

Have you reached it?

Flower Stop is continually striving to improve the convenience of ordering online. Since the Internet is truly global our challenge has been to serve the needs of different cultures and their use of flowers. A goal based on service is never "reached" but always provides direction.

How much product have you sold (dollar amount)?

Our Internet site is like a branch store. The demand is high during the holidays and follows the seasonal fluctuations normal to the flower industry. Our total electronic sales are less since we lost our position with CompuServe and AOL to the big dogs. Our Web site continues to grow, but at a decreasing rate.

What is the best marketing strategy you've learned in the past year?

The Internet is becoming flooded with vendors large and small (mostly small). Individually they don't present much competition, but collectively we all get lost in a sea of "florists." The market is changing rapidly and we are finding that our international business is increasing significantly. Our best marketing strategy is to offer our customers more than just a selection of arrangements. They want more information about flowers and we are in the process of supplying that.

What is the best way to get people to come to your site?

We have found that almost all "banner" advertising is way overpriced. You have to make a lot of $40–$50 sales to justify the going rate for traditional advertising on the internet. Since Flower Stop has been online longer than almost all other florists, we have hundreds of links that we have established over the past two and a half years that continue to bring in customers. It is a constant job to update our site information and to get the exposure needed to justify the expense of doing business online. We put as much effort into it as we would a branch location.

What is the best way to get people to return to your site?

With the mammoth number of sites on the Internet, I feel that once a customer finds a good "store" they will stay with that company until something goes wrong and they are forced to look for another source. The better we take care of our customers, the more they come back. Sound familiar?

1997 Update

Have you reached your goal for going online?

In October 1994, Flower Stop opened its Web site. Our goal has always been to make ordering fresh flowers easy and accessible. Since the Internet is truly global, our challenge has been to serve the needs of different cultures and their use of flowers. Our very first order was a birthday arrangement from Hong Kong to Manchester, England. A goal based on service is never "reached" but always provides direction.

What is the best way to get people to come and eventually return to your site?

The better we take care of our customers, the more they come back. We have hundreds of links that we established over the past two and half years that continue to bring in customers. We put as much effort into it as we would with a branch location. We have to make a lot of $40–$50 sales to justify the going rate for traditional advertising on the Internet. With the mammouth number of sites on the Internet, I feel that once a customer finds a good "store" they will stay with that company until somethng goes wrong.

Case Study: WorldWeb Supplies & Accessories, Inc.

Figure 5–4. WorldWeb Supplies removes the risk of buying by pointing out its pledges on the opening screen. Copyright 1997, WorldWeb Supplies and Accessories, Inc.

WorldWeb Supplies and Accessories, Inc.

Michael A. Berger

1103 High Vista Lane

Richardson, TX 75080

(original interview 1995)

mberger@intex.net

www.wsa-supplies.com

214-437-2538

Who is your primary audience?

Computer, fax, and printer owners—both business and personal.

How will they benefit from your product?

They can shop online. We have a large ($30-million) inventory. The prices are discounted. Delivery is next day, anywhere in the USA—at discount shipping rates.

How does your product differ from others?

The large inventory, next-day shipping, and VERY experienced sales personnel at the 800 number.

Is this business an offshoot of your existing business or does it exist only on the Internet?

Only on the Internet.

Where is your office?

Home office.

What is your background and training?

Physicist with more than thirty years computer training and twenty years computer supply experience.

Getting Started

When did you start your business?

March 1995.

Did you create a business plan before going online?

Yes.

How much time did it take to get up and running?

Four months.

Did you create the pages yourself or did you get help?

I got help.

How much did it cost to get started?

About $12,000 for getting online (pages, graphics, etc.). Setup of inventory (consigned) and administration was about $20,000.

Did you need to go to an outside source for start-up capital?

Outside source. Wrote and presented business plan.

How did you promote your site?

Search engines.

How much did it cost to promote your site?

Not done yet. About $20,000 over six months.

How long did it take until you got your first sale?

One week after site up.

How much has your company made?

First order, $90.

How much money do you expect to make?

About $300,000 first-year sales.

What mistakes did you make that you wish you hadn't made?

Bad site and programmers.

What advice would you give someone starting a similar business?

Hire your own people or contractors.

What skills would a person need to conduct business?

Marketing and technical.

What special qualities are needed to run your site?

MBA would help!

My Day

What does your average day look like?

Check site.

Write checks.

Devote about two hours to marketing (plans, etc.).

What does your job entail?

Everything (one-man company).

How much time do you spend conducting business, marketing, selling, and upgrading your site?

Forty hours per week. Administration 25 percent; marketing 25 percent; dealing with vendors 15 percent; working on site programming, etc. 15 percent; other (?) 20 percent.

What was the hardest aspect of the work in the beginning?

Getting the initial site running properly.

What do you like most about your work?

Selling!

What do you like the least?

Dealing with incompetent programmers, etc.

What was your greatest moment?

The first sale.

How did the start-up phase affect your personal life?

No personal life!

Are you glad your store is on the Web?

Yes. Cutting edge....

Given what you know now, would you do it again?

Yes.

The Future

What is your next venture?

Expand product line. More fully automate sales process.

What else would you like to say?

The most important part of doing this if you want to keep employees to a minimum is to systematize and automate the process from order-taking to shipping to payments for inventory.

Case Study: Bears by the Sea

Figure 5–5. Easy navigation to its key shopping areas helps shoppers find products they want quickly. Copyright 1997, Bears by the Sea.

Bears by the Sea	*bears@callamer.com*
Kitty Wilde	*www.callamer.com/bears/*
680 Cypress Street	805-773-1952
Pismo Beach, CA 93449	fax 805-773-5869
(original interview 1995; update February 1997)	

What does your company do?

Sells teddy bears and other collectibles

Who is your primary audience?

Teddy bear collectors.

Is this business an offshoot of your existing business or does it exist only on the Internet?

Offshoot of our retail store—generates income as well as funnels people to actual store.

What is your background and training?

BA in education. Registered nurse. Have started several businesses.

When did you start your business?

Bears by the Sea began in 1992.

Getting Started

Did you create a business plan before going online?

Business plan was created before going online.

How much did time did it take to get up and running?

Ninety hours.

Did you create the pages yourself or did you get help?

Got help creating pages.

How much did it cost to get started?

Cost of creating Web pages, storage online, maintenance—complete package for one year, $1,500.

What advice would you give someone starting a business?

Shop around. Pay attention to potential hidden charges. Get an all-inclusive package. Make sure you are listed in the right directories.

What skills would a person need to operate a business?

Open mind. Willing to learn new technology. Patience—it takes time.

What special qualities are needed to operate the store?

Artistic and business skills.

How did you promote the site?

URL on business cards and literature. Word of mouth.

How long did it take to get your first sale?

Two weeks.

My Day

How many hours a week do you spend working on your site?

Four hours a day.

What was the hardest aspect of the work in the beginning?

Time to get established: two weeks.

How much time do you spend marketing the site?

One hour per day.

What do you like most about your work?

Challenge of new ideas.

What do you like the least?

Time spent.

What was your greatest moment?

Seeing it all come together online and having people respond.

How did the start-up phase affect your personal life?

You do not have one while you are setting this up!

The Future

What else would you like to say?

We are helping other people put their businesses on the Internet. It is a great, innovative, inexpensive way to do business. Every business needs an Internet presence to be competitive in this changing world.

1997 Update

What was your company's goal for going online?

To increase sales.

How do you know you have reached that goal?

Twenty-five percent of my sales are from the Internet.

How much did it cost to get started?

$1,295.

What makes your site special?

Updates, online forums, voting polls, and great information for collectors.

How to do you get people to come to your site?

Listings in search engines.

How do you get people to return to your site?

Updates and good information.

How do you move people from window-shoppers to paying customers?

Updates.

What is the most important thing you learned in the past year about marketing on the Internet?

Keeping my sites fresh with updates.

How much money have you made?

25 percent of my sales are from the Internet

Case Study: Marinemart

Marinemart   *silvermn@marinemart.com*

Albert Silverman   *www.marinemart.com*

PO Box 472   617-862-6507

Lexington, MA 02173

(original interview 1995)

Marinemart proves you can sell big-ticket items on the Internet. The company provides a virtual mall for vendors who sell products of interest to consumers who love the water world.

Who is your primary audience?

Boaters and people interested in boating.

How will they benefit from your product?

They will receive a better understanding of what is available in the sense of products and services.

How does your product differ from others?

Our mall is run by people with a marine background. We have a better understanding of the needs of both the marine industry and the boating public, having been in the pleasure boat industry for over a quarter of a century as a marine distributor selling globally.

Is this business an offshoot of your existing business or does it exist only on the Internet?

It is a new venture based on our past experience and exists only on the Internet, but we are tying this in with the varied marketing approaches of our clients, so that the varied marketing approaches augment each other. It is driven as a business to be revenue generating.

Where is your business located?

Home and office.

What is your background and training?

Education is four years in graduate school. Work experience is twenty-five-odd years in the marine business as a manufacturer and distributor of pleasure boat marine products and three years as an independent marketing consultant.

When did you start your business?

1995.

How much money has your company made online?

Confidential.

Getting Started

Did you create a business plan before going online?

Yes.

How much time did it take to get up and running?

This is an evolving process. It took a short period of time to get on the Internet, but our business is evolving to meet the needs of our customers and viewers, the marine providers, and the boating public. Every viable business, if it is to grow, must constantly reinvent itself.

Did you create the pages yourself?

Initially I got help, but later on we did our own creating. I had done marine catalogs and flyers for some fifteen years prior to this.

How much did it cost to get started?

Because this is a service industry there are no merchandise costs. This evolved and is still part of our consulting business so that start-up costs were shared by both, i.e., computer hardware and software costs, office, salaries, etc. Estimation for start-up just for this would be $25,000 for just capital investment, no salaries.

How did you obtain your start-up capital?

Self-financed.

What mistakes did you make that you wish you hadn't made?

Too early to tell, but I try to learn from my mistakes, and so they become an education tool. If you do not try and fail, you do not learn and cannot succeed.

What advice would you give to a similar start-up?

The Internet is a new medium and not everyone understands or is comfortable with it. Use it in conjunction with more conventional types of marketing approaches. Too many people think of it as an end in itself and see how far they can go with it as a means to its own end, i.e., technology for its own sake.

What skills are necessary to run a business?

Understand business concepts, your customer, and your marketplace.

What education is needed to run your site?

A background in business, especially from the experience side, with experience in marketing and advertising.

What special qualities are needed to run your site?

An understanding of the industry and the boating consumer, from having worked in the industry and having been a boating consumer oneself; the ability to create your own structure and to adapt the old to new and innovative approaches.

How did you promote your home page?

Directories, links from other sites, and having customers promote their own presence, which brings people to the mall in general, press releases in general and trade-specific publications.

How much did it cost to promote your site?

Time and more time.

How long did it take until you made your first sale?

Immediately to get first commitment, but process is slow in getting people prepared to enter cyberspace. First commitment still not on, but later commitments are up and running.

How did the start-up phase affect your personal life?

I have always worked for myself, so this is not new. We were always doing things differently than the pack and looking at old positions through a different mind-set. Although starting up can be frustrating, trying to convince someone to see something that is obvious to you but hidden to them when finally accomplished can be very exhilarating.

My Day

What does your average day look like?

Work 6:30 A.M. to 10 A.M., but my day was always like that.

What does your job entail?

Everything—marketing, graphic arts, sales, reading, etc.

How many hours a week do you spend working on your site?

Seventy to eighty.

What percentages of time are spent on each task?

It varies; because we do not fill orders we have other job requirements, like prospecting for marine providers to join our mall.

What was the hardest part of the job in the beginning?

Getting someone to accept your concept as being viable and willing to buy into it, through a sale.

How long did it take to get established?

I am never established, because I always create new goals.

What do you like most about your work?

Exciting, trying to sell a new concept.

What do you like least?

It is hard trying to sell a new concept to people who do not see it.

What was your greatest moment?

When someone sees what you see for the first time—the "aha" concept.

Are there any hazards to running your site?

The hazard of failing because I didn't do something that someone else did and I failed and they succeeded. Legal, financial, and other hazards are not a major concern to me now.

How much money do you hope to make?

Now, break even or a small profit, and later a larger profit commensurate with other industries.

Where can people find advice for running a business?

Talk to people who are doing it, read about it, work for one.

General

Are you glad to be on the Web?

Yes.

Given what you know now, would you do it again?

Yes.

The Future

What is your next venture?

Write another novel.

Case Study: World-Wide Collectors Digest

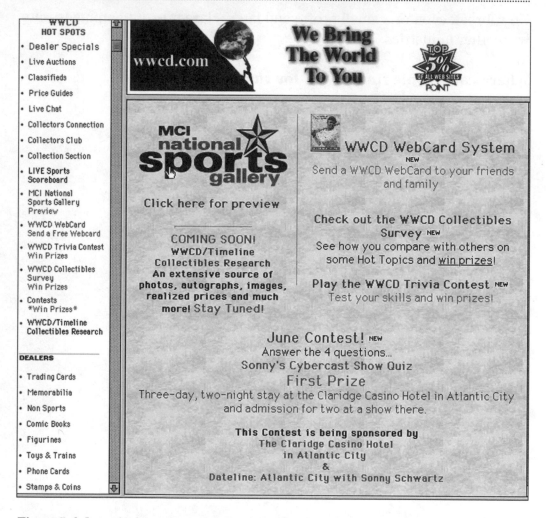

Figure 5–6. Lots of information and links make this site a joy for sports fans. Copyright 1997, World-Wide Collectors Digest, Inc.

World-Wide Collectors Digest, Inc. *steve@wwcd.com*

Jack Stern, Steve Schall   *market@wwcd.com, http://wwcd.com*

2 Railroad Avenue, Suite 203

Glyndon, MD 21071

(original interview 1995; update February 1997)

World-Wide Collectors Digest, Inc. sells collectible items like sports memorabilia, comic books, and toy trains; offers price guides; posts classified ads; and features live auctions.

Who is your primary audience?

Hobbyists and collectors. Ages ten to sixty.

How will they benefit from your product?

One stop for collectibles.

How does your product differ from others?

Complete digest, not just dealers and manufacturers.

Is this business an offshoot of your existing business or does it exist only on the Internet?

Offshoot.

If it is an offshoot, was it meant to generate income on its own or to steer people to your other outlets?

On its own.

Where is your workplace?

Office.

What is your background and training?

College graduate.

When did you start your business?

February 1990.

How much money has your company made online?

N/A

Getting Started

Did you create a business plan before going online?

Yes.

How much time did it take to get up and running?

Three months.

Did you create the pages yourself?

Many graphic artists [contributed to their creation].

How much did it cost to get started?

$60,000.

How did you obtain your start-up capital?

N/A

What mistakes did you make that you wish you hadn't made?

None so far.

What advice would you give to a similar start-up?

Lots of preparation and money. Get the best people.

What skills are necessary to run a business?

Business, marketing, computer, telecommunications experience.

What education is needed to run your site?

College.

What special qualities are needed to run your site?

Business, marketing, legal, artistic skills.

How did you promote your home page?

On the Internet and in trade magazines.

How much did it cost to promote your site?

$10,000–$20,000.

How long did it take until you made your first sale?

Two weeks.

How did the start-up phase affect your personal life?

What personal life?

My Day

What does your average day look like?

In at 9 A.M. Answer questions from everyone till 6 P.M.

What does your job entail?

Everything. Overseeing the operation.

How many hours a week do you spend working on your site?

On the site, fifty hours.

Answering mail, three hours.

What was the hardest part of the job in the beginning?

Turning the picture into reality.

How long did it take to get established?

Three or four months.

What do you like most about your work?

Taking part in the creating of new accounts.

What do you like least?

Answering e-mail.

What was your greatest moment?

Our first account.

Are there any hazards to running your site?

Not any more. There were personal.

How much money do you hope to make?

Millions!

General

Are customers concerned about security for their credit cards?

Yes.

Are you glad your company is on the Web?

YES.

Given what you know now, would you do it again?

YES.

Where can people find advice for running a business like yours?

Hire the successful people that have done it.

The Future

What is your next venture?

Building this, then building this, then....

What else would you like to say?

This is FUN!

1997 Update

What is the most important thing you learned in the past year about marketing on the Internet?

Not to have all the glitz. You would think that most of the sites you visit are in the graphic design business, or that is what they are trying to sell. Keep it simple and to the point!

What is the most effective way to get people to come to your site?

Cross-advertising, search engines, and, most importantly, word of mouth!

What is the most effective way to get people to return to your site?

CONTENT! CONTENT! CONTENT!

What is the most effective way to get people to buy products or services?

CUSTOMER SERVICE is by far #1, #2, and #3.

How much money have you made?

Growth has been 225 percent. Successful, but it takes a lot of work.

T-shirt Business

Overview

Because of the large number of college students who have free Internet accounts, vendors of T-shirts have reported brisk sales since the Web first began to be used as a commercial medium. The general public has also adopted the T-shirt as an acceptable garment for vacation and weekend wear.

Rewards

T-shirt makers face a very low cost of entry to the marketplace. A high quality T-shirt can cost a merchant about $2 and can sell for $16 or more. Sweatshirts also can be sold at even greater margins. You can even get a free software program called T-shirt Maker from Austin-Brett. The files can be downloaded for free from CompuServe's Graphics Forum (Go Graphics) or America Online's Software Section (search for *T-shirt*). You'll have the ability to design T-shirts, import artwork, add text that can be rotated, print on the front and back, and add color. The artwork is sent directly to a factory via modem or on a disk via the mail. The factory sends the high-quality T-shirt to you or your customer. While anyone can get into this business because of the low overhead, the field remains wide open to people who have good ideas, funny sayings, and intriguing artwork.

Risks

Merchants must be aware of rip-offs of their ideas so they should copyright their works. They also must constantly market their products.

Special Marketing Considerations for the Home Page

T-shirts need to be seen to be ordered. You will have to take photos of the products, scan them, and attach them to the home page. Because photos take a long time to display on the screen, great care must be taken when deciding how many pictures to place on a page. A good menu structure will help here, as you can ask customers to select T-shirts by category.

ARTS AND CRAFTS

Overview

Arts and crafts companies can find a market full of hobbyists of one sort or another.

Rewards

You can turn a hobby into a source of income.

Risks

Normal business risks.

Special Marketing Considerations for the Home Page

Pictures of products must be shown so people can see what they are getting. See other portions of this chapter for advice.

Case Study: Whiffle Tree Quilts

Whiffle Tree Quilts

the user-friendly quilt shop in the heart of Silicon Valley

May – August 1997 -- Vol. 7 Issue 2

Hello to all our friends:

WTQ is filling with wonderful new fabrics, as well as full stocks of your favorite basics.

- We have a great new group from Benartex -- designed by Pat Campbell. (A challenge is sponsored by Benartex -- come in and pick up an entry form.)

- We are eagerly awaiting the rest of the full line called "The Fabric Sale" produced by In the Beginning Fabrics. It is full of vibrant colors, geometrics and stylized prints. A book by the designer, Mary Lou Weidman, is forthcoming from The Patchwork Place.

- We also have a luscious group of linen-cotton plaids and stripes --wider width--perfect for summer garments as well as quilt projects.

Figure 5–7. Whiffle Tree Quilts prints a newsletter on the Internet and gets orders from around the world. Courtesy of Whiffle Tree Quilts.

Whiffle Tree Quilts   *tq@aol.com*

Marsha Burdick and Louise Horkey   *www.danish.com/wtq*

10261 S. DeAnza Boulevard   408-255-5270

Cupertino, CA 95014

(original interview 1995; update February 1997)

What does your company do?

We sell 100 percent cotton fabric, books, patterns, notions, have classes relating to making quilts, garments, dolls, etc. It is part of the soft craft industry. Quilting is a very large segment of the craft and art market.

What were you hoping to accomplish on the Web?

We wanted to go on the Internet because I had experience using e-mail when I worked at Lockheed, knew many people used e-mail and Internet, and wanted to differentiate ourselves from the other quilt shops around. It is a way to make ourselves known to others and also project the user-friendly and modern image—not just country crafts, as often associated with quilting.

How has being on the Internet helped you?

It has gotten us noticed by people around the world who have written to say they liked our home page, and customers who have come in the [actual] store because they discovered our home page and read our newsletters. It gained us respect and appreciation that we are "avant guard," as one customer's husband put it (a tourist from Asia).

1997 Update

What is the most important thing you learned in the past year about marketing on the Internet?

We have had orders from around the world—including a huge one from Japan.

What is the most effective way to get people to come to your site?

We just put up our store newsletter and class schedule.

What is the most effective way to get people to return to your site?

I don't know. We do not track hits.

What is the most effective way to get people to buy products or services?

I guess they respond to the descriptions and/or pictures in color. Basic marketing.

How much money have you made?

Our store's sales have increased 14 percent over last year and I believe some of the increase is related to our Internet exposure to our merchandise and classes.

Case Study: The Rubber Stamp Queen/Ace Stampworks

Figure 5–8. High tech meets high touch at this home page. Courtesy of Rubber Stamp Queen.

The Rubber Stamp Queen/Ace Stampworks

Moira Collins

320 S. Jefferson
Chicago, IL 60661

(original interview 1995)

rsqueen@aol.com

www.dol.com/queen

800-998-2627 for
brochures
800-239-9328 for orders

What are you hoping to accomplish by being on the Web?

We sell beautifully designed quality rubber art stamps along with practical, useful custom stock stamps and logos. Because of the visual nature of our artistic stamps—everything from dancing frogs and unicorns to beautifully rendered Japanese crests and calligraphy stamps—we felt the World Wide Web was the perfect medium to show the joys of rubber-stamping.

We are a Chicago-based company that is easily able to handle a lot of business and being on the Internet gives us access to retail and wholesale orders simultaneously.

How has being on the Internet helped you?

We have not been on the Web long—in our finished format, only about two months. We have not yet really started to advertise the site (because we are still working on pages), but it's clear we have started to be noticed—we get requests for our brochure daily from our 800 number as well as e-mail requests. The response is building, so we are planning to print our catalog a couple of months earlier than we intended, as we view this as potentially a financially rewarding environment requiring little effort. It seems like every time we are posted somewhere—perhaps we are recommended—a flurry of requests follows. For example, a week or two ago we received a notice from Prodigy that we had been listed in their arts and crafts section and in sample interviews with customers. We seem to be hitting a responsive chord; that encourages us to continue to invest in this area. We are beginning to receive wholesale requests from states our city reps would not reach.

What advice would you give an entrepreneur?

John Nesbitt wrote some years ago in *Megatrends* that "the higher the tech, the higher the touch." In other words, in a high-tech world, as it becomes increasingly technical, high-touch human products become valuable as a balance and antidote. If you have a service that is high-touch, consider how you might translate that into a high-tech environment like the Internet. Think of the orders that you expect as orders you would normally never get. At the start, don't expect to pay your mortgage or even your office rent by launching your new business on the Internet, but if you are an established business orders over the Internet in a sense are gravy. They are orders that come with little cost of advertising aside from setup costs, and if your site becomes popular you may want to learn how to market directly to this global market you are only beginning to tap into. If you are a company that actually is able to handle personal requests and phone calls believe me, you are a rarity in today's world. Take advantage of it! Advertise yourself on the Internet. Business might be slow in a local area; however, in a sense your business may be booming in another town or hamlet in the country where people don't have access to what you offer. It helps if you have a product you already know that people have wanted or a service people already requested, and believe it or not, word of mouth can work in the global neighborhood of cyberspace. It helps to have supporting printed materials until the ordering potential via MasterCard/Visa becomes easy, probably early in 1996. Not everyone is comfortable with ordering by e-mail. Although fax orders are perhaps the norm, many Internet newbies are more comfortable ordering by snail mail. Clearly it's easier to do business internationally if you take MasterCard/Visa. It also helps to offer information that you don't sell and offer a deal on the Internet that you might not offer elsewhere to encourage orders with this new medium. And don't be afraid to add a little humanness in your offering. "The higher the tech, the higher the touch."

What else would you like to say?

Perhaps you have discovered that many people aren't interested in panning for gold until it's proven to be a mother lode. However, those of us with a pioneer attitude are in keeping with the gold rush mentality that shaped our country. "Go west, young man. Go west." It's kinda fun to be exploring this cyberspace.

Site Review: FREEZ-IT

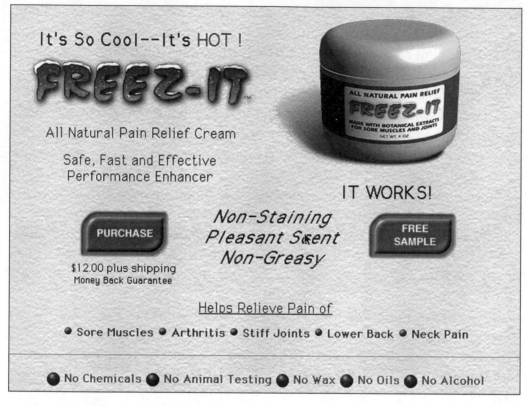

Figure 5–9. FREEZ-IT's Web site looks like a flyer. Copyright 1997, FREEZ-IT.

FREEZ-IT	*www.freezit-com*
Patricia Appleby	415-387-4883
Interactive Marketing Solutions	800-256-6461

(original interview 1997)

Dr. Nancy Charney, a successful chiropractor in San Francisco, searched South America and other exotic locations for natural healing ingredients and created FREEZ-IT, a face cream that claims to immediately relieve sore muscles and joints, improve circulation, and relieve arthritis pain. FREEZ-IT has been registered with the FDA.

The next problem was how to let people know about it. Dr. Charney contacted Patricia Appleby of Interactive Marketing Solutions. Appleby suggested that instead of spending anywhere from $25,000 to $50,000 on targeted trade advertising they use the Internet to advertise and distribute samples. Both women had such faith in the product, they knew if people tried it, they would certainly buy more. So, with a budget of $13,000, the campaign was initiated. Designed by Appleby, the Web site cost $3,000 to build and was constructed by MiraNet (415-617-4555). The site describes the product, enables people to sign up for a free sample, and is capable of secure electronic purchases. There is also an area for people to contact the doctor directly by e-mail, affording more personalized assistance. All the search engines were notified of the site and that free samples were available.

The response was astronomical! Within the first two weeks, they had over eight thousand e-mail and regular addresses of people wanting samples. By the end of the month there were an additional ten thousand requests. The doctor's staff was totally unprepared for such an overwhelming response, and there was some delay in sending out the samples. They put a notice on the Web site to please have patience—the samples were forthcoming.

The first mailing just went out and it consisted of three thousand samples with an enclosed flyer redirecting people to the Web site for purchases or to order via 800-256-6461. The cost of a four-ounce jar is $12 plus $3 shipping, or a special offer of two jars for $20 plus shipping and handling.

"It will be most interesting and educational to discover the percentage of sales from this campaign," Appleby said. "In traditional direct marketing, a successful campaign is one in which 3 percent of the total contacts result in a sale. It is projected that the FREEZ-IT campaign will generate triple this percentage, and will also benefit from repeat and additional word-of-mouth sales from satisfied customers.

"When you believe in your product and samples are viable, the Internet is the most direct medium to inexpensively and proactively locate buyers who are interested in purchasing your product," said Appleby. "The usability of your Web site is also a very beneficial tool in developing an ongoing relationship with your customers."

Case Study: Bike Pedalers

Figure 5–10. A simple design helps customers find products quickly and easily. Copyright 1997, Bike Pedalers, Inc.

Bike Pedalers	bikeped@inetnebr.com
Rich Rodenburg	www.bikeped.com
1353 South 33rd	800-728-0856
Lincoln, NE 68510	fax 402-474-7104

(original interview 1995; update 1997)

Who is your primary audience?

Bicycle enthusiasts.

How will they benefit from your product?

We have included maintenance tips, local interest, links to other cycling sites, calendars, etc.

How does your product differ from others?

We are a (regular) bike shop and offer our services online as well. We were one of the first, if not the first, to do so.

Is this business an offshoot of your existing business or does it exist only on the Internet?

We are primarily a walk-in (or ride-in) in bike shop. The Web site is a very small percentage of our business.

If it is an offshoot, was it meant to generate income on its own or to steer people to your other outlets?

This home page was set up originally to create local interest and some out-of-town recognition, but has grown into an international thing.

Where is your workplace?

In the beginning, just out of my home office, but now we have Internet access at the shop.

What is your background and training?

In cycling: avid cyclist and shop proprietor and mechanic for thirteen years. Computers: hobbyist.

When did you start your business?

1982 offline, June 1995 online.

How much money has your company made online?

(Retail) We have grossed $1.5 million a year for several years.

(Online) There was a long dry spell, with only a couple of bikes and a few minor accessories for the first six weeks, but last week I sent about $3,000 out, with more ready to ship. It is too early in the game to make predictions.

Getting Started

Did you create a business plan before going online?

It follows our retail business plan.

How much time did it take to get up and running?

About a month.

Did you create the pages yourself?

This was the idea and baby of my former partner, who is now setting up Web sites as a business.

How much did it cost to get started?

A couple thousand over the course of a year. That includes full Internet access and some hardware.

How did you obtain your start-up capital?

Wrote it off as advertising.

What mistakes did you make that you wish you hadn't made?

I should have appealed more to the top-of-the line buyer instead of the beginner.

What advice would you give to a similar start-up?

Don't count on a get-rich-quick venture.

What skills are needed to run this business?

Basic computer knowledge and expertise in your own field.

What education is needed to run your site?

Trial and error, and have a guru to help dig you out.

What special qualities are needed to run your site?

Marketing and sales. You've got to know what will get people to read.

How did you promote your home page?

Mostly by getting the links included in other sites. I also included the URL in local advertising, business cards, etc.

How much did it cost to promote your site?

No extra budget; we already have a pretty good advertising plan.

How long did it take until you made your first sale?

Several weeks.

How did the start-up phase affect your personal life?

I am spending an additional hour a day responding to questions and updating the site, answering questionnaires like this, etc.

My Day

What does your average day look like?

I am Mr. Mom until noon (my wife has her own business at home). Then off to the shop, noon–8 P.M. Then after the kids are in bed, I hit the computer for a couple.

What does your job entail?

Retail sales, personnel management (forty employees), ordering, troubleshooting, etc.

How many hours a week do you spend working on your site?

Probably about twelve hours (total).

Answering mail = nine hours; researching questions = one hour; filling orders = two hours.

What was the hardest part of the job in the beginning?

Lots and lots of responses and compliments with few or no orders.

How long did it take to get established?

Still growing on the Internet. Established as a shop in about five years.

What do you like most about your work?

I sell FUN!

What do you like least?

Dealing with the problem customers that don't want to be happy.

Are there any hazards to running your site?

Yes. I am taking Visa numbers and sending product. UPS damages some product. The extra time I spend, though enjoyable, is at a sacrifice to other projects and personal time.

How much money do you hope to make?

Eventually, $20,000 extra a year—hopefully more, probably less.

General

Are customers concerned about security for their credit cards?

Not too much.

How do you process orders via credit cards?

Already had the machine. The bank gave it to me to use.

Was it easy or hard to get a machine?

It was easy. I had all sorts of sales people trying to sell me a machine. I had been doing it by hand. The bank brought one down the next day when they learned that I was about to purchase a machine that would have routed the money through a different bank.

Given what you know now, would you do it again?

This has been time-consuming, frustrating, and has cost me more than I have made, but I think it has been worth the expense and trouble, and will just get better. Yes, I would do it again.

Where can people find advice?

They can contact my buddy Randy at *randy@zyzzyva.com*.

The Future

What is your next venture?

I wish to have my own products on the Web instead of retailing the same thing other people have.

What else would you like to say?

It is difficult to keep up with changing and dated material. Even now I have a contest that is expired. I should be changing the dates instead of responding to this.

1997 Update

What is the most important thing you learned in the past year about marketing on the Internet?

In our case, the first year we looked more for the smaller-purchase customer. We found that we were getting more of the big-ticket-item shopper, so now we are targeting more toward that.

What is the most effective way to get people to buy products or services?

Generate patter with them. Answer their questions and ask them some of your own. Encourage them to call you and talk in person on the toll-free number.

How does your site generate revenue?

Sales of bicycles and accessories.

How much money have you made?

At least one customer a day walks into the shop and mentions the Web site. At least one customer a week has us ship out a big-ticket sale. When we were one of only two or three bike shops on the Web, the results were much slower than now that we are among hundreds. This continues to surprise me—that more Web competition has not hurt our share. There must be proportionately more people buying through the Web than competing shops coming online. Either that, or our unique approach makes us stand out from the crowd.

6 Housing and Real Estate

Real estate professionals are rapidly moving onto the Internet. All the major real estate companies have Web sites, but there is still room for independent realtors as well as other service providers to the housing and real estate industries. Opportunities for profits exist with suppliers to the real estate industries, as seen in Chapter 4, with business models calling for malls and lead generation.

Affluent professionals who don't have a lot of extra time to hunt for houses are finding the Internet can help them weed out homes in a matter of minutes, not weeks. Executives who are being relocated can use the Internet to find houses in distant cities without taking unnecessary house-hunting trips. Furthermore, people looking to go on vacation can use the Internet to find time-shares, vacation villas, and other rental properties (see Chapter 15).

As a purely anecdotal incident, I used the Internet to find a realtor to sell land I had purchased many years ago in a state three thousand miles away. The realtor had a listing on the Internet that I found through an online yellow pages service. I called him on the phone and was transferred to an agent who specialized in the area where my land was. He found a buyer in a matter of days and the transaction closed in about a month. The transaction couldn't have been any easier if I still lived in that area.

Virtually every real estate–related business is represented on the Web: real estate agencies, appraisers, auctioneers, books, consultants, corporate housing, development, individual listings, investment opportunities, law firms, listing services, magazines, marketing, mortgage loan companies, office space, planned communities, property management, relocation services, software, time-shares, and title insurance.

Businesses considering going online should follow these basic steps:

1. Build credibility by listing bios and company history.

2. Ask customers to complete a form asking what kinds of properties and amenities they are considering; send the form via e-mail to reduce typing and interview time.

3. Jazz up a site with interactive features that could include a calculator that estimates moving costs, closing costs, and mortgage rates.

Let's look at a few of the opportunities for current practitioners as well as entrepreneurs. You don't have to be Century 21 to make a living selling real estate via the Internet.

ROOMMATE REFERRALS BUSINESS

Overview

Stretching money is a key point for many recent college grads as well as others. Just look at the TV show *Friends* to see an example of this trend. Sharing an apartment is a fact of life for undergrads too. You can start a business to find roommates for people. Of course, this service can help people of any age. In fact, you could specialize the service to target specific audiences, such as gays, nonsmokers, or single parents.

The Web site is essentially a database of information regarding the apartments and the potential roommates. Your main tasks will be data entry, marketing, and keeping track of the finances. You don't need a realtor's license to start this business.

Rewards

Unlimited income is yours if you can sell well and show that the site is visited by qualified customers. You can make money by charging both landlords and renters for listings. If your site gets a lot of traffic, you can sell ads to companies that need to reach this market, such as movers, rental van companies, and decorators.

Risks

Normal business risks. Check with your lawyer to make sure you can't get sued for pairing someone with the roommate from hell.

Special Marketing Considerations for the Home Page

To look substantial, the home page must show that you list a wide variety of properties and people. Because the site is essentially a database of information and pictures of apartments and roommates, it must be easy to search for houses by geographic location and personality traits of roommates (such as smoker, night person, heavy metal music listener).

Hot Site

Homebuyers Fair, *www.homebuyers.com.*

REAL ESTATE BUSINESS

Overview

Realtors can show property without leaving the office by listing properties on Web sites. From the comfort of their homes, house hunters can select properties by location, price, and amenities. Consumers can see traditional house pictures; new software programs allow views from specific locations, such as the view of the master bedroom from the hallway.

Detailed descriptions can be downloaded when consumers find houses that meet their needs. After they have explored the databases of various realtors, customers can call to set appointments for the ones they like, thus saving time for themselves and the realtors.

Rewards

Realtors benefit as consumers come to them and ask to see specific houses. These prospects should be easy to work with because they know what they want. Realtors who are used to spending money on print advertisements might find Web sites a good alternative, especially if their area is a prime relocation market—people in distant cities make good online prospects.

Special Marketing Considerations for the Home Page

Good sites show pictures. Great sites offer a video walk-through of the house. Check out the software of BeHere, *www.behere.com*, with which consumers can see 360-degree views of the house.

To draw attention to specific properties, list them under enticing buttons such as "House of the Week" or "Best of the Lot."

The site must be easy to search by keyword.

Case Study: The Serkes Real Estate Search Engine

Berkeley Real Estate Search Engine – California

Your Real Estate "Home" Page!

Rated Excellent ☆ by Internet Real Estate Directory!!!

Honored by Allen Hainge as a Real Estate CyberStar

Allen F. Hainge
Seminars
CyberStars

★

- Consider this your new "Home" Page! There's a lot of information here, and many links take you all over the San Francisco Bay Area, so be sure to **Bookmark** us for easy and frequent return.

- We've completed a massive update to the site, and have information and links on the East Bay's most pleasant neighborhoods, best restaurants, newsletters for moms, most interesting sites, and community resources (newspapers, TV, radio, movies, bookstores, books and more!) Here's a first look at our new East Bay Neighborhood & Community Resource Page

- We respect the value of your time - our site is optimized for *speed*, not graphics which slow you down!

- *We welcome your business, and value your ideas, and thoughts.* Please tell us how we can help you , and how we can make the "Home" Page even better. Email your questions, real estate needs, & comments to Realtor@home-buy-sell.com

---

Figure 6–1. Serkes Real Estate Search Engine helps people find homes. Courtesy of Ira and Carol Serkes, RE/MAX Bay Area.

RE/MAX Bay Area—Berkeley	realtor@home-buy-sell.com
Ira & Carol Serkes, Realtors	*www.home-buy-sell.com*
1758 Solano Avenue	510-526-6668
Berkeley, CA 94707	888-Buy-Berkeley
	800-887-6668

(original interview 1995; update February 1997)

Who is your primary audience?

Home buyers, sellers, realtors, corporate relocation groups, people who need referrals to great realtors in the cities they're moving to or moving from.

How will they benefit from your service?

Buyers who use a buyers' broker generally pay about 3.5 percent lower prices than a buyer who uses a conventional agent.

Our seller clients received higher sales prices, in less time, than sellers who hired other agents to sell their homes.

How does your service differ from others?

We're very organized and computerized and provide a high level of service and follow-up. In the past few years our sales (as measured by number of closed transactions as well as total closed dollar volume of sales) have been in the top 1 percent of realtors in our market area.

We provide more than just information on homes. Our site has lots of links to local communities, sightseeing, radio and TV stations, personal interests, local history and architecture.

Is this business an offshoot of your existing business or does it exist only on the Internet?

We earn our living as realtors.

Our Web site—The Serkes Real Estate Search Engine—is an offshoot of our existing real estate business. We help people buy and sell homes in Berkeley, Albany, Kensington, El Cerrito, and nearby communities, and offer referrals to other highly qualified realtors all over the United States and Canada.

Was it meant to generate income on its own or to steer people to your office?

It should generate income on its own. I hope to have more people decide to hire us after seeing the kind of service they receive from us. We also hope to help buyers and sellers by referring them to top realtors all over the nation.

Where do you operate your business?

Back rear bedroom of a two-bedroom house facing the garden and watching the cats stroll by.

What is your background and training?

Chemical engineer with two patents in research. I've been using computers for almost thirty years, and the Internet/World Wide Web is the most exciting thing I've ever seen. I once programmed in Octal on a PDP 8 Digital Equipment computer, had an Osborne for many years, and now use a Quadra 840AV Macintosh.

Getting Started

When did you start your business?

Realtor: September 1986. Online: June 1995.

Did you create a business plan before going online?

A business plan for real estate business, not Web business.

How much time did it take to get up and running?

I first saw the World Wide Web in mid-February, and hired someone to get me online. I was online within about a week.

Did you create the pages yourself or did you get help?

Initial pages were done by someone else. I had some very good leads at the beginning and then had very little response. That's when I decided to rework the page. I spent several months surfing over to other pages to see what I liked and what I didn't like. I also set up a basic template for our page design. Then one Saturday morning, I woke up early and by the end of the day had our Web pages up and running.

How much did it cost to get started?

It cost about $240 for the initial Web page. Once I went online, it cost me about $25/month for seventy-five hours/month and five megabytes of storage. It cost about $100 to register my domain name, home-buy-sell.com, with the InterNIC.

Did you need to go to an outside source for start-up capital?

No.

How did you promote your site?

I registered the site with Yahoo! and with another search engine called Submit It, which takes the information and distributes it to fifteen or twenty other search engines! We cross-link our site to as many places as possible. I've several links to local radio stations. They have our URL on their listeners' Web site.

We put our Web site URL on every piece of e-mail we send.

I put our Web address on our business cards, on every property flyer, and on open house ads.

I plan to make a sign rider for our for-sale signs so people will see our e-mail and Web address as they drive by.

We're sending out a mailing to about 3,500 people in our database—past clients, neighbors in our farm, attorneys, CPAs, newspaper and TV reporters, etc. This will be distributed the first week of August 1995.

How much did it cost to promote your site?

Except for the mailing, everything else was practically free.

How long did it take until you got your first sale?

Haven't had any sales yet. [Note: See the update for 1997!]

How much money do you expect to make?

$10,000–$150,000 a year.

What mistakes did you make that you wish you hadn't made?

I started with a different Internet service provider (ISP) than I am with now. I'd chosen an ISP that had no minimum charges and relatively low ($2–$4/hour) online charges. I didn't realize how much time I'd be spending online.

What advice would you give someone starting a business?

Ira's Tips for Setting Up a World Wide Web Page

- Make sure your home page is easy to navigate. Make it easy to return to the home page. For each page I used a template with a place for someone to e-mail me, a return to the entry page, and our name and toll-free number. I think I'll also be adding the home page address, i.e., *www.dnai.com/realtor*, so people will know how to return to the page if they happen to print it out.

- Keep graphics small so they load quickly and easily. Consider using small thumbnail graphics to get people interested, and use a larger graphic on the next page.

- Make sure that you don't need to use graphics to navigate around. Whenever you have a graphic, be sure to use text to describe what the graphic does.

- It's much faster to navigate when you have only text and no or few graphics.

- Put the date and time on each page and keep them up to date and fresh. Make each page about one screen's worth of information. It's easier to click to another page than it is to page down.

- Make the Web site wide and shallow. What this means is to set up the entry page to reach to three to eight other pages, then have each of these second-level pages point to several other pages. Think of it like a bamboo plant with wide roots that go out ten or twenty feet but go down only six to twelve inches. That way, it's easy to navigate the site. It's very difficult when you have to go down twelve levels to find something.

- Make your site interesting! Include something about yourself, your interests, your neighborhood, city, community. Give someone a reason to return to your site.

- Some tips on selecting an ISP: Find one with a local phone number for calling in and that provides lots of online time for low cost. My provider gives me seventy-five hours a month for $25.

- Obtain a reasonable amount of free storage. I have five megabytes of storage, which should be more than enough for a while.

- Get decent tech service. It's very confusing to set up your account for the first time, so be sure you've got someone of whom you can ask questions about domain name registration. Make sure you can register your domain. We registered *home-buy-sell.com* as our domain, which means you can send e-mail to realtor@home-buy-sell.com and it will come to us.

- TEST, TEST, TEST. Upload your pages,and check all the links. It's easiest to play with one or two pages or links, get familiar with the concepts, and then charge ahead. If you're a Mac user and have a CD-ROM, purchase the excellent CD *Roadside Resources* from BMUG (Berkeley Macintosh User Group),1442A Walnut Street #62, Berkeley, CA 94709 (510-540-1029).

What skills are needed?

For real estate: curiosity, willingness to prospect for new business, and contact with past clients.

What special qualities are needed to run your site?

Curiosity. The language of the Web, HTML, is very similar to the Wordstar word processing program. I'd recommend just surfing around, identifying the Web sites you like the best, and then viewing the source code to see how they did it.

My Day

What does your average day look like?

Up at 6:30–8:00 A.M.

Search the Multiple Listing Service (MLS) database for expired listings.

Determine what to do for the day. Do it.

What does your job entail?

Helping people buy or sell real estate, solving the many problems that arise, and offering referrals for people who wish to move to other communities.

How many hours a week do you spend working on your site?

About one hour a day. I often tweak the site, add more links, and add forms.

What percentages of time are spent on each task?

Don't know. Most of the online time is spent writing/reading e-mail.

What was the hardest aspect of the work in the beginning?

Real estate—the frustrations of working on a transaction and having it fall through because of problems with the house.

What do you like most about your work?

Getting paid for our services.

What do you like the least?

Frustration and unsteady income.

What was your greatest moment?

When I was selected to be coauthor of the Nolo Press book *How to Buy a House in California,* which has now sold over 35,000 copies.

How did the start-up phase affect your personal life?

Not much.

Are you glad you are on the Web for personal and business reasons?

Delighted.

Given what you know now, would you do it again?

For sure, only faster.

The Future

What is your next venture?

Giving seminars on how business people can use the Internet and World Wide Web to build their business. Letting people know how exciting it is.

What else would you like to say?

Well-done survey—lots of good questions.

1997 Update

What is the most important thing you learned in the past year about marketing on the Internet?

Design your site for the people who are visiting it. Virtually every inquiry I received came from buyers, so we did a massive update to our site designed to help home buyers learn about our favorite Berkeley/East Bay communities and find homes in their price range.

I made a list of our favorite places–movies, restaurants, cafés, bookstores, books, pubs, hangouts, parks, etc., and cross-referenced each place with the neighborhood it's in. Then I spent several days visiting about a dozen of the most livable neighborhoods in Berkeley, Albany, Kensington, El Cerrito, Oakland, Piedmont, Montclair, and Emeryville. I took lots of digital photos of the shops, parks, and amenities that make each neighborhood unique.

Next I set up a page for each neighborhood, with information, photos, and maps showing people our favorite places in each neighborhood. They know the best places to buy bagels, have dinner, or browse a in bookstore Thousand Oaks and Berkeley and the best place for soup in Kensington!

In addition, I set up a page for each grouping such as hamburger joints, cafés, etc. Our Books and Library site features our favorite bookstores and libraries and the title, author, and Dewey decimal numbers on books about East Bay and Berkeley.

Yes, it was (and is) a massive job—but lately we've been rewarded with two or three leads a week! The people who write to me say that the site is friendly and full of information

What is the most effective way to get people to come to your site?

1. Register with the search engines.

2. Tell everyone you meet about the site. Whenever a buyer or seller calls, ask him for his e-mail address, and tell (and e-mail) him your URL.

What is the most effective way to get people to return to your site?

Visitors return to my site because I've a direct link to the Realtor's Multiple Listing Service. They can find out about the latest homes in their price range.

I think the advantage of the Web is that it lets you be an expert in an extremely local area while at the same time have a worldwide presence.

What is the most effective way to get people to buy products or services?

Give them lots of information about your services so they're eager to e-mail or call you, then meet with them to make sure that they're nice folks you want to work with.

How much money have you made?

Without a doubt, I'd say that our Web site is the most cost-effective thing I've done for building my business.

By the time home buyers call us or send us e-mail, they're already sold on our service! People who really like what we have to offer are eager to contact us, and those who don't like our style don't bother. I'd say that we've met the nicest people on the Web.

In addition, the buyers often have already selected the home they want to buy, and in two of the sales we never even showed a home and another time we only showed two homes.

We've already closed over a million dollars in sales, have been paid on two outgoing referrals, have another buyer in escrow, another buyer about to go into escrow, and about two dozen other leads—all from our Web site.

One of our transactions was an international referral halfway across the globe. A home buyer living in Abu Dhabi (a United Arab Emirate in the Arabian Gulf) took advantage of our free realtor referral service and e-mailed us a request for a Hawaiian Buyer Broker. We searched our

Certified Residential Specialist (CRS) database for a highly qualified realtor, used e-mail to put them both together, and the buyer just moved into his new Hawaiian home!

Interestingly, most of our clients buy or sell exclusively within the communities of Berkeley, Albany, Kensington, El Cerrito, and Rockridge/ North Oakland. Our clients are thrilled that we know these communities extremely well. We feel strongly that home buyers and sellers should demand to be represented by a realtor with a strong local track record, one who knows what makes each neighborhood unique, not an agent who is willing to go all over the county just to make a commission.

Our sellers also greatly benefit from our strong Internet presence. We sold one charming Thousand Oaks home after the buyer surfed our Web site and viewed the many pictures we took with our digital camera when we listed the home. They realized the home would work well for them, asked their realtor to show it, their offer was accepted, and they moved into their new home in time for Thanksgiving!

MORTGAGE BROKER

Overview

People who buy houses online may use online mortgage brokers as well. Clever mortgage brokers follow the lead of the insurance industry and allow consumers to search a database for competitive bids from different lending sources. See chapter 4 for a discussion of the role of the middleman in the online world.

Rewards and Risks

The Internet can increase sales and build a network of new professional contacts. Normal business risks.

Special Marketing Considerations for the Home Page

Build credibility by showing a résumé, awards, professional designations, and testimonials from clients. Create a sense of purpose by adding articles about home buying, refinancing, and the like. Add a mortgage calculator software program that people can fill out online to see what mortgages they qualify for.

Hot Site

Mortgage Mart Information Service, *www.mortgagemart.com*, a product of Inland Mortgage Corp., offers one hundred pages on getting a loan. Consumers can prepare an application form online.

Case Study: Mortgage Market Information Services

Mortgage Market Information Services   eaton@banking.interest.com

Daniel Eaton Interactive   *www.interest.com*

53 E. St. Charles Road   800-509-4636

Villa Park, IL 60181

(original interview 1995)

Mortgage Market is one of the nation's largest suppliers of mortgage, real estate, and financial information and provides these services to three hundred of the top newspapers. The Internet projects complement the mortgage rate guides that appear in over three hundred newspapers across the country.

Who is your primary audience?

Consumers.

How will they benefit from your product or service?

When consumers are educated about available mortgage products and services, they are able to make smarter decisions that have the potential to save them thousands of dollars in interest payments.

How does your service differ from others?

The information we offer is presented in terms that are simple to understand and are relevant to the existing market conditions.

Is this business an offshoot of your existing business or does it exist only on the Internet?

The Internet projects complement our mortgage rate guides that appear in over 300 newspapers across the country.

Was it meant to generate income on its own or to steer people to your other outlets?

This project has several goals:

1. Increase company exposure.

2. Promote company products.

3. Generate revenue from ad space for lending institutions.

4. Promote our client customers.

Where is your office located?

Corporate office.

What is your background and training?

I have been involved in the real estate industry for the past fifteen years. I was educated at the University of Wisconsin and am a former president of Realty Data Systems, Inc.

When did you start your business?

Mortgage Market Information Services, Inc., was founded by James R. De Both, a former telecommunications and computer planning consultant for Arthur Young & Co. In 1987 De Both acted on his perception that the Midwest needed a consumer-assisted mortgage information service. He viewed the telephone as the ideal vehicle for providing timely comprehensive and comprehensible mortgage rate information to consumers, loan officers, and real estate agents. Expanding on this, he developed specialized mortgage rate directories that are featured in newspapers' real estate sections.

How much money has your company made online?

N/A

Getting Started

Did you create a business plan before going online?

Mortgage Market Information Services has operated a public bulletin board service (BBS), Mortgage Market ONLINE (708-834-1450), over the past four years. We were able to build on this experience for an effective Web site.

How much time did it take to get up and running?

I was encouraging management to invest in the project for about six months. Then management saw the light with all of the hoopla and press regarding the Internet and they decided to invest.

Did you create the pages yourself?

I created all of the pages myself with the assistance of our in-house graphics department and the Multimedia Graphics Network.

How much did it cost to get started?

We incurred capital equipment costs of approximately $15,000.

How did you obtain your start-up capital?

The project was funded internally.

What mistakes did you make that you wish you hadn't made?

To avoid them, we should have talked to networking experts and people that already made the mistakes.

What advice would you give to a similar start-up?

Use a turnkey solution such as Sun Microsystems Netra or SGI Indy. It will cost you more—however, it will save you time and aggravation in the future. Your time to live will also be shortened dramatically.

What skills are necessary to run a business?

VISION. The ability to see the potential—for any application.

What education is needed to run your site?

Once it is up and running, you need skills and education similar to a publisher.

What special qualities are needed to run your site?

Unique business perspective.

How did you promote your home page?

Our URL is published on our newspaper rate guides that appear in some of the nation's largest newspapers.

How much did it cost to promote your site?

Promoting costs were merely incorporated into projects we are already doing. This includes newspaper advertising, trade magazine advertising, and industry trade shows.

How long did it take until you made your first sale?

About six weeks.

How did the start-up phase affect your personal life?

You can't help but get excited over this new technology.

My Day

What does your average day look like?

Check systems (Internet, fax broadcast, online services). Review work from previous day, answer mail, review market research, build reports, distribute reports to clients, check marketing projects, check status of graphics in process, check satellite news feeds.

What does your job entail?

All phases of management.

How many hours a week do you spend working on your site?

At least thirty hours: updating—20 percent; marketing—20 percent; creating new features—40 percent; administrative—15 percent; drinking coffee—5 percent

What was the hardest part of the job in the beginning?

Selling new technologies.

We recently had a visit by some bankers (our customers). They found the demonstration interesting; however, their first questions were "How is this going to make me money?" and "What kind of results can I expect?"

The questions were reasonable and understandable. However, my observation was that they REALLY scrutinized the entire idea.

The reaction is totally different with our print product. The paper has a circulation of one hundred thousand and it costs $10 to advertise. They say, "Where do I sign?"

The print product is tangible. People like to touch and feel. They can deal with a paper product.

The comfort level just wasn't there. It is going to take time to convert business people to online benefits and time to build a track record of success.

How long did it take to get established?

This thing has a life of its own. I don't think one will ever get truly "established" because of its dynamic nature. "Recognized" may be a more appropriate term. Users need to find you either by traditional advertising or through an index.

What do you like most about your work?

The creative nature of the medium. The ability to help people in their home buying process.

What do you like least?

The difficulty in educating close-minded business people.

What was your greatest moment?

Every day when I read my mail, the comments from consumers on how much they like the service. The day a lender called and stated how many calls they received from the posting.

Are there any hazards to running your site?

Know your market. Know your product and how it fits in that market. You must do your homework. Writing HTML is only a small portion of the big picture.

Compare your site's processes with those of magazines or newspapers. They have editorial departments, sales departments, production departments, etc. Successful publishers rely upon a team of professionals to produce their final product.

How much money do you hope to make?

N/A

General

Given what you know now, would you do it again?

Absolutely.

REAL ESTATE SERVICE PROVIDERS REFERRAL BUSINESS

Overview

Realtors need a lot of support services to close deals. Buyers depend on realtors to refer them to home inspectors, pest control companies, painters, plumbers, carpenters, moving companies, and a lot of other service providers.

You can create a referral business for these service providers. Create a home page and list the providers for free or a nominal fee. Charge them more for a link to their home page, or charge them to create a home page. You can also sell advertisements to companies that want to reach these service providers.

You can specialize in your city or region or set up a national referral service.

Rewards and Risks

You will receive income from the sale of links, Web sites, and ads. Normal business risks.

Special Marketing Considerations for the Home Page

In addition to nice graphics, consider adding timely information of interest to realtors, such as mortgage rate updates, home construction figures, and the like.

Job Hunting Online

The Internet is becoming a resource center for employers seeking new workers and for employees finding new jobs. Millions of people look for work every year. You can benefit by starting businesses that match them up! This chapter will examine job banks and resumes.

The Internet can make money for career counselors, job banks, newsletters and newspapers, résumé services. Training companies can also use Web sites as electronic brochures for their classes, newsletters, software, and other services.

JOB BANKS

Overview

Headhunters have come online! Career centers, headhunters, placement offices, and the like are on the Internet. In addition, many technology companies and Internet advertising agencies place employment ads on their Web sites.

Entrepreneurs can start their own job banks, Web sites that contain information for both employers and employees. Job hunters can see job listings with qualifications and pay scales. Employers can see candidates' résumés.

This business can make a lot of sense to college entrepreneurs, as they come across hundreds of their classmates looking for work each day. You could create a career center at your university that has résumés from the general class, business students, and/or law students. You can also create a service that offers not only full-time jobs but part-time jobs and internships as well.

You can select a market and dominate it. Consider creating a site that caters to a specific market, like computer programmers, or a geographic region, like Boston. By selecting a niche, you can become known and develop a following among employers and employees.

Rewards

This business can yield income in several sources. Employers pay for the job posting at rates that start at $100 per job per month. Web sites can also make money by creating home pages for clients that include information about the company or by posting the notice in a premier location on the Web site.

Job placement centers can also conduct job searches for companies. Employers typically pay a commission of 30 percent or more of the candidate's first year's salary, so the money can be very, very good.

You should be a good salesperson to make this site work, as you will need to prove that you can attract both job seekers and employers.

There are lots of opportunities for local markets and niches. Every town or region can have its own job bank. Every vertical market can have its own local, regional, or national job bank as well.

Risks

Competition could heat up, thus driving prices down or forcing you to sell better, smarter, and harder.

Special Marketing Considerations for the Home Page

Each placement center should build credibility by printing its mission statement, noting that it makes reference checks on candidates, and demonstrating its expertise in handling job searches.

Employers and employees can be attracted to the site with solid editorial information on job hiring, interview strategies, and links to related sites.

Hot Sites

- IntelliMatch   *www.intellimatch.com*
- Career Mosaic   *www.careermosaic.com*
- SuperSite.Net/TechJobs *www.supersite.net*
- Monster Board   *www.monster.com*
- Career Mart   *www.careermart.com*

Site Review: IntelliMatch

IntelliMatch	*www.intellimatch.com*
10 Almaden Boulevard, 9th Floor	408-494-7200
San Jose, CA 94113	

IntelliMatch, *www.intellimatch.com*, a job bank site on the Internet, features an automated job search function. The job seeker uses a structured format to define specific job criteria. All jobs in the IntelliMatch HotJobs! database that meet the job seeker's preferences are automatically identified. This new job agent feature streamlines the job search process. For employers, a new search option enables employers to find candidates who have résumés containing specific text strings.

Employers can post job openings or search for candidates who have placed their résumés online. As of this writing, the job bank had fifty thousand résumés, which included forty thousand people currently employed. Employers searching for candidates can see a list ranked in order by the search criteria.

"IntelliMatch's Precision Matching Technology is a real breakthrough for online recruiting, especially in the health care industry, where having the right credentials for the job affects patient care as well as the bottom line. It will allow us to define our requirements quickly in great detail and then automatically single out the right candidates," said Ralph Friedman, president of HealthStaf, a specialist in serving the staffing needs of many of the nation's leading health care facilities and companies.

Another testimonial comes from high-tech company I-Planet's executive vice president, Vish Mishra, who said, "We hired 10 percent of our workforce through IntelliMatch. It is clearly the most cost-effective way to recruitment that gives us more control over the types of candidates we want to attract and hire. It is an incredible time-saver."

More than ten thousand users visit Intellimatch's site daily. Employers posting jobs include Hewlett-Packard, Mitsubishi, Seagate, 3Com, and Bay Networks.

Site Review: The Black Collegians

A perfect example of selecting a niche audience is the *Black Collegian's* online National Job Résumé Database, an electronic version of the twenty-six-year-old publication. The *Black Collegian* presents job opportunities in all corporations, and in government, academic, and nonprofit organizations. Employers post the notices; job hunters search for jobs by keyword, employer name, geography, and experience requirements.

Giving the site a healthy editorial focus are articles on career planning and job search information as well as commentary by leading African American writers and lifestyle/entertainment features.

RÉSUMÉ WRITING BUSINESS

Overview

With people being laid off—excuse me, downsized—in large numbers, résumé writers should have a large base of customers on the Internet. Entrepreneurs can start businesses that target select markets, like graduating students, teachers and professors, and college administrators, or offer a general service. Several sites ask customers to fill out forms that list the traditional job information (companies, positions, dates, responsibilities), which the business uses to write the résumé.

Rewards and Risks

Let's face it, the barriers to entry aren't high! If you can write your own résumé, you can pick up money writing résumés for other people. Because of the ease of entry into this field, you need to position yourself as different from the rest and be up on the latest résumé formats and buzzwords. Nothing reads worse than last year's buzzwords! Prices for writing résumés can range from $65 to $150 each. Additional income can be garnered from writing cover letters and follow-up letters.

Résumés written for the Internet are taking a new look and feel because companies scan them into computers. When a job opens, the computer searches for keywords, like UNIX or programmer. This means the flowery prose used in paper résumés (e.g., dynamic, well-rounded, self-starter) will not be read or acted upon. To impress the computer and make the first cut, a good online résumé must have plenty of keywords.

Special Marketing Considerations for the Home Page

Differentiation is the key here. Lots of people are getting into this field, so the consumer must be able to see how your services differ from your competitors'. At the very least, you should have your own résumé online as well as samples of work you have done. Testimonials from satisfied clients would help too. Articles about job hunting and interview tactics would be a bonus, as would links to companies that offer jobs on their home pages. To prime the pump, consider offering a free critique of a person's existing résumés. One site even offers a guarantee. If the résumés it writes doesn't land the applicant a job, the fee will be returned.

Hot Sites

- Guaranteed Résumés, *http://users.aol.com/GResumes/index.htm*, shows how to create a useful poage for getting business.

- Resumail Network, *www.resumail.com*, hopes to set a new standard in résumé writing. By offering software that helps create online résumés, they hope employers will find candidates faster than by scanning traditional résumés cut and pasted from word processors. This business plan requires a massive shift in the way people write and read résumés. Time will tell if this is too big a hurdle to cross.

8 Information Services

If information is power, there are a lot of powerful people and companies on the Internet. Information providers can use the Internet to promote their regular businesses or to create virtual businesses that exist only online—an ideal situation for a start-up or moonlighter. This chapter explores information brokering and providing businesses you can start online.

INFORMATION BROKER

Overview

With the vast amount of data available on the Internet and the commercial online services, like CompuServe, Prodigy, and America Online, as well as business-to-business services, it isn't surprising that a new breed of online librarian has come to the fore. Called information brokers, these researchers find information requested by their clients, which can include large corporations that need voluminous material to support their marketing programs or financial analyses and start-ups that must have statistics to bolster new business plans.

You must have good research skills, work well under deadlines, and have extensive knowledge of resources on the Internet and other online services. Not only must you be able to understand a client's requests but also you must be able to add value to a search by identifying possible avenues of research the client hasn't thought about because you knew they existed and the client didn't. To get started, read a good book about this field, such as *Information Brokers' Handbook* by Linda Rugge and Alfred Glossbrenner (McGraw Hill, 1997), or contact the Association of Independent Information Professionals, 609-730-8759.

Rewards

Prices for services can vary widely depending on the scope of the project, deadline, or part of the country you live in, as well as your background. Fees generally range from $25 to $125 an hour; a rush job can command higher fees. Someone starting out or doing this part time can charge less. We've seen prices as low as $10 an hour from a retired librarian. Entrepreneurs can start this type of business either full time or part time and can subcontract work as demand for services increases.

Risks

Normal business risks.

Special Marketing Considerations for the Home Page

The Web site can contain credibility-building devices like résumés, testimonials from clients, and articles you've written about trends in an industry you want to mine for prospective clients. As a way to build relationships with clients, search newsgroups and mailing lists for people who ask questions that you can find the answers to. Post the answers and let people know about your services through your signature file. You'll build credibility with them immediately. Consider offering a free proposal that outlines what you would do.

Case Study: Smartbiz

Figure 8–1. Information centers like Smart Business Supersite attract people by presenting them with a vast array of useful information. Copyright 1997, Smart Business Supersite.

Smart Business Supersite, The How-To Resource for Business

Irv Brechner   *irv@smartbiz.com*

88 Orchard Road, CN 5219   *www.smartbiz.com*

Princeton, NJ 08543

(original interview February 1997)

What does your company do?

Develop and operate "how-to" supersites that provide a wealth of free information and also offer how-to books, tapes, reports, etc., for sale.

What expertise/background do you draw on to operate your business?

Eighteen years of direct marketing experience, two years of Internet marketing experience, a lot of common sense.

What was your company's goal for going online?

To learn how to attract traffic and sell products.

How do you know you have reached that goal?

We have because our site has received a nice amount of traffic. We've won dozens of awards and are profitable.

How much did it cost to get started?

Prefer not to reveal.

What makes your site special?

It's the only site with such an extensive collection of how-to resources. It is extremely easy to navigate and posts new columns every month, news briefs and tips every day.

How to do you get people to come to your site?

Registering with search engines, word of mouth, postings to newsgroups, etc.

How do you get people to return to your site?

Additional content every day, free reminder service.

How do you move people from being window-shoppers to paying customers?

By offering appropriate products based on what they're looking for and by making it easy to order—via credit card, over the Internet, 800 number, fax, or snail mail.

What is the most important thing you learned in the past year about marketing on the Internet?

You've got to do your homework in terms of defining a unique selling proposition, understanding what's out there and what you're up against, and having enough capital to see you through twice as many months/years as you think it will take.

What is the most effective way to get people to come to your site?

Search engines.

What is the most effective way to get people to return to your site?

New and updated content, special services

What is the most effective way to get people to buy products or services?

Give them something free and then offer to sell them more information on the same topic.

How much money have you made?

Site is profitable. Orders and advertising sold per thousand page views is high and growing, thanks again, for your help!

MARKET ANALYST

Overview

Every industry has experts who conduct research and sell the results. Entrepreneurs can create a new online business analyzing business data ranging from the computer chip market to the purchasing habits of coeds in Midwest colleges. You must have the qualifications and background to be an analyst, just as you must be trained to be a doctor. It is essential that you have a good background in marketing, finance, and analysis as well as the dynamics of the industry you study.

Rewards

By having fixed costs for creating materials, your income is limited only by your ability to convince companies to buy. If the material is highly valued, companies can pay tens of thousands of dollars. If you have good material, it can be resold to many companies.

Risks

If your material is not valued or is poorly researched, you will not sell many reports; if you do, their buyers will not come back for more.

Special Marketing Considerations for the Home Page

Credibility is the key to making sales. You have to prove that you—a virtual unknown in a virtual world—have the insight and experience to forecast the future and make sense of the present. Consider writing short articles, press releases, and position papers that give away the highlights of your report. This strategy might sound like heresy to you can—after all, why would anyone buy the cow if they can get the milk for free? However, analysts have been doing this for years. They write a press release that entices the market, which then turns around and buys the whole report because they are number junkies and detail-oriented perfectionists who need your facts to justify their multimillion-dollar marketing campaigns or company acquisitions.

To add value to your site, add links to companies in your industry as well as to newspapers and magazines covering the field.

Hot Sites

- AP Research   *www.apresearch.com*
- Frost & Sullivan   *www.frost.com*
- Dataquest   *www.dataquest.com*

Case Study: AP Research

AP Research   *aprophet@apresearch.com*

Andrew Prophet   *www.apresearch.com*

19672 Stevens Creek Blvd., Suite 175

Cupertino, CA 95014-2464

(original interview 1995)

What do you do? Who is your primary audience?

AP Research (APR) is a firm dedicated to providing market research and custom consulting services to the PC Card (PCMCIA) and SCSI industries. This is a small subsegment of the portable computing industry. The client base is very broad. APR offers custom advice and reports to corporate management, venture capitalists, marketing managers, financial analysts, strategic planners, product planners, procurement executives, and public relations firms. The company was founded in 1982.

How will they benefit from your service?

I research niche markets, review product plans, evaluate product portfolios, prepare competitive analyses, and offer seminars. AP Research concentrates on PC Cards (PCMCIA cards), SCSI adapters, and the underlying semiconductor technology.

In addition to market research, we publish *Baseline Analysis of PCMCIA Card Markets*, a low-cost executive overview of the PC Card markets, and recently, a more focused briefing entitled *Baseline Analysis of Wireless PC Cards*.

How does your product or service differ from others?

AP Research concentrates on the PC Card industry, thus providing in-depth market analysis at a very low cost.

Is this business an offshoot of your existing business or does it exist only on the Internet?

Like any other specialized consulting firm, AP Research seeks client engagements using all the traditional means, including the Web. The Web page is designed to stimulate interest in our services and market research.

What is your background and training?

I was associate director of semiconductor consulting at Dataquest, a high-technology market research firm. My consulting projects covered a wide range of strategic business issues involving semiconductors and personal computers. I am founder of the ASIC segment of the Semiconductor Industry Service and gained wide prominence as its principal analyst. My academic training includes a masters in business administration from Santa Clara University, a B.S. electrical engineering from Illinois Institute of Technology, and M.S. electrical engineering from San Jose State University.

What advice would you give to a similar start-up?

Answering this question is difficult. The diversity of products/service on the Web is very broad. I think it largely depends on the infrastructure of the industry. For consulting services such as mine, I think the prospective client needs to feel comfortable with AP Research and the specific type of market research/consulting services available. Obviously, for other enterprises the message may be different.

What skills are necessary to run a business?

I think the skill set depends on the type of business. In my case, a strong background in semiconductor market research and consulting is mandatory. I believe this is more important than knowledge of the Internet or the Web.

What education is needed to run your site?

I believe my background as an engineer and market researcher are critical to the success of my practice.

Are you glad you are on the Web for personal and business reasons?

I believe the Web offers my firm the opportunity to cast a wider net and demonstrate expertise.

Given what you know now, would you do it again?

Yes.

COLLEGE SERVICE

A great many college students have free accounts on the Internet, courtesy of their universities. They comprise a great potential audience for marketers of products that appeal to young adults. They are also candidates for services that help improve their lives as students. These can seed new ideas for additional businesses to serve this large market.

Case Study: CollegeNET

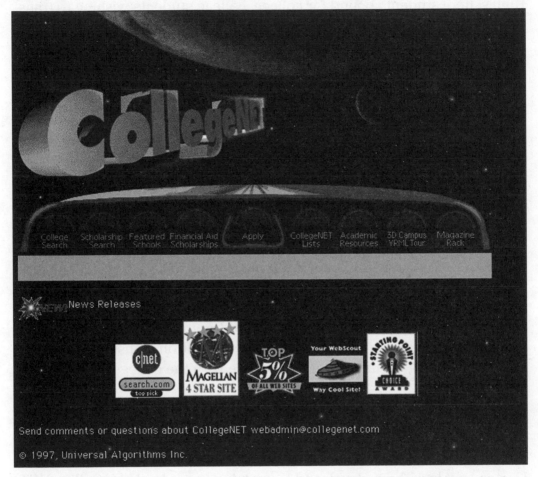

Figure 8–2. CollegeNET's innovative graphics appeal to its target audience—high school and college students. Copyright 1997, CollegeNET.

Universal Algorithms, Inc.   *jim@unival.com*

Jim Wolfston   *www.collegenet.com*

One SW Columbia, Suite 100   503-227-2790

Portland, OR 97258

(original interview 1995; update March 1997)

Who is your primary audience?

High school students bound for college, college students wishing to transfer to other schools, college students looking for graduate schools.

How will they benefit from your service?

CollegeNET provides quick and easy access to information about colleges and universities. The CollegeNET database contains the most accurate, up-to-date, and complete set of links to college and university home pages. College-bound students can easily generate lists of colleges by tuition, enrollment, and geography. In the fall of 1995, CollegeNET will introduce online college applications

How does your service differ from others?

It is easier to use and navigate. It has more links to colleges and universities than any other site. It has more schools and other academic resources backlinked to us. The links are set up to financial aid information and other resources. It uses the new ANSI-approved Electronic Data Interchange (EDI) definition for college application transmission to the college, ensuring accuracy. It is compatible with the colleges' information systems.

Is this an offshoot of an existing business or does it only exist on the Internet?

Universal Algorithms developed, maintains, and markets CollegeNET. CollegeNET exists only on the Internet.

Getting Started

When did the business start?

Universal Algorithms, Inc., was started in 1977. CollegeNET was announced in April of 1995.

Did you create a business plan before going online?

Ready, fire, aim!

How much time did it take to get up and running?

Site is being continuously developed (started).

Who created the Web pages?

Our software developers.

How much did it cost to get started?

Confidential.

Did you need to go to an outside source for start-up capital?

Company proceeds.

How is the home page being promoted?

Direct mailings, professional conferences, public relations, etc.

How much does it cost to promote the site?

Confidential.

How long did it take to get the first sale?

Within one week of product announcement.

How much money have you made?

Confidential.

What mistakes did you make that you wish you hadn't made?

Of Kourse not!

What advice can you give to someone starting a business?

It depends upon what kind of page.

What skills are needed to run your business?

UNIX, Perl, graphics design, strong writing, logical organization of information, hardware knowledge, competitive spirit, pioneering spirit.

My Day

What does your average day look like?

An impossible selection of thousands of good choices. I try to cover the most pressing of the thousands of selections and cajole others into helping me with the others.

How many hours a week do you spend working on your site?

Ten to twenty hours.

What's the hardest aspect of your job?

Coping with negativism.

What do you like the most about your work?

Watching people get pumped.

What do you like the least?

Countering and coping with negativism.

What was your greatest moment?

Smoking the Graduate Record Exam.

How did the start-up of this business affect your personal life?

I had none at the time I started.

Given what you know now, would you do it again?

Of course.

The Future

What's the next venture?

Starting a social/philosophical revolution.

What are your long-term goals for this home page?

CASH FLOW.

What else would you like to say?

Watch out!!!

1997 Update

CollegeNET gets hundreds of thousands of page views each day. It has added a feature that allows students to fill out college applications online. It also has a financial aid search service. The Web site has won several major awards from C/net, an online news service that also produces a syndicated TV show, and others.

COLLEGE FINANCIAL AID SERVICE

Overview

Did you find scholarship money online to fund your education? Then the information can be just as valuable as you find sources of cash for others. Several companies in the offline world offer this kind of database service. You might want to work with them to run an online version. That way you won't have to search for information from scratch; you'll be able to tap into their resources, which will reduce your start-up costs.

Rewards

Your fee can be charged hourly or fixed.

Risks

You might have to fill out the forms for the less able, but you can charge for that service. Competition can come quickly.

Special Marketing Considerations for the Home Page

Your Web site should tell your story without giving away your trade secrets—where the money is buried.

ADVICE COLUMNIST

Overview

Dear Abby hasn't hit the Internet yet, so the field is wide open for enterprising know-it-alls. Do you have common sense and a kicky writing style? Then you could be the next advicemeister. Hey, if Psychic Friends can be a hit on an infomercial, can this be a bad job?

This business doesn't have to be limited to the lovelorn. How about creating a similar service that draws on your expertise on such topics as car repair, computer solutions, household repair, interior decorating, and parenting? You can also specialize in different groups of people, like teens, gays, and seniors.

Here's how the business works. You create a home page and tell everyone about it (see Chapter 3). Show you are an expert in a given field. List types of questions you answer. You might show previously answered questions.

Rewards

You can make money by charging questioners, readers, or advertisers.

Risks

Normal business risks.

Special Marketing Considerations for the Home Page

If you decide to charge readers, you'll need to set up a password or registration system (see Chapter 4). You should consider creating a persona or alter ego for the character you portray online. No one will ask questions of an ordinary Joe, so create a vivid character that people will want to confide in and read replies from.

Hot Site

America's Brightest, *www.americasbrightest.com*, will answer questions about tax, travel, and other topics for its subscribers, who pay between $9.95 and $49.95 a month.

REVIEW SERVICE

Overview

If you are the type of person who is always giving your opinion on restaurants, movies, books, and the like, then consider starting a review service. Write reviews and post them on your Web site. Qualifications should include good writing style and the ability to write lots of reviews in a timely manner.

Rewards

You could make money from selling advertising space or subscriptions. You just might be able to get free meals, books, and movie passes.

Risks

Normal business risks. Competition may arise quickly on national issues, like books and movies. However, you might have the field to yourself by specializing in local restaurants, clubs, and bands.

Special Marketing Considerations for Home Pages

Your home page should show you to be the expert that you are. Consider giving away old copies of your reviews so people can get a sampling of the quality of your work. Remember, online, no one knows if you have a Ph.D. in literature from Yale or if you are a sixteen-year-old who can sling a great phrase.

Hot Site

Larry Chase's Web Digest for Marketers, *www.wdfm.com*, presents weekly reviews of business Web sites. The site sells advertising.

BACKGROUND CHECKING AND CREDIT RATING AGENCY

Overview

You can never really be sure who is honest and who is a con man. That might be even more so on the Internet, because you don't see anyone face to face. Because frauds can prey on people on the Internet, you could create a business that checks people's credit ratings. This could be useful to any Internet business that must enter into relationships involving significant amounts of money, such as roommate referrals, apartment rentals, equipment purchases, singles dating services, and the like. Qualifications for this job include the ability to know how to use online services to tap into legal databases of credit information (such as TRW), bankruptcy court records, databases of criminals.. It is amazing how much information can be gathered legally from public records or inexpensive credit rating services.

Rewards

This service can be performed on a project or hourly basis at whatever rates your client feels comfortable with.

Risks

Normal business risks.

Special Marketing Considerations for the Home Page

Home pages should stress confidentiality, professionalism, and prompt completion of assignments.

BUSINESS PLAN WRITER

Overview

The Web is full of small start-up companies operated by people with varying levels of experience in business. Of the forty or so case studies in this book, a mere handful created business plans before going online. Perhaps that shows why some entrepreneurs, are not doing as well they had hoped. If you have good writing and research skills, there could be an opportunity to start a service to write business plans for online entrepreneurs, as well as to use the Internet to promote the service to offline businesses.

Rewards

Fees for writing business plans range all over the ballpark. You could get thousands from a large company and hundreds from a home-based business.

Risks

Deadbeats. All consultants and writers should get a significant part of their fee in advance and upon completion of a first draft. Nothing devalues faster than a service after it has been performed.

Special Marketing Considerations for the Home Page

Build credibility with your bio, testimonials, and partial samples of your work. Attract people to your site by writing and posting articles of interest to new businesses. Link to and from sites relating to your potential customers. Alert people in relevant newsgroups to the articles and information available for free. Don't hype your business by announcing its opening in a newsgroup.

GRANT WRITER

Overview

Grant writing is a field that will never go out of business. Colleges, researchers, and laboratories live on their ability to get funding by the grants offered by the government, foundations, and businesses. Writing grants is an intricate art that must be mastered, just like playing the flute. Grant writing has its own language and ways of phrasing words and requests to make a point and get the attention of the grantors.

Rewards

Because of the specialty of this work, you won't be swamped with competitors. Prices for services vary by the type of agency you deal with and the complexity of the application.

Risks

Normal business risks.

Special Marketing Considerations for the Home Pages

Prove your credibility by posting your bio, testimonials, and writing samples.

Hot Site

Dr. Pat Rife, *www.maui.net/~envision.html*, can write grants for you, or you can buy her grant-writing software!

9 Writers and Books

It is truly amazing how many people want to be writers. *Writer's Digest* has 225,000 subscribers who would love to find someone to publish their novels, screenplays, and poems. Unfortunately for them, book publishers don't have the budget to print all those new works and bookstores don't offer these writers shelf space. What's a would-be writer to do?

Welcome to the World Wide Web, everyman's printing press. For a small price (see start-up costs in section 1), you can post your poem, novel, or short story on your home page and let the world read it and discover the talent you have.

What's that? You want to get paid? Okay, let's look at how writers can make money on the Internet.

This chapter explores ways to make money if you are an entrepreneurial writer, book publisher, freelance writer, advertising copy writer, technical writer, newshound, or bookstore. Additional opportunities for writers can be found in Chapter 19.

BOOK PUBLISHER (SELF-PUBLISHED, REAL WORLD)

Overview

Can't get a publisher for your masterpiece? Publish it online! Here are two strategies. (1) Upload the first two or three chapters onto your home page. Take orders for the full copies, which you can send through e-mail or snail mail. Hint:—email is cheaper! (2) If you have a full line of books or a garage full of printed copies, the Web is a great place to advertise. I've gotten orders from Canada, Germany, Israel, and Australia, as well as throughout the United States

Rewards

You can sell books to people all over the world and take home all the money. You don't have to split the income with a publisher, bookstore, or book distributor.

Risks

You'd be amazed at how inexpensive a book can cost to print—as low as $2 a unit for a two-hundred-page book—but you have to order three thousand copies to get a good price. You're also investing your time and effort in writing the book, and paying a proofreader and an artist to design the cover and interior pages.

Special Marketing Considerations for the Home Page

Consider offering the first few chapters for free online. People can read the work online or print it out. If they want to read the rest of the book, they can send you a check!

Publishers should supply an overview of the book, a table of contents, reviews and testimonials, a sample chapter, the author's bio, as well as info on how to order the book online and offline.

RESEARCH REPORTS, MONOGRAPHS, BOOKLETS

Overview

Books take a long time to write and edit. They are costly to produce. Writers can instead produce research reports, monographs, booklets, and special reports of eight to twenty pages.

Rewards

People are willing to spend $5–$10 on this type of work. Your per-unit profit might even be higher for reports than for a book. If you send the work out via e-mail, or let people see it if they have a password, then your material costs are next to nothing. As you create more and more booklets, you could have the basis for a book. You will be making money as you are writing.

Risks

Normal business risks.

Special Marketing Considerations for the Home Page

Consider giving a report away for free as a method of attracting visitors and for proving your credibility.

Case Study: Herman Holtz, Writer

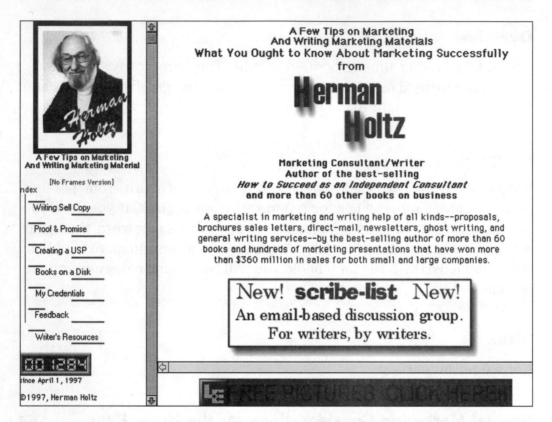

Figure 9–1. Marketing wxpert Herman Holtz offers lots of free advice on his site. Copyright 1997, Herman Holtz.

Herman Holtz   *holtz@paltech.com*

PO Box 1731   *www.bellicose.com/freelance*

Wheaton, MD 20915   301-649-2499

(original interview 1995; update February 1997)

How effective is the Internet for selling your reports?

I have offered a free report on freelance writing and am getting quite an enthusiastic response—i.e., requests for the report, which I e-mail to the respondent. The report includes a catalog of my reports and an order form.

It is too soon to judge the total results, but the early results are encouraging. The reports are how-to monographs of five to eight pages each (a few are longer) that sell for an average of about $3 each. I also have collections of the most popular reports and one book on disk, each at approximately $10.

The most popular of these reports—there are approximately thirty of them—deal with freelance writing. Most of those are not about how to write as much as they are about how and where to market. The reports that are not about writing are on a wide variety of topics: government grant programs, how to use OPM (other people's money), marketing, how to start and run a singles club, and bartering, to name a few.

I have been advertising these on the USENET (newsgroups), and I am still planning a Web presence. I have been publishing these reports for nearly twenty years, mostly by mail until now. I am still probing ways to market online.

My own claim to fame is based on my reputation as a guru on consulting, largely the result of my highly successful book, *How to Succeed as an Independent Consultant* (John Wiley and Sons), plus a continuing series of books for the independent consultant.

1997 Update

What is the most important thing you learned in the past year about marketing on the Internet?

The need for diversity in order to gain a sufficiently large presence.

What is the most effective way to get people to come to your site?

Announce it everywhere in terms of some specific benefit to be gained by visiting.

What is the most effective way to get people to return to your site?

New, useful information.

What is the most effective way to get people to buy products or services?

Show the reward in direct terms.

How much money have you made? Is your site profitable?

The site serves my need. It was not and is not intended to be a major marketing tool; it is only one of many efforts, more than a few experimental, with tools of market research.

DIGIZINE

Overview

A digizine is a *digi*tal maga*zine*. Get it? You can use a digizine to report on areas of interest to you and your audience that can't be seen anywhere else. One of the Internet's great strengths is the ability to let you publish your own work and seek representation for your views or interests. Although there are thousands of special interest print magazines and tens of thousands of special interest newsletters and professional publications, none can be produced as inexpensively as one published on the Internet. Whereas the economics of publishing a hard-copy newsletter might be prohibitively expensive, a digizine can be a money maker.

Rewards

To make money on a digizine, sell subscriptions, advertisements, or links to related pages. Other benefits of publishing a digizine include increasing your credibility and stature in your industry, which could lead to paid speaking engagements and new clients.

Risks

Normal business risks.

Special Marketing Considerations for the Home Page

If you want to make money on advertisements, then make the page free to subscribers, who can provide a minimal amount of demographic information in return for the privilege of free issues. You need the demographic information to sell advertisements to companies who want to be sure they are reaching their desired target audience.

Hot Sites

- Suck   *www.suck.com*
- Stale   *www.stale.com*
- Hot Wired   *www.hotwired.com*

FREELANCE WRITING BUSINESS

Overview

Freelance journalists and writers can prospect for new clients on the Internet.

Rewards

Writers can show and sell their works to potential clients all over the world. Having a home page is like having a portfolio that people can see whenever they want to view it.

Risks

Normal business risks.

Special Marketing Considerations for the Home Page

Post old articles online so prospects can see your writing style and command of the material. Resumes, bios, testimonials also help.

TECHNICAL WRITING BUSINESS

Overview

If you're a geek, proud of it, and can write, then you can start a technical writing business. Your home page can show examples of your work and testimonials from clients as well as your rates and preferred subjects. You can operate a solo firm in this manner or grow a business.

Rewards

Increased income.

Risks

None, beyond normal business operations.

Special Marketing Considerations for the Home Page

Show examples of your work and testimonials from clients. A résumé would also help build creditability and a list of your interests would help clients learn your strong suits.

NEWS SERVICES

Overview

Do you have insatiable curiosity about a certain topic that other people care about? If you said yes, then you can start your own news service on the Internet. You must be able to find information (which is a snap on the Internet and commercial online services), find sources (use Yahoo! or another search engine), get comments from newsmakers, and write up the material. You can send your digizine to people who subscribe to your homegrown mailing list. Remember, e-mail is free. Subscribers can also read daily updates at your home page.

Rewards

Increased income from sales of subscriptions, advertisements, or links to related pages.

Risks

Normal business risks.

Special Marketing Considerations for the Home Page

Your home page should extol the benefits of your service. The actual newsletter probably should be sent via e-mail.

BOOKSELLING

Overview

So you have a couple hundred or thousand books from college and you want to sell them on the Internet? And you figure if you sell those, then why not sell more? You're in the right place. Booksellers have reported brisk sales. Book publishers have their own sites (including my publisher, Van Nostrand Reinhold, *www.vnr.com*), where people can place orders online or by phone or fax.

Remember, you don't have to own a bookstore—you can join the new band of booksellers that don't have a storefront but exist only online. These companies might or might not have inventory. They mainly function as a front end for a drop-shipping business. In other words, they place information online about the book, such as title, topic, overview, and price, and then wait for the orders. When someone calls, they process the order information and then call their supplier, who ships directly to the consumer.

In either case, your bookstore can offer collections of books that appeal to specialized audiences, such as business books, comic books, romance novels, art books, oriental literature, or Judaica.

Rewards

You'll benefit from sales. You minimize your risks by not carrying inventory. The only costs you incur are for running the home page.

Risks

Normal business risks.

Special Marketing Considerations for the Home Page

The strength of a bookseller's Web site lies in the power of a database engine that can find books quickly and display the information attractively to the viewer. You'll want to allow the consumer to choose books by category (romance, sports, adventure, etc.) as well as by title and author. Building the database is a task that can be performed by talented database programmers (of which there are a few). The hardest part is to edit the information for the database. Of course, you'll have to negotiate purchases from the publishers or from local bookstores that agree to work with you. Publishers generally will give discounts beginning at 40 percent for single-copy sales. A local bookstore might take the order and ship it for you for a lower discount to cover their costs.

Hot Site

Amazon.com, www.amazon.com, sets the standard for booksellers on the Web. With an easy search tool, e-mail updates on your favorite authors and genres, and an associates plan to pay customers for sending their friends, Amazon raises the barrier for all booksellers on the Web.

10 Dramatic Arts

As time goes by and technology advances, actors will give performances on the Internet on a pay-per-view basis, or for free to get exposure for their services. Today the Internet can be used as a talent agency, a way for actors to promote their services directly to corporations (yes, corporations. Many actors make their living by doing presentations at trade shows and conventions, or starring in corporate videos!) and the entertainment industry. Screenwriters, too, can promote their services online. You can also start a talk radio business. If directing is more your style, see the business opportunity for coaching people who participate in online videoconferences in chapter 19.

TALENT AGENCY

Overview

Entrepreneurs can start a talent agency for local actors, mimes, street musicians, entertainers, children's party entertainers, models, and others.

Rewards

You could make money by:

- Creating a home page and selling ad space to actors.

- Creating home pages for actors and charging for your services.

- Selling links from your home page to theirs.

- Acting as an agent charging a commission for actual bookings.

Risks

Normal business risks apply.

Special Marketing Considerations for Home Pages

Post pictures, video clips, and résumés of your clients. Add keywords to résumés so producers can easily search for people with specific talents and characteristics. Promote the site to casting directors as a means of finding talent quickly.

Hot Sites

- World Wide Stars   *www.worldstars.com*

- CenterStage@Buzz   *www.buzznyc.com*

- Screen Test Online   *www.screentestonline.com*

- Theatre Central   *www.theatre-central.com*

ACTOR, ENTERTAINER

Overview

Actors and entertainers can post their own home pages in the hopes of landing jobs.

Rewards

By listing your talents and promoting them to the world, you might be able to get jobs.

Risks

Time and setup costs.

Special Marketing Considerations for the Home Page

Your online marketing materials should include the basic package you have probably already created for getting jobs right now. That includes a professionally taken photo, a description of your acting experience, and desired roles, fees, travel restrictions (if any), and the like.

To make your page come alive, draw on your creative resources.

You can also include short audio and video files of your best scenes, which viewers can retrieve and play on their computers.

SCREENWRITER

Overview

It seems like everyone is writing a screenplay. Why not promote your ideas on the Internet?

Rewards

You might reach the person who can bring your characters to life.

Risks

Someone could steal your idea. You wouldn't have any way to prove it was stolen, either.

Special Marketing Considerations for the Home Page

Your home page should tell the world who you are and describe your previously published and produced works. You might want to limit the number of creative ideas you give away to protect your scripts. However, you do need to show readers that you have compelling ideas.

INTERNET PERFORMER

Overview

Why not start your own Internet Web radio show? You can do drama, comedy, or even singing. Go to the Audio Net company, *www.audionet.com*, and see how you can create a show and have them broadcast it over the Internet. If you currently conduct a show on a local radio station, people all around the world will be able to hear you—and your advertisers' commercials!

Rewards

Charge people on a pay-per-view basis. If they want to attend, they must type in a password that is good for that night's show. No one does this now, so you would be the first and get a lot of publicity. You can also sell sponsorships, ads, and links from your home page or show.

Risks

Technology is imperfect, so productions might be similar to the quality of a 1950's TV show. People might forgive this to be part of a new venture, or they might say it isn't MTV and tune you out.

Hot Site

AudioNet, *www.audionet.com*, is the *TV Guide* of online radio programs as well as the technical hub that makes it all happen.

11 Visual Arts

Because the first stop for many Internet newbies (new Internet subscribers) is the Louvre, the majestic Parisian art museum, you'd think art galleries would do a thriving business on the Internet. Visual artists have an appreciative audience awaiting them online This is not surprising because the Internet is a visual medium. People like graphics, art, pictures, and the ability to ponder their significance.

This chapter shows how entrepreneurial artists can sell paintings and clip art, operate an art gallery, market photographic services and art photographs, and merchandise cartoons on the Internet.

Visual artists making money online include photographers, designers, and purveyors of supplies and equipment.

Case Study: The Borderline

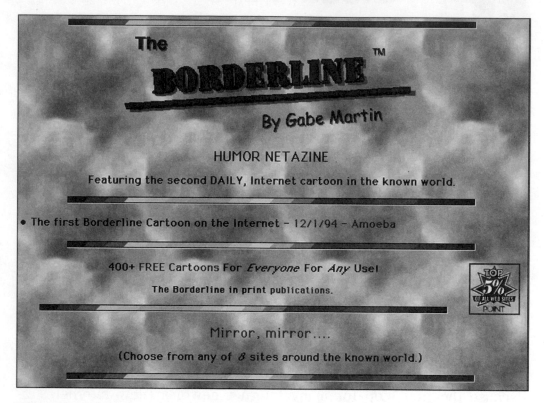

Figure 11–1. *Borderline*'s free cartoons landed Gabe Martin a top daily newspaper! Copyright 1997, *The Borderline*.

The Borderline

Gabe Martin

PO Box 262272

San Diego, CA 92196

borderln@cts.com

www.the-borderline.com

(original interview 1995, update February 1997)

The Borderline *netazine is the home page for cartoonist Gabe Martin, who at age seventeen is one of the youngest entrepreneurs on the*

Internet! He uses the site to show his cartoons, which can be viewed by anyone for free. He hopes to sell cartoons to "anyone who appreciates the Far-Sideish slant of my humor [and who wants] a small humorous lift in their day. I like to think that my cartoons are funnier than some of the others on the Web. But of course, I'm prejudiced. :-)"

Is this business an offshoot of your existing business or does it exist only on the Internet?

I tried submitting my cartoons to national syndicators, but as of yet I haven't gotten an offer. However for the last year and a half I have been doing a monthly cartoon for the San Diego Gas & Electric Company newsletter. This work can be quite challenging due to the conflicting goals of making a cartoon that is specific to a given article in the newsletter as well as something that can be used for the more diverse audience on the Internet. It is a paid gig, however.

I assume that within a year or so there should be a general mechanism on the Web for charging small amounts (1 cent?, 1/10 cent?) for access to information on the Web (including cartoons). At that point I may decide to charge a nominal fee for the monthly updates or maybe access to the cartoon archive. My primary focus at this time, however, is to get exposure for my work and to prove to any potential syndicator that I can reliably produce cartoons on a daily basis.

Where do you run your business?

I operate from home using the computer in my bedroom for producing the cartoons. I use the computers in the dining room for e-mail, Web browsing, etc.

What is your background and training?

I have no formal training in cartooning or art. Since I was very young I've been making birthday cards for relatives. Along the way I decided that they were more interesting if there was a humorous twist to them. That's basically how I got started.

The cartooning side obviously required years of practice along with some innate talent inherited from my mother. I probably inherited my particular sense of humor from my dad. Animated cartoons and cartoon strips also had a large influence on me. My dad is currently handling the business side of things. His experience with computers and business in general has been a real asset.

When did you start your business?

I had been creating cartoons sporadically for a couple of years when my dad decided that we should put the cartoons up on the Web. Starting December 1, 1994, I began putting a daily cartoon up on the Web. I had a cushion of thirty or so cartoons that I had already produced. This allowed me to ease into the routine of daily production without too much trouble.

How much money has your company made?

I currently make nothing off of my daily cartoon on the Web, although I do have a couple of minor offers for use of specific cartoons. I do make $50/cartoon/month from the San Diego Gas & Electric Co.

How much money do you hope to make?

Eventually in two to three years enough for a good living.

Getting Started

Did you create a business plan before going online?

No. There were too many unknowns at the time. Going online was basically an experiment to see how much exposure I could get for my work.

Figure 11–2. *Borderline* prints its cartoons online and hopes to sell reprint rights to companies. Copyright 1997, *The Borderline*.

How much time did it take to get up and running?

It took approximately a month to get everything together. My Internet service provider normally didn't let individuals start their own home pages, but because this was just a hobby page, they decided to allow it. However, they made it clear that if I started to make money on the page then I would have to convert to a business (i.e., more expensive) account. Thankfully, after a few months, due to the popularity of my site (judged by the access statistics that they collected), they gave me a FREE upgrade to a business account. Their reason for doing so was that my site brought visitors to their server; visitors that might stick around to see what other services they had to offer.

Being nominated as the "Cool Site of the Day" also helped get their attention.

Did you create the pages yourself?

My dad, who is a PC analyst, took care of most of the technical details. He had to learn HTML and some UNIX, but all of the information was available on the Web (once he knew how to search for it). He also made sure that I knew everything about what he was doing so that I could run the whole process by myself should that become necessary. We still take turns updating the home page just to make sure that I can still do it.

How much did it cost to get started?

As I already had a computer, the only cost for start-up was the Internet access account. That cost about $75 for start-up fees and the $23/month for access to the Web, e-mail, FTP, etc. I've recently run up against my limit for file storage so I will have to decide to whether to remove some of the older stuff or continue to pay the additional storage fee (30 cents/MB/day).

What mistakes did you make that you wish you hadn't made?

I wish I had gotten onto the Web even sooner than I did. There is always more attention given to the first success in any endeavor. Although I was the second (as far as I can determine) daily Internet cartoon, the guy who did the FIRST daily Internet cartoon (Dave Farley—Dr. Fun) continues to get most of the attention/respect/etc., on the Web and recently signed a contract with a major syndicator, United Media. United Media had its Web site up for only a month or so when it picked up Dr. Fun.

What advice would you give someone starting an Internet business?

Move fast! Don't take too long to make decisions. The Web is a moving target; decisions that make sense today may not make sense next month or even tomorrow.

What skills would a person have to conduct business?

Because everything is funneled through a PC, you should have a good working knowledge of computers and computer accessories.

How did you promote your home page?

I signed up with all of the major lists of sites that I came across. I also spent considerable time searching for sites that already had cartoon-related information on them. The Web Crawler and Lycos search pages were invaluable for this type of searching. Most people that I contacted were very receptive to adding a link to my cartoon page. The plan was to get as many sites as possible to put up a link to my page. This not only got the owner of the page to check out my site, it also would hopefully get some of the visitors to his site to also come.

Although the cold calls were productive, they were also time-consuming. My dad got the idea of starting a contest on my page. The idea of the contest was that a visitor could enter the contest if she put up a link to *The Borderline* on HER home page. If the link was on her page when her name was drawn then she would win the prize. The contest was set up with a weekly prize of a *Borderline* T-shirt and a grand prize of $1000 (at the end of six months). My dad paid for the T-shirts and shipping (approximately $250) and I put up the $1000 from my own money (as an investment in my future). So far (halfway through the contest) I've gotten over five hundred valid entries for the contest. At the start of the contest I decided that a thousand entries would make the contest a marketing success. If it is a success, my dad has promised to sponsor another bigger and better promotion.

How much did it cost to promote your site?

Nothing, other than the contest mentioned above.

How did the start-up phase affect your personal life?

Long hours. Very little personal life during the start-up.

What was the hardest part of the job in the beginning?

Uncertainty as to what might come of all this work.

How long did it take until you made your first sale?

Two weeks. I negotiated my first deal (for money) with someone who publishes a newsletter and wanted to use several of my cartoons that he had seen on the Internet. I hope this is just the beginning.

How long did it take to get established?

It took about a month to get a steady flow of daily visitors to the page.

My Day

What does your average day look like?

Six to eight hours Monday through Friday working on producing the cartoons—usually later in the day. My dad spends another three to four hours a day working the business end of things. He recently received a layoff notice from the company where he has worked for six years and now plans to work with me full time for at least six months to see if we can work *The Borderline* into a full-time job for one or, preferably, both of us.

What does your job entail?

Drawing cartoons.

How many hours a week do you spend working on your site?

Thirty hours/week between my dad and myself:

10 percent updating site (daily)

60 percent e-mail (fans, promotions, business contacts, etc.)

20 percent contest management

10 percent miscellaneous

What do you like most about your work?

Making people laugh.

What do you like least?

Investing all the time and effort of putting out a daily cartoon and (as of yet) getting very little in return. Put it down as the impatience of youth.

What was your greatest moment?

Recently I faxed one of my cartoons to Art Bell (a national radio talk-show host). He said that even though he didn't normally like cartoons, he really liked this one. He liked it so much that he described it to his listeners (not an easy task for radio). I trust that wasn't my fifteen (five?) minutes of fame.

Are you glad you are on the Web?

It's a fun place to be and it's the right place to be.

Given what you know now, would you do it again?

Sooner, bigger, better.

The Future

What is your next venture?

I plan to expand the monthly features into a more full-fledged humor magazine.

What else would you like to say?

The Web is the perfect place for entrepreneurs—a huge and growing customer base, little regulation, a level playing field (my page is the same "size" as IBM's!!), and limitless possibilities for the inventive mind.

Where can people look for more advice?

The information is all over the Web. The best places to look are on the home pages of the major Web browser companies. Most of the browser software comes with direct access to the company's home page built in. They have detailed information on how to start Web pages, servers, etc.

1997 Update

What is the most important thing you learned in the past year about marketing on the Internet?

The Internet allows marketing to be done on a shoestring budget, but you have to be patient. It can take months or years to build up a group of regular visitors to your site. It takes just as long to form the links with other people's pages that bring new visitors to you.

What is the most effective way to get people to come to your site?

From the beginning I've offered free viewing of the daily cartoon that I produce. After the first year, I started to let people actually use the cartoons for free, and for anything they wanted. Borrowing from the well-established software shareware concept, I decided to call my free cartoons *sharetoons* (What's a marketing concept if it doesn't have a name? :-)).

My long-term objective was simply to gain name recognition for myself and my work. With that in mind, it was obvious that the more people who saw my work, the sooner I would be able to break into the lucrative newspaper/magazine market. In my view, people who used my cartoons were providing me with free advertising for my work.

What is the most effective way to get people to return to your site?

A Web site must have something that will bring people back on a regular basis. A daily cartoon was the perfect thing for this. I've had many people say that they have my daily cartoon as the first thing that comes up when they log onto the Internet every day. And with that repetition comes name recognition.

What is the most effective way to get people to buy products or services?

Because of some of the uncertainties and bad press surrounding Internet commerce, a Web site has to offer something too good to pass up—something where there's little or no risk involved for the buyer yet still offering substantial benefit to the seller.

With this idea in mind, I started selling my book of cartoons (which has the same free-use offer) on my Web site. To make the offer risk-free, I offered to send the book to anyone who ordered it WITHOUT asking for payment first. Once the buyer received the book, he was to send back only what he thought the book was worth (full price suggested, of course).

As crazy as this approach may sound, it has turned out rather well for me. I not only reached my goal of maintaining a (modest) profit, I also gained a bit of a reputation as an Internet pioneer in this area (OK, no jokes about the pioneers getting the arrows. :-)).

This selling strategy not only allowed me to sell books outside the traditional book-distribution channels (read expensive channels), it also provided a way to get the cartoons into the hands of people outside the Internet. Again, I look at it as people paying me (buying my book) to advertise my work.

How much money have you made?

Since my venture into the Internet was mainly to gain name recognition, I would have to say that I have succeeded very well for a seventeen-year-old (started at fifteen). My cartoons are now in a major metropolitan newspaper (San Diego *Union-Tribune*, circulation 370,000), on America Online ($$$), and many other newspapers, magazines, etc., around the world. I have a book in print that has been accepted by a national book distributor. And, I've been exposed to a lot of entrepreneurial activities that would have been difficult to experience had it not been for the accessibility of the Internet, experiences that I'm sure will serve me well regardless of where my future lies.

Case Study: Little-Raidl Design Studios

Figure 11–3. Stained art images show up beautifully on the Little-Raidl Design Studios Web site. Copyright 1997, Little-Raidl Design Studios.

Little-Raidl Design Studios

Roy E. Little, Artist/Designer

Jim Raidl, Marketing/Sales/Production Assistant

6145 Austin Creek Road

Cazadero, CA 95421

(original interview February 1997)

cazguy@sonic.net

www.sonic.net/little-raidl

707 632-5569

What does your company do?

Create and fabricate totally original custom-designed art glass treatments for residential and commercial clients around the world. Treatments include windows, privacy screens, lightboxes, skylights, light fixtures, mosaic tabletops and wall hanging pieces, fireplace screens, mobiles, and window accent pieces called cut corners (a concept we created and have published articles on).

What expertise/background is necessary to operate your business?

Roy Little, for twenty years a television art director, has a fine arts degree and thirty years of experience as a painter, muralist, brass etcher, and stained-glass artist. He was schooled in both America and Europe. Jim Raidl, with a business marketing degree, worked as a manager in the fashion retail business and owned and operated an antique business for several years in San Francisco.

What was your company's goal for going online?

To reach more people worldwide who enjoy high-quality art and living in a beautiful environment.

How do you know you have reached that goal?

Several existing clients are telling others about our site [networking on the Internet] so they too can have access to our top-quality and unique art. Also, others who never heard about our glass work are contacting us after looking at our site and asking for more information.

How much did it cost to get started?

$3,000–$4,000

What makes your site special?

The focus of our site is on the visual, which is what we do, and the copy is precise and informative. The site also shows the diversity of our technique and design range.

How do you get people to come to your site?

When the site first went up, all of the major search engines were contacted and we sent out new business cards telling our clients and new potential client contacts that we had gone global with a new Web site.

How do you get people to return to your site?

Our work is so exciting and unique that they come back on their own so they can take it all in a little at a time, each time. They also bring others to it through word of mouth or through e-mail messages.

How do you move people from being window-shoppers to paying customers?

They contact us directly and ask for more information. Once this personal contact is made, they are on their way to an enjoyable, interesting, and totally satisfying creative process.

What is the most important thing you learned in the past year about marketing on the Internet?

We have only been up since late October 1996, but in that time we can see that we are now accessible to so many, so fast, and that everyone is very excited about our work.

What is the most effective way to get people to come to your site?

Our work speaks for itself. When people hear about our site, they visit it again and again and spread the word to others to do likewise. Also, people who have been surfing the Web for a long time know when a site is hot or not.

What is the most effective way to get people to return to your site?

Once people visit us, they realize that our site is all that one should be—colorful, informative, quick-loading, and easy to move around on. The site was created very thoughtfully and carefully with the intent to make people feel comfortable about looking at us and to give them the desire to keep coming back to us on their own—and they do!

What is the most effective way to get people to buy products or services?

People who understand totally custom work that is not readily available anywhere else open their checkbooks and tell us to do our thing. They want and expect quality and they get it!

How much money have you made?

Too soon to tell, other than the fact that each week brings more and more hits, phone calls, and new potential clients. Check back with us in a year, if you can even get through to us. We're expecting big things to happen and are confident that they will.

CLIP ART

Overview

Clip art and stock photography are used to illustrate slides that accompany speeches, brighten company newsletters, or act as the focal point of advertisements and brochures. The market for these products is unending, as tremendous numbers of people give speeches every day and seek to illustrate their ideas. Although many software programs come with clip art, speakers want their presentations to look unique. Those people are your potential customers.

You can sell clip art on the Internet, including line drawings in black and white or color and photographs based on timeless themes such as cars, and nature. However, virtually every topic could be considered for your portfolio.

You can set your own prices for clip art, with higher prices going for more talented work and unusual topics. Commercial clip art, sold in software stores, can be quite cheap—about $2 per dozen images. Remember that you can make money by selling in volume.

To succeed in this business you need artistic skills, a wide repertoire of samples, and marketing ability.

Rewards

Creating newsletters and brochures is one the major uses of computers; therefore, you will find a large potential audience. You can make incremental income by creating the artwork once and selling it many times. Your cost of goods and time remains the same whether you sell the work one time or one hundred times.

Risks

As with any business, people can steal your work and not pay your fee. Further, you might not have any way of knowing they used your work unless it comes to your attention by accident. You therefore need to take precautions to protect your work. Consider these two options:

1. Create a portfolio of clip art that is limited in number but that shows your talent and personality traits (such as humor). If people like your style, they will order your portfolio.

2. Disable the art in some way, such as putting your signature in a key portion of the viewing field. Alert your prospects that these are samples and the versions they buy will have a clear viewing area.

Special Marketing Considerations for the Home Page

To help protect their work, artists' home pages should always contain prominent notices about copyright laws and the penalties for violation.

Artists' home pages will be held to a higher standard than those of other vendors. If your home page isn't visually attractive, then what can a consumer expect from the rest of your work?

Artists can create online résumés by listing their exhibitions and dates, reviews and testimonials from critics, and clients.

Content for the home page should include portfolios of your work so people can get a feel for your style. The work should be displayed in small, postage-stamp sizes so they can transmit quickly to the viewer's screen. To prevent widespread copying and theft, don't include larger versions that would fit neatly into newsletters. Save those for the paying customers.

Hot Site

PhotoDisc, *www.photodisc.com*, drives traffic to its Web site with a forty-page catalog sent via direct mail.

ART GALLERY

Overview

You don't have to be an artist to sell art on the Internet. Entrepreneurs can start a home page gallery of works they arrange to show on consignment.

That way there is no out-of-pocket expenditure for inventory. You could also charge the artist for the space you provide and the promotion you create that attracts connoisseurs to your site. You could charge artists for creating home pages. Finally, you could charge local galleries for advertisements on your page or for links to their pages (or you might do this in exchange for a link from their site to yours). The site can also sell art books.

Rewards

Increased sales and exposure.

Risks

You can put art on the walls of the Internet for people to admire, but will people buy it there? Fortunately for artists, paintings aren't cheap. I think of the old joke about a blind man selling pencils on the street corner. He holds a sign saying "Pencils, one million dollars." A passerby says, "Hey, you aren't going to sell many pencils at a million dollars apiece." "Mister," the blind man replies, "I only need to sell one." Lots of entrepreneurs are trying. Competition should not be a problem, given the variety of styles and schools of art, prices, and consumer tastes.

Special Marketing Considerations for the Home Page

For all artwork on the Internet, copyright notices should be posted prominently. Strict warnings should be placed regarding the prohibition of copying artwork on the Internet and offline. Some people actually think they are doing you a favor by posting your art on their sites—even if they give full credit—because they think they are publicizing the work. Tell them they cannot do this!

Artwork, by its nature, will comprise a large file. This can be a problem, as large files take a long time to appear on people's screens. You might consider offering a postage-stamp-sized view of the painting that people see at first and a larger view that they can see only if they really want to invest the time.

To attract people to your site month after month, consider posting news of interest to the local art community, like gallery openings, exhibits, and classes, and bios of artists that include their exhibitions.

ARTIST

Overview

You don't need a gallery to sell art on the Internet. An entrepreneurial artist working in any medium—watercolors, sculpture, clay, mixed media, photography, and so on—can create a home page and sell works directly to the public.

Rewards

By selling art directly you cut out the middleman, the gallery. You'll keep more money. However, galleries that market correctly will be able to draw more people to see your work.

Risks

Normal business risks.

Special Marketing Considerations for the Home Page

See discussion of art galleries above.

SEMINAR BUSINESS

Overview

Photographers can teach others how to become better shutterbugs by hosting online seminars. See the seminar information in Chapter 23.

Hot Sites

- Barnstorm IX—The Eddie Adams Workshop, *www.s2f.com/ eaworkshop/*, is a workshop put on by Pulitzer Prize–winning photographer Eddie Adams in upstate New York.

- Great Lakes Institute of Photography, *www.glip.org*, offers basic to advanced classes for people involved in professional photography.

- Maine Photographic Workshops, *www.meworkshops.com*, provides information about film, television, and photographic workshops.

- Santa Fe Workshops, *www.sfworkshop.com*, offers photographic and digital media workshops.

12 Music

The success of entertainment sites for rock stars and the first virtual concert, featuring the Rolling Stones, shows that rock and roll is here to stay on the Internet. A large portion of Internet users are in college, recent graduates, or involved with music as a business or hobby, so there is a large and growing online market for all things musical.

This chapter looks at how lyrical entrepreneurs can create new businesses on the Internet. Bands can sell records, music stores can sell new and used equipment or build actual store traffic, and independent record producers can create an empire—all online.

Many areas of the music world are gaining or serving clients online. Sellers of CDs, records, tapes, musical equipment, and memorabilia are online. Service providers such as instructors, disk jockeys, managers, agents, and producers are on the Web, as are publishers of music magazines, classified ads, and software. All types of music are represented, from Christian to karaoke.

DISK JOCKEY

Overview

Disk jockeys can promote their business online by pointing out what kinds of events they perform at (weddings, parties, etc.), their favorite music, the geographic areas they serve, professional affiliations, testimonials, videotapes, guarantees, and insurance coverage.

Hot Sites

- A Sound Investment Mobile DJ, Inc., *asoundinvestment.com*, is a mobile DJ music entertainment for wedding receptions, company dinner dances, and other events.

- Dancing D.J.s, Inc., *www.dancingdj.com*, says its sounds create excitement at any wedding, bar/bat mitzvah, dinner dance, or any kind of outrageous party.

- DJ Jiten, *www.nexx.com/dj-jiten*, features the latest Hindi remixes.

SONGWRITER

Overview

Songwriters can find new clients online. Your home page should show sample works, credentials, testimonials, and rates.

Hot Sites

- Education Through Music, *www.etm.co.uk*, writes educational music for children.

- I Write the Songs, *www.safari.net/~pianoman*, creates professionally recorded custom songs composed and arranged with musical background for weddings, bar mitzvahs, engagements, and special events.

MEMORABILIA

Overview

The alternative crowd on the Internet can fill out their wardrobes and jewelry needs online. If you went to a concert last night, you could be selling T-shirts tonight.

Hot Sites

- Blues Stuff Market Place, *www.vivanet.com/~blues/stuff.html*, offers a collection of unusual blues-related merchandise including framed 78s, stamps, posters, books, videos, and T-shirts.

- ArkStar, *www.arkstar.com*, sells rock-and-roll memorabilia specializing in Grateful Dead merchandise.

- Merit Adventures, *www.csmonline.com/~merit/intro2.html*, favors Led Zeppelin memorabilia and has thousands of items including tour programs, CDs, books, T-shirts, and posters.

- Woodstock 1969, *www.woodstock69.com*, is dedicated to the 1969 Woodstock Art and Music Festival.

SELLING MUSIC ONLINE

Overview

Musicians have embraced online services with a frenzy that is matched by some groups' music. Because many young people are on the Internet, musicians find a natural audience online. Most major music studios promote their top new releases online before the albums are released in stores.

Groups that don't have contracts with major studios can benefit greatly by posting their audio files on the Internet. They can reach a worldwide audience for only a few hundred dollars by creating a home page and promoting it by linking to other music home pages. They can take orders directly and keep the money that agents, distributors, and music stores would have siphoned off!

The strategy goes like this: Post audio files of the songs on your home page that people can download and hear on computers equipped with speakers. Cuts can be for thirty seconds so people get a good feel for your sound. However, you might decide to give away the title cut in the hopes of people buying the entire album. Experiment to find which approach works best for your group. You can collect money by mail or credit cards delivered over the Internet, fax, or phone.

Rewards

Unknown local bands can reach a worldwide audience with the Internet. Consumers can hear snippets of songs and read lyrics before buying the disk. Because the cost of mastering a CD is pretty low and home page design pricing is reasonable, this strategy can be a good one that bands can't beat.

Risks

To prevent widespread copying, groups might want to load only a thirty-second preview of their best song.

Special Marketing Considerations for the Home Page

Several songwriters place the lyrics to their songs online as well, even for songs that aren't available online, so people can get a feel for the tone and texture of the album. Musicians also include biographies or messages to their listeners that show the tone of the performer—a sweet folksinger or a tear-your-eyes-out heavy metal group. These tactics help to create a presence for the artist and a bond of kinship and rapport with the consumer.

MUSIC STORE, RECORD STORE (NEW AND USED)

Overview

Operators of stores selling new and used musical instruments can find a ready market on the Internet. Entrepreneurs can start their own business, without a storefront, by listing ads for used musical instruments. They can find instruments by perusing bulletin boards at record and music shops, pawnshops, garage sales, and flea markets. Entrepreneurs can use one of four business models:

1. Buy equipment that you like. This step ensures you will have inventory, but it could hurt your cash flow.

2. Sell equipment on consignment (i.e., you don't pay for anything until you sell it. You receive a share of the sale price—as much as 50 percent—for your efforts).

3. Sell advertising space on your home page to the owners of the instruments. An ad could sell for $25 a month. If you had a hundred ads, you'd pocket $2,500.

4. Obtain a broker. You can get money when the instrument is purchased.

Rewards

Retailers and entrepreneurs benefit from the low cost of advertising their wares to a worldwide audience on the Internet.

Risks

Sellers must beware of rip-offs from people trying to steal equipment. Profits might also be squeezed by the cost of mailing, insurance, and returns from dissatisfied customers.

Special Marketing Considerations for the Home Page

Because your inventory changes continuously and people's needs change as well, you need to draw people to your home page on a regular basis. This can be done by increasing its educational and entertainment value. Include articles on how to be a better drummer, how to form a band, and the like. Post sheet music from local artists who give you permission. Also, consider posting photos of the instruments so people can see that the products are not damaged. Consider giving a warranty or guarantee of satisfaction for a stated period of time.

Hot Sites

Some stores are specialized, like Anacortes Music Company, *www.cnw.com/~anamusic*, a full-line music store specializing in Celtic music and Celtic instruments, or Anaheim Band Instruments, *www.abimusic.com*, a retail musical instrument store specializing in brass, woodwinds, percussion, and strings. You'll find medieval and Renaissance bagpipes at Ancestral Instruments, *www.gmm.co.uk/ai*. G. Finkenbeiner, Inc., *www.finkenbeiner.bcn.net*, offers glass harmonicas and musical instruments made of spinning quartz crystal bowls.

RECORD PRODUCER

Overview

Future recording moguls and independent record producers can get their start through the Internet. By rounding up promising talent and placing the music online, entrepreneurs can hope to create a musical empire. You must be able to find top talent and arrange for all technical recording operations as well as promotion.

Rewards

Build an empire and entertain people.

Risks

Instead of finding the next Cher you discover the next Sonny Bono. Also, because most start-up bands have little money, you might have to front all the cash for creating the CD and promoting it online and offline.

Special Marketing Considerations for the Home Page

Pictures, biographies, and fan club materials for the groups would be a good way to create personalities for the rockers and relationships with their soon-to-be fans. See other overviews in this section for ideas on selling records online.

FAN CLUB

Overview

Operating a fan club can be a fun, rewarding business that can be started and operated part time while keeping your day job or going to school. This business can be run online and offline. You can use the online service to send messages to members and offer products. The best bet is to sell memberships and give people access codes to see more information on the home page than nonmembers can see.

Rewards

Income.

Risks

Check with a lawyer to learn about copyright infringements. What can you do without getting a nasty note from the lawyer of the objects of your enthusiasm claiming you are stealing their famous mark?

Special Marketing Considerations for the Home Page

Give something away for free to encourage people to join the fan club. Allow nonmembers to see a certain amount of information, but cut them off from the really good stuff. Only members who have registration numbers or passwords will get in to the neat stuff.

Hot Site

Industry.net, *www.industry.net*, isn't really a fan club, but it does show you how to offer different levels of service and information to registered members and newcomers.

13 Food and Dining

For many Americans, their first exposure to the Internet came from a news report that Pizza Hut was letting people order pizza on its Web site. The story ran on the front page of many newspapers, including *USA Today*, as well as on the national news broadcasts.

Today, not only can you order food online, including lobsters, peanuts, and hot sauces, but you can also learn of new restaurants and bars in your area or in places you hope to visit.

All sorts of food vendors are online selling baked goods, condiments, dairy, drinks, desserts, meats, noodles, vegetarian dishes, pizza, oils, organic ingredients, seasonings, and snacks. Caterers, consultants, cooking schools, and cookbooks also are racking up sales online. Delivery services, franchises and restaurants for sale, software, magazines, and other organizations are marketing on the Web.

For additional online resources, read *Food and Wine Online*, Gary Holleman (Van Nostrand Reinhold, 1995).

GOURMET FOODS AND WINES

Overview

Because the Internet audience is largely affluent and worldly, gourmet foods and hard-to-find items can be good groups of products to sell. Merchants are selling everything: lobsters, chocolates, hot sauces, peanuts, and even garlic.

Rewards and Risks

Established food merchants, especially local and regional producers, can open a new line of distribution through the Internet. Companies that can't get widespread distribution in grocery stores or national outlets can find willing customers online.

On the downside, merchants need to be careful about returned products that don't match the expectations of consumers. Consider using an overnight delivery service (with packed ice, if necessary) to ensure that foods arrive unspoiled.

Special Marketing Considerations for the Home Page

Show accurate pictures of products. Increase sales by selling gift baskets of related products to raise the price of the average order. Develop your relationship and level of interaction with customers by asking for their recipes and cooking tips and printing them in a newsletter distributed either online or via snail mail.

Site Review: Mozzarella Company

Mozzarella Company	*www.dreamshop .com*
Paula Lambert	*www.foodwine.com*
2944 Elm Street	214-741-4072
Dallas, TX 75226	

(original interview January 1997)

Mozzarella Company, of Dallas, has been selling gift baskets of cheese selections on the Internet since June 1995.

"Over Christmas we had ten to fifteen orders a day, which we thought was great," said Paula Lambert, owner and president, *http://mozzco.aol.com.* The company can be found on two sites on the Internet, Time Warner's Dreamshop, (*www.dreamshop.com*), and the Electronic Gourmet Guide, (*www.foodwine.com*). Most orders range in price between $50 and $75. "It is a definite way to increase your sales in a new market. We've loved it."

Most orders are from the United States.

The site is successful because of the wide assortment of information for cooks, Lambert says. "We have tons of information about our company, recipes, and serving suggestions. I think that has really helped us. Our customers have something to see and learn."

Mozzarella Company accepts credit card orders online. "We have had the same problems as with mail order," she reports. "We verify each order either by e-mail or on the phone."

The company handles all orders and credit card verification in-house. It pays a royalty of 15–20 percent to the mall operators.

Case Study: Lobster Direct

Order your Holiday Lobster or send a lobster dinner gift to a loved one

 ORDER PAGE and PRICING

Figure 13–1. Lobster Direct puts its toll-free order line high on the home page. Copyright 1997, Lobster Direct.

Lobster Direct   *lobster@fox.nstn.ca*

Jeff Morris   *http://novaweb.com/lobster*

109 Ilsley Avenue, Suite 3   800-NS-CLAWS

Dartmouth, N.S. Canada B3B 1S8

(original interview 1995)

Who is your primary audience?

Seafood lovers, people with cooking/recipe interests.

How will they benefit from your product?

Fresh product delivered overnight, quality information about lobster and salmon, including recipes, cooking tips, etc.

How does your product differ from others?

Lots of content on our Internet site, including pictures and text on how to crack and eat a Nova Scotia lobster.

Is this business an offshoot of your existing business or does it exist only on the Internet?

It is an offshoot of our wholesale business, but our first venture into retail and delivery direct to the consumer.

If it is an offshoot, was it meant to generate income on its own or to steer people to your other outlets?

Generate income on its own. We have no actual retail outlets.

Where does your business operate?

Office.

What is your background and training?

Attorney/entrepreneur.

When did you start your business?

January 1995.

How much money has your company made online?

Confidential, but we are shipping lots of orders every week across North America.

Getting Started

Did you create a business plan before going online?

No.

How much time did it take to get up and running?

One month.

Did you create the pages yourself?

We decided to make a computer friend who can do HTML code and graphics our partner in the business.

How much did it cost to get started?

Cost was under $2,000.

How did you obtain your start-up capital?

No comment.

What mistakes did you make that you wish you hadn't made?

No major mistakes so far—we hope this continues!

What advice would you give to a similar start-up?

Do not expect instant profits or revenues. Shopping on the Internet is still in its early days and you should look at a five-year window if you are not selling Internet-related products. Develop a marketing strategy to attract attention and traffic to your site and to try to establish a following.

What skills are needed to run this business?

Obviously, computer skills and running a retail store.

What education is needed to run your site?

Read and write.

What special qualities are needed to run your site?

Imagination and creativity.

How did you promote your home page?

We established in a number of Internet malls, indexed on What's New, Yahoo!

How much did it cost to promote your site?

About $200/month.

How long did it take until you made your first sale?

About three weeks! We thought we would never sell a lobster. Then we got our first order and our sales keep building.

How did the start-up phase affect your personal life?

No comment.

My Day

What does your average day look like?

Two hours answering mail and processing orders and shipping.

What does your job entail?

As above, writing our newsletter that goes out to about four hundred Internet users each month.

What was the hardest aspect of the work in the beginning?

Developing a streamlined system to obtain the order and to ship it on time.

How long did it take to get established?

Two months.

What do you like most about your work?

Creativity in our newsletter.

What do you like the least?

Sending out our newsletter—we have to set up a mail server soon!

What was your greatest moment?

Being in *Internet World*, June 1995 issue, in an article on doing business on the Internet. Never thought we would be mentioned in an international magazine.

How much time do you spend conducting business, marketing, selling, and upgrading your site?

Fifteen hours a week.

Are there any hazards to running your site?

None.

How much money do you expect to make?

We would like to net $75,000 a year.

General

Are customers concerned about security for their credit cards?

Yes.

How do you process orders via credit cards?

We write out slips by hand.

Was it easy or hard to get a machine?

Mail-order credit cards take time to obtain and require personal contacts with banks.

Are you glad your store is on the Web?

Yes. It has opened up a new world of communications.

Given what you know now, would you do it again?

Yes.

Where can people find advice about running a site like yours?

Call us.

The Future

What is your next venture?

We just opened Skyscrapers International Network, a sophisticated Web site for professionals only, *http://novaweb.com/sky*. It is a virtual reality office skyscraper designed by an architect, like a cybermall.

Can you share your cooking tips with us?

Why not try grilling lobster during barbecue season? What's better than surf 'n' turf! Precooked lobster only needs to be heated on the grill and lightly browned, perhaps one or two minutes at most. Try using an olive oil, garlic, or lime juice baste while heating.

RESTAURANTS

Overview

Restaurants are a natural business for the Internet. Those that appeal to young, hip, Internet-savvy audiences are popping up all over the Internet, especially in college towns and on the West Coast, including San Francisco, Seattle, and Portland. Restaurants should market on the Web because travelers and vacationers always ask for recommendations. This is only logical, as numerous people use the Internet to make travel plans and reservations.

Rewards

Restaurants can increase sales in several ways by using the Internet.

- They can sell meals for takeout or pickup.
- They can mail order prepared foods.

Risks

It can be hard to measure the effectiveness of advertisements without careful controls or surveys.

Special Marketing Considerations for the Home Page

Restaurant home pages should show their boîtes are cool places to visit as well as sources of good food. Home pages should include a map, menu, hours, and bio of the chef (they each have foodie fans who follow them around). For added value, include favorite recipes and coupons. To create a coupon, simply design one for a page and ask people to print it out. Put an expiration date on the coupon so you don't give away discounts forever. Test various coupon offers with different expiration dates so you can judge their effectiveness.

Case Study: The Virginia Diner

The Virginia Diner   *vadiner@infi.net*

Bill Galloway   *www.infi.net/vadiner*

PO Box 310

Wakefield, VA 23888

(original interview 1995)

Founded in 1929, the Virginia Diner sells gifts and peanuts around the world.

Getting Started

Who is your primary audience?

Our audience consists of anyone interested in gourmet gifts and other peanut products.

How will they benefit from your product?

The benefits of ordering our products or visiting our restaurant.

Did you create your home page, or did you get help?

The folks at *www.infi.net* were a tremendous help in getting us started. As the Web is a relatively new medium, it takes time to develop and as time goes on so does our growth. Despite being new on the Internet, we've done rather well, but it will still take time to develop. So far there aren't any real mistakes to speak of.

What advice do you have for other entrepreneurs?

My advice to someone starting up is that the Internet is a good place to do business, but don't expect an immediate return on investment (ROI), as it, like any new business or medium, will take time to develop.

What qualities are needed for success?

With any business, education is a must, and of course the qualities needed are those that would relate to your business, such as dealing with the public, marketing your products, etc.

My Day

My day starts by getting catalog inquiries and orders and of course answering these inquiries and mail. My job entails the marketing of our products both on and off the Internet. Dealing with online business takes a couple of hours a day. The hardest part of doing business in the beginning probably was becoming computer literate.

As always in the restaurant and now on the Internet, I still love meeting new people from all over the world and dealing with them in business. We like the Web and it's a good place to do business at this time. Given what I know now, of course I'd do it again, but of course I'd do it better.

For now, we are looking for a wonderful ROI and hope that the response from the Internet will always continue to grow.

The Future

I wish the best of luck to everyone in business, and if you need some great gift ideas, check us out at *www.infi.net/vadiner*, or if you're in the Wakefield, Virginia, area, stop in—our chicken and ham dinner will definitely make it worth your while.

INTERNET CAFÉS

Overview

For all those people who think Internetters like to hang out by themselves, think again. Dozens of restaurants and bars from New York to San

Francisco and Seattle have begun offering Internet access as well as burgers and beers. People pay for their food and their online time as well, about $10 an hour. These elite eateries get a lot of publicity for their owners. As an added draw, Internet cafés feature guest speakers (I spoke at the @Café in New York as a Japanese TV crew was in another part of the bar interviewing patrons).

Rewards

As there is a lot of competition in the restaurant business, the Internet gives a café a chance to be different and stand out. Also, the longer people stay, the more money you make from their online access time. Normally, restaurants don't like people gabbing at the tables after a dinner when the table could be used for a new set of paying customers. At an Internet café, the meter is always running.

Risks

Internet cafés are prone to the same pressures as other restaurants. Good content on the Internet must be matched by good food and atmosphere; otherwise, people will stay home.

Special Marketing Considerations for the Home Page

See information for restaurants in the preceding case studies. Internet cafés can hold online seminars as their special real-world speakers conduct online conferences. Copies of the tapes can be stored as files that can be downloaded by interested viewers.

Hot Site

Internet Café, *www.bigmagic.com*, in New York City, lists its menu for food and entertainment in a clean design.

COOKING SCHOOL

Overview

You have your recipes, you've taught all your roommates, kids, or sister-hood how to cook, so now you're ready to go public. Start a cooking school online. See Chapter 23 to see how people are selling seminars and course materials.

Owners of cooking schools can promote their business or offer classes online. The additional exposure can result in enrollments in your classes or visits by tourists to your store, which sells your own branded products and cookbooks.

Rewards

Increased income, additional exposure for your established business, books, or the like.

Risks

Normal business risks.

Special Marketing Considerations for the Home Page

Consider linking to related home pages of cooking schools in different cities as well as Internet sites offering restaurants, recipes, travel and tourism, wine, beverages, and so on. Add value to the page by offering recipes and cooking tips for free. Also, list newsgroup and mailing lists devoted to your specialties.

Hot Site

Sante Fe School of Cooking, *www.intac.com/~avalon/SANTAFE8.HTML #welcome*, shows its courses, fees and schedules. It also sells chili, salsa, sauces, pasta and herb gift baskets, beans, posole, flour, corn meal, nuts, cooking tools, dinnerware, and cookbooks.

SELLING RECIPES AND COOKBOOKS

Overview

When you look in the back of fine periodicals like *Star* and *National Enquirer*, you always see offers for Granny's special homemade sauces— send $2 and you'll get the secret recipe. That was then. This is now. Welcome to the Internet, where this same tactic can conceivably work for epicurean entrepreneurs.

You'll need a host of recipes, a home page, and marketing savvy to draw people in and make them salivate. If you've ever wanted to write your own cookbook, this is your chance.

Rewards

You could sell books or recipes and make money from material you've already created. Several Web stores, such as Ragu, the spaghetti sauce company, offer recipes as an added value for viewers. You might be able to sell your recipes to other home pages that want to add high touch to high tech.

Risks

Out-of-pocket expenses.

Special Marketing Considerations for the Home Page

Because people can't taste or smell your recipes on the Web, you need to describe these wonders with the flair of a restaurant menu writer. French fries become "succulent and golden." You can also make people's mouths water with small pictures of the completed meal. If you are a noted chef at a famed restaurant, tell people and post your bio!

SELLING HOMEMADE CHEESECAKES AND DELICACIES

Overview

Do all your relatives love the cheesecake you bake for their birthday so much they lie and tell you they have two birthdays a year? If so, you might have a dessert that is so good you can sell it on the Internet.

Rewards

Income.

Risks

Normal business risks.

Hot Site

Appetizer.com, *www.theappetizer.com*, serves Chicago and Boston. It offers secure ordering and payment via the Internet and remembers your information so you don't have to retype it when you come back for seconds.

14 Professional Services

While service providers like lawyers, accountants, and doctors can't practice their professions online, they can advertise and promote their services to an audience that can contract with them for work to be performed in the real world.

This chapter looks at how the Internet can help professionals and service vendors promote business.

LAWYER

Overview

Lawyers learn to use computers and online services in law school as they research Lexis and other online legal and governmental databases. It is only natural for this group to move to the Internet.

Rewards

By placing material on the Internet lawyers can attract new clients and referrals from lawyers with clients who need to consult an expert or to retain someone to handle matters outside their lawyer's normal scope of business. For example, a lawyer might represent a client for a business transaction and then need to find a criminal defense lawyer to provide further assistance.

Risks

Lawyers should check with their state bar association concerning its policy on advertising. Although Internet marketing has not clearly been defined as advertising in the traditional sense, there is reason to believe that it will fall under the same ethical considerations as advertising in other media.

Special Marketing Considerations for the Home Page

Home pages for lawyers should contain information about their specialty or primary area of practice, the cases they handle, and their educational and professional credentials. Extra value is added by lawyers who post information files, such as articles they've written for legal publications or papers presented at legal conferences.

Links to legal resources and experts who have home pages will also be appreciated.

Hot Sites

- Seamless.com, *www.seamless.com* is a starting point for information about lawyers and legal resources. It contains links to lawyers in many specialties in most states.

- Steven L. Kessler, Esq., *www.janal.com/kessler/html*, is the country's leading expert on civil forfeiture and racketeering laws. His site includes articles he's written for the *New York State Bar Journal*.

- Jerome Mullins, *www.seamless.com/alawyer*, is a lawyer in San Jose with a marvelous home page; his local number is 408-A-LAWYER. He's a very savvy marketing guy!

ACCOUNTING AND TAX PREPARATION

Overview

Professionals involved in accounting can use the Internet to find new clients and to consult or subcontract from others. The Internet could help these professionals: independent accountants, bookkeepers, tax preparers, accounting firms, and auditors.

Rewards

New clients and referrals.

Risks

Normal business risks.

Special Marketing Considerations for the Home Page

Accountants can post their areas of expertise, résumés, and articles of interest to target markets. Professionals who seek to do tax returns for small businesses, for example, could write an article called "Ten Ways to Cut Your Taxes" and post it on their home page.

Hot Sites

Secure Tax, *www.securetax.com*, lets people fill out tax forms online and file them. The site is promoted with banner ads on other sites and in print publications. The company makes money by charging for the service and by selling ads. For a good example of a local tax practitioner, see Taxland, *www.taxland.com*.

HEALTH CARE PROVIDERS

Overview

Entrepreneurial professionals can use the Internet to market their services by telling the world about their skills, backgrounds, and specialities. Home pages can be used to show the range of services performed, arrange appointments, and create both visibility and credibility. Additionally, there are many sites for preventive and alternative health care.

Rewards

Health care professionals can gain new clients and referrals from their peers.

Risks

Ethical considerations dictate that each caregiver check with state and professional association officials regarding regulations on advertising to see where the Internet falls in their codes. Special care should be given to announce disclaimers that advice given to one patient might not apply to others, as each person is different.

Special Marketing Considerations for the Home Page

Healers can use Web sites to establish their credibility by listing degrees, awards, and affiliations with hospitals and clinics.

To encourage people to make appointments, the home page should list office hours, a map, and telephone numbers, and perhaps include coupons. Dentists, for example, place ads for low-cost cleanings in every print advertising mechanism available, from TV guides to direct mail, so why not advertise a one-time discount on the Internet?

Physicians can also build credibility by writing articles that help all readers lead healthier lives. Topics can inlude such useful and noncontroversial themes as "Ten Ways to Reduce Stress" or "Ten Steps to a Healthier Heart."

Hot Site

Dr. Alan Green, *www.drgreen.com*, a pediatrician, ads value to his site by answering medical questions from parents.

Case Study: Infertitlity Resources

Infertility Resources

According to a Chinese saying –
Babies are found inside the flower of the Lotus plant.

Developed and maintained by Internet Health Resources Company

Welcome to Infertility Resources. This Web site is designed for:

- **People experiencing infertility** - provides information about IVF, GIFT, TET, ICSI, egg donor, infertility clinics, donor egg and surrogacy services (e.g., surrogate mothers), sperm banks, infertility books and journals, infertility newsgroups and support organizations, Metrodin, Pergonal, Clomid, and adoption
- **Infertility physicians and embryologists** - provides technical, research, and infertility product information
- **News media** - provides a list of experts who can be contacted

We would like to hear your comments or suggestions for additional information to be listed. Feel free to email us. Thank you.

What's New

MSNBC's show, "The Site," would like to interview a woman in the San Francisco Bay Area who has had infertility difficulties, found helpful infertility information on the Internet, and had a successful pregnancy through medications and/or IVF. If you are interested, please read further.

Figure 14–1. Infertility Resources provides information that draws readers to its Web site and potential customers for its health care provider clients. Copyright 1997,.Internet Health Resources.

Cliff Bernstein, Ph.D.   *cliffb@hooked.net*

1133 Garden Lane   *www.ihr.com/infertility*

Lafayette, CA 94549

(original interview 1995; update February 1997)

Infertility Resources began in 1995 as Internet Health Resources. Site owner, Cliff Bernstein changed the focus to reflect his own personal interest and attract a more highly focused audience.

What does your company do?

We provide Internet marketing for infertility organizations.

What expertise/background do you have to operate your business?

Nine years of computer systems analysis work and a Ph.D. in psychology.

Who is your primary audience?

Internet Health Resources (IHR) has two audiences. First, IHR provides health and fitness information to Internet users who want to take more responsibility for their health care. Secondly, IHR builds Web sites for health care organizations that want to deliver well-organized, user-friendly information.

How will they benefit from your product or service?

Internet users can gain practical health information for both their general interest and for effective health care decisions. Health care organizations can gain a low-cost medium for effectively distributing service and product information to the rapidly growing Internet market.

How does your product or service differ from others?

IHR provides one of the only Web sites devoted exclusively to a wide range of health care topics and builds Web sites *exclusively for the health care industry*. We understand the needs of health care organizations.

Is this business an offshoot of your existing business or does it exist only on the Internet?

Exists only on the Internet.

Where does your business operate?

I operate from my home office and from my Web service provider.

What is your background and training?

I worked nine years in health care as a psychotherapist and evaluation consultant. The work settings were hospital psychiatry departments, community mental health centers, and private practice. I also worked nine years as a computer systems analyst, including two and a half years on a medical cost containment system. My current work as president of IHR is an opportunity to bring together my health care and computer science interests.

When did you start your business?

November 1994.

How much money has your company made?

N/A

Getting Started

Did you create a business plan before going online?

I did not create a formal business plan before getting started. However, I did have a clear business model of what I intended to do.

How much time did it take to get up and running?

It took about one month from the time I thought of the project until I finally put the IHR Web site online in December 1994.

Did you create the pages yourself?

I created all the pages myself.

How much did it cost to get started?

The initial start-up cost very little. In November/December 1994 I did all the HTML using my existing hardware and software. However, since that time, as I have obtained customers, I have had to beef up my hardware and software. I purchased a gigabyte hard drive ($400), a tape backup system ($260), and a computer to serve as my Web server ($760). There are also hidden costs, such as the time I now take off from my previously full-time job. This results in a loss of one fifth of my salary income.

Did you need to go to an outside source for start-up capital?

No, I did not need this.

What mistakes did you make that you wish you hadn't made?

One early mistake was to not establish a domain name as early as possible. My previous Web service provider said they could provide a domain name but then was unable to do so. I did not want to market my site with an address that was hardwired to my Web service provider.

What advice would you give someone starting a business?

First, if you are serious about growing a business on the Internet, I think it is very important to get a domain name. This serves two major purposes: It shows the Internet community that you are serious about what you are doing and it gives you portability. That portability allows you to move to another Web service provider, if you need to, with no disruption in your URL.

Second, I would advise finding competent people to work with whose compensation requirements fit with your budget. It is impossible to do all the work by yourself; you cannot develop all the skills to do everything well. You may need to work with Web site administrators, graphic artists, CGI programming experts, database specialists, marketing people, etc. By being creative, you can work within a start-up budget. Think about advertising for students who are graphic artists or database specialists, then make sure that the work you give them is within their sphere of competency.

Third, because the Internet offers so many possibilities for developing a Web site or providing services, it is easy to get lost or spend time in nonproductive activities. I recommend always asking yourself, "How will this activity further my short-term or long-term business goals?"

What skills would a person need?

Developing an Internet business requires many skills, including computer software (HTML authoring, graphics, etc.) and hardware, graphic design, sales and marketing, project management, finance, and overall business savvy.

What kind of education is necessary to run your site?

I don't believe someone would need a formal education; however, she would need the skills listed above.

What special qualities are needed to run your site?

I think the main qualities for me are vision, persistence, and sticking to my business model. Vision allows me to develop a road map of where I am headed and lets me know when I am off course. I constantly have to move from the details of my work back to the vision. Persistence keeps me moving forward in the face of the inevitable frustrations and difficulties. I have to keep reminding myself why I got started in this in the first place. And sticking to my business model helps me to stay on course. Staying on course can be tough in the face of the awesome number of possibilities and distractions there are on the Internet. I try to keep things simple, focus on the business, and not get too caught up with all of the new technology.

How did you promote your site?

I requested to be listed on large directories such as Yahoo!. Also, I have been fortunate in that the June 1995 issue of *CompuServe* magazine selected the IHR Web site as one of the three notable health Web sites on the Internet. Other print publications have also listed the IHR Web site.

How much did it cost to promote your site?

I hired a marketing person to promote the IHR Web site on the Internet. That work is projected to cost $200 to $300.

How long did it take until you got your first sale?

It took about four months from the time my site was up in December 1994 to the first sales agreement from a customer.

How did the start-up phase affect your personal life?

IHR has very much affected my life. Basically, although it does not cost a lot of money, it tales considerable time and attention. This means little time with my wife and friends, very little time enjoying weekends, and no personal time. I often sit indoors on sunny weekend days. It is a *major* sacrifice of my personal life. This is the biggest cost in developing the business. Additionally, I am earning less money now due to cutting back in my salaried computer systems work.

My Day

What does your average day look like?

I work four weekdays as a salaried systems analyst, leaving one weekday to devote to IHR. I also devote most evenings and weekends to IHR. My one IHR weekday consists of sales demos in the morning and then dozens of phone calls in the afternoon. In the evenings and weekends I answer e-mail, build customers and IHR's Web sites, and do administrative work.

What does your job entail?

The job entails lots of phone calling, HTML authoring, e-mailing, Internet surfing, demos, meetings, doing financials (billing, etc.).

How many hours a week do you spend working on your site?

About forty hours a week:

- phone calling—17 percent

- demos—8 percent

- HTML authoring—15 percent

- e-mail (including reading e-mail newsletters)—30 percent

- Internet surfing (for business objective)—10 percent

- miscellaneous administration (meetings, financial)—20 percent

What was the hardest aspect of the work in the beginning?

Putting all the pieces together (i.e., building the infrastructure), marketing, building the Web site, learning all the new software and HTML, administrative work, demos, etc.

How long did it take to get established?

I cannot say that I am yet established but I do feel more confident that the pieces are falling together and that I am working with the right business plan.

What do you like most about your work?

I enjoy building the Web sites, doing demos, being a pioneer in new technology and business processes, and making sales calls to tell people about the IHR services.

What do you like the least?

The frustrations of dealing with technology that is not always consistent or plug-and-play. For example, my backup tape drive software did not work, my Web server TCP/IP stack kept crashing, and getting a dialup script to work correctly was difficult.

What was your greatest moment?

My first sale.

Are there any hazards to running your site?

There are potential legal liabilities when operating a Web site devoted to health care resources. I do not, though, give medical advice.

How much money do you expect to make?

I expect to make over $70,000 a year.

General

Are you glad you are on the Web for personal and business reasons?

I enjoy the excitement of the business. I do not like the time away from my personal life.

Given what you know now, would you do it again?

Definitely yes.

The Future

What is your next venture?

This is it for now.

What else would you like to say?

The Internet affords exciting opportunities both for business potential and for operating on the cutting edge. However, anyone getting into this should know up front that this requires a lot of time and attention to do it right. Thanks for the opportunity to share some of my thoughts. I hope others will find this helpful.

1997 Update

What makes your site special?

Specialized information.

How do you get people to come to your site?

Register in search engines and get listed on Web sites.

How do you get people to return to your site?

Provide helpful information.

What is the most important thing you learned in the past year about marketing on the Internet?

Just keep at it.

What is the most effective way to get people to buy products or services?

Provide helpful information in a user-friendly manner. My customers (i.e., the fertility clinics) have been very successful in obtaining patients via their Web sites by providing helpful information for Internet users.

How does your site generate revenue?

Fertility clinics pay me to market their services.

How much money have you made?

Sales on my Web site are up.

INSURANCE AGENT

Overview

Insurance agents selling all types of products can find an audience online. Look at all the rich high-tech executives who use the Internet, as well as the company employees who need to stash their retirement plans somewhere. Lots of work-at-home executives (like me) could use disability coverage. (I've already got mine, please don't call. Yes, I bought it offline but that was before I knew about the Internet).

Rewards

People who don't want to talk to pushy salespeople are using the Internet to buy policies.

Risks

Please check with your attorney and state agencies regarding the dispensing of advice and your ability to sell policies in states in which you do not live.

Special Marketing Considerations for the Home Page

Lots of information about the practical needs and uses of insurance could draw people to your home page. Remember, we aren't talking about the normal gloom-and-doom brochures that have marked the insurance industry. Be creative in telling people new reasons for buying insurance. Then show them why they should buy from you.

Hot Site

Quotesmith, *www.quotesmith.com,* is setting a new standard in how insurance policies are sold on the Internet. Consumers fill out a form with their needs and Quotesmith shows them the prices offered by dozens of companies. Consumers click on the link to see the details and have a local agent call them to answer questions and sign the policy.

FINANCIAL PLANNER OR STOCKBROKER

Overview

Look at the demographics of the Internet. There are a lot of rich people out there! They could all use your advice. This could be a great service for the right person who can create custom-made portfolios. People could track their investments on a daily basis.

Rewards

New clients.

Risks

Check with your lawyer regarding rules and regulations. If you house portfolios on the site, be sure to protect the data with passwords.

Special Marketing Considerations for the Home Page

Online citizens know there is a sucker born every minute and they don't want to be the next one who get picked. You must create an atmosphere of trust. Show your credentials in your heading, such as Joe Smith, CFP. Present articles on financial planning, along with tips and strategies. By giving away free information, you can attract an audience. With credibility and good advice, you might be able to get a new client.

PRIVATE INVESTIGATOR

Overview

Sam Spade has come to the Internet! Round up the usual suspects, sweetheart. Private investigators and other members of the criminal investigation services can find new clients and network with peers in related fields by using the Internet (i.e., bail bondsmen need private investigators; lawyers need process servers). By using public documents, you can perform background checks on clients., and find out where people live and their phone numbers and e-mail addresses.

Rewards

Benefits include increased exposure and opportunity to build a business.

Risks

Normal business risks.

Special Marketing Considerations for the Home Page

List special interests and abilities, such as speaking foreign languages, gun permits, special training or contacts, background (such as law enforcement positions), and state-registered license numbers. Add biographies on staffers to show depth to the service. For entertainment value, consider a game or contest. This field is ripe with possibilities!

15 Travel and Tourism

Travel services have always been popular on the commercial online services, and that is true of the Internet. People like the convenience of reading about travel destinations in the comfort of their own home. Many travel agencies have taken advantage of this need by creating Web sites that offer free information and pictures of exotic destinations. Hotel chains, too, have gone online to post information and pictures about their rooms and rates. Some futurists predict that the travel agent business will be completely reworked as online services give consumers the power to make reservations directly with hotels, airlines, and car rental services.

Travel services are among the hottest commercial activities on the Internet, according to surveys by Forrester Research, *www.forrester.com* and others.

More than in any other area of electronic commerce, consumers and business travelers feel totally comfortable placing orders online to purchase airline tickets, hotel reservations, and other travel-related services.

Entrepreneurial companies in the travel industry are using the Internet to break new ground in online marketing. Companies like TravelBids (see Chapter 4, under Service Auctions) and Hotel Discounts, an online reservation station, are using the Internet to sell travel services in ways that were not possible before the age of electronic commerce. These Web-based businesses are siphoning off customers from traditional travel agents, who should be concerned about the future of their industry and jobs.

Entrepreneurs can create travel or geographic malls and sell space, advertising, and links to businesses in that targeted area. See Chapter 4 for more information on malls and their relatives, aggregator sites.

TravelWeb, *www.travelweb.com* claims it handled $1 million worth of Internet-sourced hotel reservations in November 1996. "This is a clear indication of the acceptance of electronic commerce on the Web," said John F. Davis III, CEO of the Web site's owner, Pegasus Systems "Even more encouraging is the pace in which it is growing. November's bookings represent nearly 20 percent of TravelWeb's total volumes for the year, and we're seeing this trend continue in our December bookings as well. This is phenomenal growth." Pegasus Systems shareholders are large hotel companies, including HFS, Hilton, Hyatt, ITT Sheraton, and Marriott.

The Internet offers opportunities to sell books, magazines, and videos as well as for specialists in boat charters, cruises, limousines, and shuttles.

This chapter explores ways to make money on the Internet as a travel agent, tour provider, and travel magazine publisher. The examples show opportunites for entrepreneurs even as major hotels, airlines, and tour operators go online.

Bon voyage!

TRAVEL AGENT

Overview

The Internet offers travel agents opportunities to sell tours, tickets, and adventure to a worldwide audience. This field will get increasingly crowded as agents realize the Internet is a gold mine. Winners will be those companies that specialize in niche markets, or have expertise in a specific area, like Disneyland, Europe, or wilderness tours.

Other entrepreneurs can make money by gathering new clients for travel agents. This can be accomplished by creating a travel mall, adding a brochure to a related site, or any number of other creative ways. Travel agents can pay them a fee based on the actual sale. The agent benefits by gaining additional business without having to spend time and money hunting for clients.

Rewards

Travel agents can promote their business to people around the country.

Risks

Normal business risks.

Special Marketing Considerations for the Home Page

People buy destinations, adventure, and romance. Show them pictures of your featured vacations; add music and recipes for exotic foods. Spark their imagination by showing calendars with dates of festivals and special events, like Carnivale in Rio de Janeiro, or local celebrations that add color to a city, like Oregon's Eugene Days, which features the Slug Queen parade and a typewriter throwing contest. Consider selling links to related services, like restaurants, hotels, and city home pages. Sell advertising on your page to airlines, hotels, and rental car agencies. Consider adding audio and video clips to capture the charm of the destination.

Hot Sites

- TravelAssist Magazine   *www.travelassist.com*
- Travelocity   *www.travelocity.com*
- TravelBids   *www.travelbids.com*

TRAVEL MAGAZINE

Overview

Many people are looking for resources to help them enrich their lives. Whether it be travel, cooking, sports, or professional information, an online magazine full of links to other sites and solid editorial matter can help attract an audience.

Rewards

If you do this business correctly, you can make money by selling ads. Travel agents can use this business model to make reservations from Internet travelers.

Risks

Normal business risks.

Special Marketing Considerations for the Home Page

Create a special marketing hook that makes the magazine speak the same language as its audience. Add an online concierge to help then find information; that word is a lot friendlier and more relevant than "search engine." Also, try to convey a sense of fun, adventure, and relaxation by your choice of words and art.

Hot Site

Biztravel.com, *www.biztravel.com*, is an online magazine for business travelers.

Case Study: TravelBank Systems

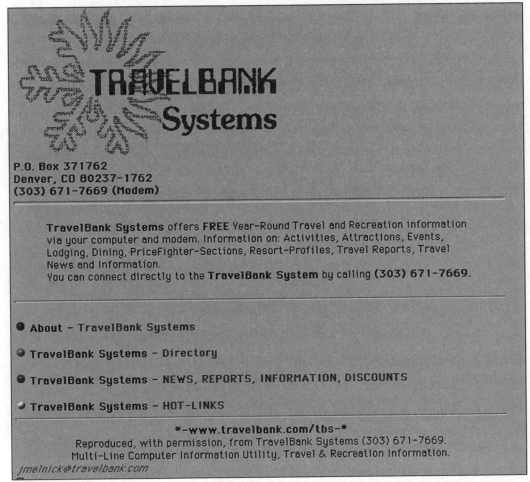

Figure 15–1. TravelBank provides lots of information for the jet set. Copyright 1997, TravelBank Systems.

TravelBank Systems

H. Jay Melnick

PO Box 371762

Denver, CO 80237-1762

(original interview March 1997)

jmelnick@travelbank.com

www.travelbank.com/tbs

What does your company do?

TravelBank Systems provides computer users online, real-time, year-round national travel and recreation information—reports on weather, roads, lodging, events, dining and entertainment, activities, fishing/hunting, skiing, etc., as well as access to message areas, and the ability to talk with other computer users across the country.

The TravelBank is a menu-driven system, which means that at each menu the reader is presented with a list of items from which to select needed information. Upon pressing the appropriate key(s), the requested information is displayed. The user has the ability to save and or print out this information from his computer.

Over 91,000 computer users (both home and office) have connected with the TravelBank from all over the United States, Canada, Mexico, Europe, and Japan. 1,782 travel agents, agencies, and clubs connect to Travel-Bank. There are 492 callers, on average, each day. The average reader is a thirty-four-year-old male, with a college degree, a professional occupation, and an annual income of $35,000+.

What expertise/background do you draw on to operate your business?

Over twelve years of on-line operation experience. Over twenty-five years of advertising, marketing, journalism experience.

What was your company's goal for going online?

To see how we can make use of the evolving technology.

How do you know you have reached that goal?

Continuing!!! In 1992 we were awarded the Colorado Tourism Achievement Award for Individual Business by the Colorado Tourism Board.

How much did it cost to get started?

$250.

What makes your site special?

Quality and level of information.

How do you get people to come to your site?

Promotion, promotion, promotion.

How do you get people to return to your site?

Ease of use, access, quality and level of information.

What is the most important thing you learned in the past twelve months about marketing on the Internet?

That it is an ongoing enterprise.

What is the most effective way to get people to come to your site?

Participate on the Internet, newsgroups, and at other Web sites.

What is the most effective way to get people to buy products or services?

Offer something of value.

How does your site generate revenue?

Selling advertising.

How much money have you made?

Profitable for the past ten years.

HOTEL, BED AND BREAKFAST, INN, LODGE

Overview

The hospitality industry is coming onto the Internet as fast as Super Bowl victors go to Disneyland. By advertising its services and taking reservations on the Internet, your stately inn in England can be seen by tourists in Sri Lanka. If you own such an establishment, you are already facing serious competition from the national chains as well as from moms and pops who saw the light years ago. The hotel industry is wired!

Rewards

Promoting your services on the Internet can expand your client base. Be sure to have data ports on your phones to please e-mail users!

Risks

The only risk of being online is *not* being online as your competitors eat your lunch.

Special Marketing Considerations for the Home Page

Major hotel sites are showing maps and pictures of rooms and offering toll-free reservation numbers. You must compete on this level. Most home pages feature photos of the establishment, rooms, and smiling staffs. They list rates and include reservation numbers and e-mail reservation forms. To add value, you could include links to home pages of local tourist attractions, cities, shopping and entertainment centers. Links from these sites can help your business grow (e.g., "Coming to Sante Fe? Stay at the Inn of the Animal Tracks! Click here for a tour!"). To help add more flavor to your site, list menus, recipes, and afternoon snacks.

Hot Sites

- San Francisco Hotel Reservations, *www.hotelres.com* lets consumers check and make reservations.

- Hotel Discounts, *www.hoteldiscounts*, lets consumers find hotels at deep discounts and make reservations online or via a toll-free number.

TRAVEL GUIDE AND TOUR SERVICE

Overview

Travel guides offering tours of Hawaii by helicopter, river canoeing adventures, and the like can be found on the Internet. You can create a tour that takes advantage of your favorite activity, like biking along country roads, wine tours of Napa Valley, or walking tours of delicatessens in New York. Create a home page and then market the site.

Rewards

Creating a tour business can be a nice sideline to your current job—and you'll get paid for doing what you like to do. As some kinds of tours can accommodate large numbers of people, you can make a decent day's income. For example, a walking tour of your town's architectural district can accommodate thirty to forty people (more if you can project your voice above the urban roar). If each paid $15 a head, you'd make $450 for a mornings or afternoon's work on a weekend. Other groups that must be kept small for safety's sake, like a bike tour, can charge slightly higher fees. A helicopter tour of Hawaii, in contrast, might be able to fit only four people, but can command $150 a seat!

Risks

Ask your insurance agent about liability for injuries.

Special Marketing Considerations for the Home Page

Pictures and written descriptions of tour highlights, comments from previous tourists, and menus of restaurants to be visited would add visual appeal. Prices, times, and itineraries should be included. For an added marketing boost, consider creating a game of the places you'd visit, such as a treasure hunt. You could also charge for links to sites you visit, or create home pages for them.

Hot Site

International Adventure Brokers, *www.2buysell.com/iab/*, offers safaris, swimming with dolphins, and exploring Antarctica with naturalists.

VACATION RENTALS LISTING AND LISTING SERVICE

Overview

Owners of vacation rentals, time-shares, and other properties can list them on the Internet. Tourists can find the listings on the owner's page or a page rented from a travel agent, travel mall, or geographic mall. Consider developing these advertising vehicles and charging for creating new pages, linking to existing pages, or selling advertisements to companies that want to reach a target market.

Rewards

Income from sales.

Risks

Normal business risks.

Hot Site

CyberShare Mall, *www.cybersharemall.com*, presents listings for time-shares, travel, and yachts. The entry page flashes pictures of resorts and a marquee shows a message for advertising on the site. The page shows each location name, contact (with e-mail address), and price in a menu list. The consumer can click on the listing to see a picture and description.

Case Study: Hale Lea Beach House

"Hale Lea Beach House"

Puako, Hawaii

ID*HI4Vpuako1ta

Hawaii Vacation Rental

Hale Lea (House of Joy) is a lovely Hawaii beach vacation home with mountain and ocean views. It is very comfortable with high vaulted ceilings throughout, lovely tile work in the kitchen and baths. The large front lanai overlooks the ocean, a great spot to dine and take in the magnificent sunsets. Complete with hammock, chaise lounge and outdoor dinning. One of the best snorkeling reefs on the islands is right across the street from our house. Located directly across a quiet residential street from the ocean, this vacation home is serene, yet is surrounded by some of the most fun and fine hotels on the island. These provide great meals, entertainment and wonderful collections of Asian and Hawaiian art and artifacts.

SIZE: This vacation home sleeps 6 persons. 3 Bedrooms and 2 bathrooms with fully equipped kitchen and linens provided. Children are welcome.We're sorry no smoking or pets allowed.

BEDS: 2 Singles, 2 Queens, 1 Sofabed, 1 Portacrib

Vacation Rental Features:

- Phone, Ceiling Fans throughout the home
- TV , VCR, Stereo, CD/player, Tape deck
- Yard, View, Lanais
- Microwave, Washer/Dryer, Dishwasher
- Large front lanai with ocean view, perfect for dining or lounging
- Garage, Parking

Figure 15–2. The Hawaiian paradise Hale Lea Beach House shows that a picture is worth a thousand words. Copyright 1997, Jane Rachel Kaplan.

Hale Lea Beach House

Jane Rachel "Kini" Kaplan

1496 Solano Avenue

Albany, CA 94706

(original interview 1997

kinik@aol.com

www.com/puako1.htm

What does your company do?

Market and rent our vacation home (owned by three couples) on the beautiful Big Island of Hawaii.

What expertise/background do you have to operate your business?

We all have successful other businesses (psychologists, counselor, physician) that we have each run an average of sixteen years.

What was your company's goal for going online?

To increase exposure.

To let interested people all over the country and the world know about our house.

To increase rental of house.

How do you know you have reached that goal?

People all over the country and the world have e-mailed us to inquire about the house. We recently rented the house for a week based on our Web site.

How much did it cost to get started?

We spent several hundred dollars to make up and send pages. Our print ads in the paper cost several hundred a year too. Our page on the WorldWide Travel Exchange, *www.wwte.com*, costs only $100 a year.

What makes your site special?

We let the people from Travel Exchange make our site, but we added our own copy, descriptions, pictures, etc.

How do you get people to come to your site?

They enter through Travel Exchange. Now we also print our Web site address on our flyers, which we mail to people who hear of us through the newspaper or by word of mouth.

How do you move people from being window-shoppers to paying customers?

We do this by mail and on the phone by calling them about the house and finding out the dates they want and booking them.

What is the most important thing you learned in the past year about marketing on the Internet?

It's fun! Usually I am the serious psychologist Jane Rachel Kaplan, but on the Internet, I get to be "Kini" and answer questions about a beautiful place. It's interesting to reach a wider audience and lots of interesting people.

What is the most effective way to get people to buy products or services?

To give them a sense of what it might be like if they vacationed there—give them a "your house" feeling.

How does your site generate revenue?

People inquire and sometimes book. It's great marketing.

How much money have you made?

We booked a week at $1,100. After expenses (20 percent goes to our agent in Hawaii) gross profit is $880, but we pay cleaning, maintenance, utilities, and mortgage. The house does not yet pay for itself (it was expensive), but we're getting there and the Web site helps.

16 Software and Computer Consultants

SOFTWARE PUBLISHING

Overview

Software sales are among the largest categories on the Internet. After all, *everyone who uses the Internet uses a computer!* What a great demographic match.

Rewards

Selling software through the retail channel can cost $250,000–$500,000, which is way too much for most midnight engineers (and small software companies). The Internet can give these entrepreneurs the exposure they need to make it in either the virtual world or the real world. More than a dozen multimillion-dollar software companies got their start posting shareware (software you can try before you buy it) on the commercial online services. Numerous other publishers have used this marketing method to make a good living and to supplement their daytime job. Today it seems like every software publisher from Microsoft to start-ups puts time-trial versions of its software on its Web site to build an audience. People can try out the software and, if they like it, pay for it when the time limit is reached. Companies that have followed this method successfully from start-up to a presence on retail shelves include PointCast, C-U-See-Me, McAfee's Virus Scan, and Web Whacker.

Risks

Software publishers the world over live in fear of having their works pirated (copied without permission). This could happen on the Internet. However, publishers can take precautions such as posting files that lock after a given period of time, or won't work unless the files have been paid for and registered.

Special Marketing Considerations for the Home Page

Software publishers should be sure to let people know the benefits of their products, which too often are shrouded in a set of meaningless features. Reviews in online publications like *C/Net*, *ZDnet*, and others are instrumental in getting the word out.

Case Study: Sausage Software

Sausage Software *www.sausage.com*

Steve Outtrim

(original interview 1995; update 1997)

Sausage Software of Australia used the Internet to promote and distribute its HotDog HTML editing program in 1995. HotDog is now available in computer stores around the United States and is usually ranked at or near the top of reviewers' lists. This business started as a one-person venture. Today its operations span the globe and involve a network of dealers, distributors, and salespeople as well as loyal customers.

Here is the first in-depth interview with HotDog founder Steve Outrrim, reprinted from the first edition of this book. He responded within five hours of my first interview request back then.

Who is your primary audience?

People who want to create HTML documents for the World Wide Web.

How will they benefit from your product or service?

HotDog provides a graphical interface to the HTML command language. In simple terms, people can click a few buttons instead of typing a slew of obscure commands.

How does your product or service differ from others?

HotDog is a 100 percent commercial venture. Most other HTML editors have been created as shareware or freeware, written in the author's spare time. Obviously, someone working on her program whenever she get a free minute is going to find it much harder to produce great software than a company that can devote much more time, money, and resources to development.

The feedback we've got from our users is that HotDog is easier to use, more pleasant to look at, and much more useful than its competitors.

Is this business an offshoot of your existing business or does it exist only on the Internet?

We exist only on the Internet (well, we sell through CompuServe and by fax, but because we're selling Internet software, we'd be dead without it!).

Where does your business operate?

I run the business from an office at home. Sausage Software is structured very much as Charles Handy described the Shamrock Organization in his book *The Age of Unreason*.

I am (at the moment) the sole full-time employee of Sausage Software; any work I can't handle is subcontracted out globally via the Internet. These subcontractors work for me, but they're not technically employees.

Some are people working from their bedroom in their spare time, some are professional consultants, and some are employed by organizations we contract work to, so they work on HotDog as part of their job.

What is your background and training?

I have a degree in accountancy and management. I've been programming since 1981 (self-taught). I've had only two full-time jobs—systems programmer on a Unisys mainframe for the New Zealand Inland Revenue Department and office manager for a food-industry business here in Melbourne. Part of my role at the latter job was to develop a financial system for them. I left with the intention of starting my own business to sell this package, but the accountancy market is pretty mature and the barriers to entry are high.

I spent three days thinking about how the world is going to change in the next few years, and almost every idea I could come up with was in some way tied to the Internet. I should qualify this by saying I was by no means an Internet junkie or guru —most of my time on the Internet was spent talking to my cyberbuddies in *alt.drunken.bastards*.

But I really believe that the Internet is going to change dramatically over the next couple of years, and the opportunities for making money here are phenomenal.

Anyway, I settled on HotDog quite by accident. I was creating some HTML pages for my personal account, just to say who I am, what I like, and all the other stuff that no one really gives a damn about.

I spent a while looking for a good editor and eventually found a program. This was functional, but not brilliant. It was written in Visual Basic, which is my programming language of choice. I thought "Hell, I must be able to do better than this," so I spent a few days banging together a little program.

When I was finished, I decided to test the waters on the Internet. I posted a single message in comp.infosystems.www.authoring.html asking if people were interested in helping to test a new HTML editor for Windows. I expected I'd get maybe ten replies. Within three days I had 150 testers (by the time HotDog was released, I had over 800). I'm not stupid—I realized very quickly that I was onto something here. There was (and still is) an enormous pent-up demand for decent HTML tools, and it seemed like there were a lot of people very unhappy with the current software.

Getting Started

When did you start your business?

March 1995 (but the idea for HotDog came in May 1995).

Did you create a business plan before going online?

Yes and no. The business plan was there, but I didn't specifically create a plan like "OK, this is how I'm going online, this is who we should use, this is how many hits a day we're going to get, etc." This information was in my head. The business plan is more useful to tell the bank, accountants, and other nontechnical people what my business is about. These people don't want to know about projected transfer volumes, hits per week, or indeed anything about the Internet (which, as they see on the news every night, is full of rapists, terrorists, and pornographers!).

This is actually one of the difficulties I've found. Because my business is totally centered around the Internet, it's not easy to explain to someone who doesn't know what that is.

How much time did it take to get up and running?

Well, it's hard to define "up and running." Getting a virtual Web server took two to three weeks, but I'm still waiting for some of the things I require here. Development of HotDog, from the day I decided to write an HTML editor to the day it was officially released, took eight weeks.

Did you create the pages yourself?

I created the initial pages myself, but they're now being done by a professional company.

How much did it cost to get started?

- virtual domain (three months) U.S. $130.

- permanent Internet connection (28800 PPP): AUD $1,200, including modems and phone lines (this is a luxury that's starting to become a necessity for me).

- development software: U.S. $1500 (approximately; I already had most of this).

- PC: AUD $5500 (I'd had this for two years).

- general start-up expenses: $10,000, but I'm paying these as I go; I didn't have to have $10,000 in cash to start the business.

How did you obtain your start-up capital?

I funded everything myself. All of the money has been spent from sales. I didn't have any money at all when I started the business!

How did you promote your home page?

By announcing the product in appropriate newsgroups and registering with Yahoo! and the other search sites. Now people who like the product are linking to our site from theirs.

How much did it cost to promote your site?

N/A

How long did it take until you made your first sale?

This is probably different for us than for a lot of people you'll be directing this survey to. We didn't put up the Web site, then wait for people to buy the program. We presold a number of copies to people testing HotDog, so our first sale came a week or so before the product was officially released.

How much money has your company made online?

In the three weeks since the product was released, about $19,000. I was expecting about a third of that.

How much money do you hope to make?

My goal for the year is $1 million in turnover (that's Australian dollars). We're not actually selling anything physical, so we don't have a cost of goods sold. Probably 30 percent of turnover will go towards research and development of future products. I'm hoping for a 50 percent net profit before tax ratio.

What mistakes did you make that you wish you hadn't made?

Our alpha program was way too open. We got people who joined but weren't interested in testing the program; they just wanted to evaluate a new editor. This meant we had to field a lot of e-mails along the lines of "How dare you release a program with so many bugs!" The whole point of the alpha program was to fix the bugs, so when people actually evaluate the product it's relatively bug-free.

It was pretty depressing to get these negative comments instead of constructive criticism, but, more importantly there's a lot of people out there who don't understand what alpha and beta testing is, and will never buy our product because of all the bugs they found when they tried an earlier version.

Our alpha program for our new product, HotDog Pro, is closed. The only way to get into it is to purchase the program in advance. This means that the people using it are genuinely interested in helping us fix all the bugs because they've made a financial commitment to the product themselves.

What advice would you give to a similar start-up?

DO IT! There's no formula for being successful on the Internet. You need to understand the basic rules of doing business on the Internet, like don't send people junk e-mail, don't repeatedly post advertising material to newsgroups, don't make inappropriate posts, and try real hard not to flame anyone no matter how much they piss you off. But if you think you have a great idea, try and bounce it off people in newsgroups or mailing lists (which is effectively free and a very rapid market research). If you get an encouraging response, go for your life!

What skills are needed to run a business?

Well, programming skills obviously, and you need to understand the syntax and the theory of HTML. I'm finding that I also have to be responsible for other companies' bugs. We get a lot of people blaming us for bugs in Netscape, Trumpet Winsock, and Windows.

You can't really say "Talk to Microsoft. I don't want to know." But it's frustrating when you get the "Your product is a load of crap" messages because of something completely out of your control! So I guess a thick skin is a useful skill.

I think a high standard of ethics is very important—a lot of people are wary of doing business over the Internet, particularly with someone in another country; in my experience, this is more of a problem for Americans than anyone else, but I guess that's because the rest of us get used to purchasing things from the States. You need to do everything in your power to reassure them. If your customers are impressed with your integrity and service, then they'll tell their friends or vouch for you in public forums like newsgroups, when people express concern.

I find writing skills to be very useful, too. I think if your English and general grammar skills were below average, you could alienate a lot of people and just generally give an unfavorable impression of your professionalism.

What special qualities are needed to run your site?

I think graphic design skills are important (that's one of the reasons why someone else is doing our site). An understanding of basic principles of business law and copyright is useful.

My Day

What does your average day look like?

Get up 9–10 A.M.

Answer e-mail for two hours.

Have lunch for an hour.

Program until about 7:30 P.M. Watch some TV, have dinner.

Either program or answer more e-mail.

I work on the business seven days a week.

How many hours a week do you spend working on your site? What percentages of time are spent on each task?

Twenty to thirty. Hard to say, I haven't really measured it.

What was the hardest part of the job in the beginning?

Learning to use the Internet—mailing lists, UNIX, PGP, things like that.

What do you like most about your work?

I can run the business whenever it suits me, and really from anywhere in the world. I guess you'd call this "freedom."

What do you like least?

Waking up in the morning to find two hundred e-mail messages waiting for replies, then finding that most of them say "Your program doesn't work. How could you do this to me?" 8*)

What was your greatest moment?

Well, some of the reviews we're getting have been pretty nice. I guess the greatest moment was my first sale. It's an amazing feeling, to know that you can create something out of thin air and people will pay you for it. It's very, very satisfying.

How much time do you spend conducting business, marketing, selling, upgrading your site?

Not much (but a lot of time on upgrading the product). I'm planning on hiring some full-time programmers very soon; this will free me up to concentrate most of my time on marketing.

How did the start-up phase affect your personal life?

The fact that I had no money made me cranky! Other than that, there weren't any major effects.

Are you glad you are on the Web for personal and business reasons?

Absolutely. I've never been happier. Not only am I making money, I'm having a helluva lot of fun! As far as business reasons go, I think I'm in the right place at the right time with the right product.

Given what you know now, would you do it again?

In a second.

The Future

What is your next venture?

We're going to continue building the business as providers of authoring and design tools for the information superhighway. I also want to diversify into multimedia programs for the educational market. I think making interactive Dr. Seuss–style books would be an incredible amount of fun.

What else would you like to say?

Hey, I've enjoyed talking about myself! I would like to say that I believe the Internet needs some sort of regulatory body to ensure that businesses that get "wired" behave properly. In Australia we have a Fair Trading Act that prevents you from making false statements and generally enforces ethical behavior. There's nothing to stop a competitor from publicly denigrating my product in a newsgroup; neither is there anything to stop a business from taking orders but never delivering the products. Sure, you could prosecute them under their local laws, but who wants to fly to Taiwan to sue a Taiwanese company?

This idea could be implemented like a chamber of commerce, an elected body that hears complaints from consumers about businesses. If you're not doing the right thing, you can't be a member of the chamber of commerce. That way, consumers who are wary of doing business with a company can check with the chamber of commerce. If the business is a member, then you're probably a lot safer dealing with them. I'd happily pay to join an organization like this.

1997 Update

The first version of HotDog was officially released for sale on the Internet on June 29, 1995. Since then, HotDog has become something of a phenomenon on the Internet, with more than thirty thousand users in more than eighty countries worldwide. HotDog is marketed, distributed, sold, and supported over the Internet and in retail outlets in North America. The company also develops and distributes Snaglets, small applications that provide webpage enhancements such as animation, sound, and interactivity. "The experience of Sausage Software demonstrates the opportunities that the Internet offers for newcomers to business," says Outtrim. "When you consider the implications of communication between scores of millions of people around the world and realise that the network is growing every month, the business possibilities are enormous. The ability to act quickly is one of Sausage Software's greatest strengths. Selling over the Internet means we can bring fresher, hotter new technology to the market sooner than any traditional retail-based company. To this end, I encourage an environment of 'structured anarchy,' which allows employees to be innovative and creative." HotDog has received five-star reviews from the Internet community and has often been cited as the best product of its kind. Among its users are scores of U.S. and overseas government departments, Fortune 500 companies, and major universities.

ONLINE RETAILER

Overview

Hardware and software retailers can benefit from selling products online because they have lower overhead and costs than traditional stores. You don't even need a storefront, as the case study on software.net will show. Please see the notes on software.net in the chapter 4 discussion of the virtual store model for starting this type of virtual business.

Real-world retailers like Egghead, *www.egghead.com*, also are using the Internet as an effective sales tool.

Rewards

Increased sales via online ordering and increased traffic to your store. Companies that do drop-ship ordering will not need to carry large amounts of products in inventory. Entrepreneurs can target special audiences, like parents, teachers, and accountants, to offer a one-stop shopping solution and resource center for customers.

Risks

Normal business risks. Be careful about fraudulent credit cards. Interview subjects have told me that many crooks try to use stolen cards to pay for computers. Routine credit card checking and address verification will save you from shipping products to criminals.

Special Marketing Considerations for the Home Page

Because you don't have a salesperson online to answer questions, the home page becomes your salesperson. It should contain a mountain of information about each product, its features, benefits, audience, and system requirements. It should also include payment options and information about return privileges, if any. People have many questions about compatibility between systems and brands; be sure to answer as many as possible online through printed matter or FAQs (lists of frequently asked questions) so as not to burden your live staff or incur returns for unwanted products.

Case Study: software.net

Figure 16–1. Sales items are displayed prominently at software.net's cyberstore. Copyright 1997, CyberSource Corporation.

software.net

William S. McKiernan

1050 Chestnut Street, Suite 201

Menlo Park, CA 94025

billm@software.net

www.software.net

415-473-3067

(original interview 1995; update February 1997)

Who is your primary audience?

Corporate, government, university users.

How will they benefit from your product or service?

Electronic distribution of software of over 8,000 software titles and 35,000 pages of product information.

How does your product or service differ from others?

Electronic distribution.

Is this business an offshoot of your existing business or does it exist only on the Internet?

Only on the Internet.

Where is your business conducted?

Office. We have ten people right now with plans to grow to thirty by first quarter 1996.

What is your background and training?

President of public software company (took them public—McAfee Associates), Harvard MBA, CPA.

Getting Started

When did you start your business?

April 1994.

Did you create a business plan before going online?

Yes.

How much time did it take to get up and running?

Six months.

Did you create the pages yourself or did you get help?

Engineering team.

How much did it cost to get started?

Approximately $100K (including merchandise).

Did you need to go to an outside source for start-up capital?

Self-funded to begin.

How did you promote your site?

Through traditional public relations and reciprocal links.

How much did it cost to promote your site?

$25,000.

How long did it take until you got your first sale?

Few hours.

How much has your company made?

$15,000 per week.

How much money do you expect to make?

Lots—plan is to do $3 million this year.

What mistakes did you make that you wish you hadn't made?

Nothing catastrophic yet.

What advice would you give someone trying to start a business?

Focus on customer needs.

What skills would a person need to conduct business?

No fear.

My Day

What does your average day look like?

Not for the faint of heart.

What does your job entail?

A little of everything.

How many hours a week do you spend working on your site?

Sixty.

What percentages of time are spent on each task?

Hour each on sixty million different things.

What was the hardest aspect of the work in the beginning?

Working without sleep.

What do you like most about your work?

Inventing a new channel, being independent.

What do you like the least?

Lack of support infrastructure.

What was your greatest moment?

Turning the server on and then seeing the site the next day on the floor of Comdex.

How did the start-up phase affect your personal life?

Fortunately, I have an understanding wife.

Are you glad you are on the Web for personal and business reasons?

Yes.

Given what you know now, would you do it again?

Definitely.

The Future

What is your next venture?

Distributing digital content besides software via the Internet.

What else would you like to say?

This is not a business for committees and task forces. You do. You make mistakes. You learn. You do again. It's like working in a giant laboratory.

1997 Update

Software.net is the largest Internet-based electronic software superstore, providing customers with the ability to electronically purchase and download software in a simple and secure online environment. We have over 20,000 software titles available to ship to our customers and over 1,800 of them available for immediate electronic delivery over the Internet. software.net offers by far the most quality products of any software store.

Combining great prices, a great selection, and not a lot of hype, software.net aims at providing real value for its customers.

In addition, we feature various product centers that focus on specific user-community interests. For example, we have a Corporate Product Center, an Internet Product Center, a Windows 95 Product Center, a Macintosh Product Center, and more! Users view only the products they are interested in and won't waste their time on products they don't care about.

COMPUTER CONSULTANT

Overview

What better place to look for a computer consultant than on the Internet? A home page could be the ideal marketing tool for the consultant who can write software from scratch, install a network, and provide myriad other services for the home, small business, large business, government, or educational marketplaces.

Rewards

You could find new clients.

Risks

Normal business risks.

Special Marketing Considerations for the Home Page

Show people you know what you are doing by posting your bio, testimonials, and qualifications. To cut down on the number of tire-kickers, you might want to list your prices and specialties.

Hot Site

See Chapter 17 for a case study of the Walter Shelby Group, an Internet tools developer.

SOFTWARE GAMES TIPSTER

Overview

You might not want your coworkers to know that you are an expert gamesman (who learned the finesse while on the company clock). However, you can tell the Internet world about your prowess and your ability to provide answers to the thorny questions that help people unlock the mysteries of Myst and other games.

Rewards

You can make incremental income from creating a tip and selling it many times. The cost of distributing the answers on e-mail is nothing. This field can be a good one as there are dozens of tip books on the retail shelves. This proves there is a market for advice.

Risks

Normal business risks.

Special Marketing Considerations for the Home Page

You need to establish credibility.

17 Internet Technical Services

A whole new field of jobs has been created by the Internet to provide services to people who want to do business on the Internet. These businesses include:

- Internet service provider
- digital mall landlord
- Webmaster
- Web site creator
- demographics and database marketer
- Internet software tools developer
- multimedia conference coordinator

Chapter 18 looks at service providers for sales and marketing positions. Chapter 19 explores opportunities for creative people and artists.

Let's look first at an overview of jobs related to the Internet with an interview with one of the premier placement firms serving the high-tech industry.

Interview: Judy Cushman

Judith Cushman and Associates

Issaquah, WA

What are the opportunities for people who want a career in Internet-related industries?

The Internet is creating a lot of new jobs in new fields. This is great news for job seekers, as these new job descriptions are vague because no one really knows what qualifications are needed. That also means there are fewer barriers to keep people out. There aren't any warnings saying "five years' experience" because no one has five years of experience.

I see a lot of opportunity. As these jobs move from getting the infrastructure state and move into strategic, impactful positions, the jobs will pay more money. The folks who are doing the jobs now will move up the ranks.

Jobs today are being filled by people who have traditional backgrounds and can adopt new technology. In a few years people who have a technical marketing background in college will become qualified and take these jobs.

Traditional jobs are evolving to include online responsibilities. Currently, there is a demand at an incredible level, which makes it possible for some positions to pay well into the six figures.

Two types of Webmaster jobs are being created:

- Content Webmaster—if the job involves decision making, the salary can go into the six figures. If the person is just coordinating and acting as a facilitator, it is a mid-range job, between $60,000 and $70,000.

- Technical Webmaster—maintains links and provides technical skills; can make $60,000 to $70,000. Jobs to design Web sites are now being done by lower-paid people. However, highly creative agencies pay well into the six figures. Small businesses pay a lot less.

What other related fields will grow?

Intranets and Extranets, as well as virtual companies.

Virtual companies will be increasingly accepted. We think that's a very viable route. It works very well. More and more companies understand that, especially consulting companies. There is going to have to be some interface (between companies and consultants, and teams of consultants). We'll also see more virtual partnerships. You'll find three people who are experts and they don't have to be in the same cities. They scatter and do client calls and problem-solving sessions.

SALARIES FOR WEB SITE PROFESSIONALS

Here are average base salaries of selected Web site professionals in 1996, according to Buck Associates of New York City.

- Web site general manager $75,400
- director of online sales and marketing $75,400
- manager of Internet operations $63,900
- Web site engineer $58,500
- Web site artist/layout editor $46,600
- Web site programmer $46,200

INTERNET SERVICE PROVIDER

Overview

This company provides the local telephone number connection for consumers to access the Internet and to host business Web sites. Although many companies are large, there are a phenomenal number of one- and two-person companies. They do best when they operate along the back roads of America where a long-distance call to connect to the Internet is a very expensive proposition. *Boardwatch* magazine says 3,100 Internet access providers are now operating in the United States, twice the number at this time last year. The magazine says the average ISP has 2,200 customers.

Qualifications

Superb technical skills. Operating this equipment is not easy. Additionally, you should be good at marketing, hiring, and managing people.

Rewards

Recurring income from leasing space on your T-1 line.

Risks

Heavy start-up costs. Lots of competition.

Case Study: Catalyst Data Systems

Welcome To
Catalyst

- Frequently Asked Questions...
- For Sale

- Test Site...
- Changes are taking place on our Web server!

Web page design by Jim Stilwell

Catalyst Data Systems is an Internet Service Provider (ISP) based in Sacramento, California. We offer both dialup access and web page hosting services. We operate on the basic principle "keep it simple". We assume that not everyone is an expert, nor does everyone have the lastest and greatest computer hardware and software available. Catalyst Data Systems is owned and operated by Carlton Brown. Send suggestions and requests for additional information to: carlton@catalyst.net.

If you are new to the Internet, please note that some of the phrases above appear in color. This denotes a phrase which is linked to related information, on another web page. If you move your mouse pointer to the highlighted phrase, you can click the left mouse button, and you can go view the linked, additional information. Most web browser programs also have a 'back' button, which will allow you to return here, when you are finished reading the linked information.

If you are a new advertiser or publisher on the web, you might want to examine some of the links, to help you to understand the difference between using written media, as you may be accustomed to doing, and using the web.

Figure 17–1. Entrepreneurs with technical expertise can make money operating the toll gate of the informtation superhighway. Copyright 1997, Catalyst Data Systems, Inc.

Carlton Brown

PO Box 161734

Sacramento, CA 95816

(original interview January 1997)

carlton@catalyst.net

www.catalyst.net

What does your company do?

Catalyst Data Systems offers dialup and dedicated access to the Internet; Web page hosting, design, and Internet market consulting; voice-mail service; and has historically provided computer consulting services, software engineering, and hardware sales/support. Today I concentrate on dialup access to Ethernet, and I do Web sites as my users ask for them. Voice-mail and consulting service, I pretty much just maintain my installed customer base.

What expertise/background so you draw on to operate your business?

I have some 170 college units, primarily in computer science/engineering, business, and electronics, and about ten years of varied experience in the software engineering industry. I found that this was only a good foundation, however; I still had to put considerable time and energy into learning UNIX system administration, Web design, data communications, and quality customer service to be effective—and I am still learning.

What was your company's goal for going online?

Truth be told, I initially went online to help out a friend who needed a job. He was a professional salesman who was having trouble finding a good job because of his age. We set up a Web server and he started selling Web marketing services. He later moved to Denver, where he now runs the Denver Internet Mall, *www.denver-internet-mall.com*—hosted on my Web server, incidentally. I started providing dialup access, primarily in response to requests from our Web customers, and then I found that I was really good at making the Internet seem simple to people with little technical background. So I went into the dialup business in a serious way. Now I host sites for other Web designers,who don't have their own equipment and sell dedicated access to those who do. I contract out Web design and support my existing consulting and voice-mail customers, taking on new business in those areas only by referral. But I digress.

How do you know you have reached that goal?

My friend is doing very well, in Denver, having become very well known locally and somewhat known nationally. I'm making a decent living (one of my main goals in business), I'm not working very hard, and I'm enjoying what I do. There is a commercial on television which depicts a woman working from her home in her bathrobe (no long commute, no morning ritual of getting ready for work, no special dressing up). That's really the way life works for me!

How much did it cost to get started?

I am a one-horse show, so payroll is not a serious issue for me. I started up on $23,000 with an eye to serving up to two hundred dialup users and trying some Web consulting/hosting (keeping in mind that there was only me to sell sites). I spent it on three things, primarily: equipment, advertising, and education; about a third for each. Nowadays, I sell franchises for $25,000, on the same general concept. Because my Web site is really secondary to providing dialup access, very little of my costs relate directly to my having set up the Web site.

What makes your service special?

I offer a very personal service. When you call for support, you get me. When you sign up for service, you talk to me. I go out to customers' homes and set up the software for them on their computer. When you have a problem, and you talk to me, and our first effort fails to resolve it, you can call back and not have to explain the problem all over again to another support tech. You'll still be talking to me. You will NOT spend forty minutes on hold. While I'm at the customers' homes, I give some tutorial education on the Internet, and how to use it to the users' advantage. I check out their computer for hardware/software problems and advise them on proper solutions—I often pick up extra business that way, selling them a faster modem, or software, or some such. I focus on making the Internet simple, and I learn about the user and the machine that they have in the process. I am NOT professional. I am personal. Maybe that's bad for business, but I prefer to make my customers also into my friends.

What makes your Web site special?

Password access to some areas (for security, and subscription areas); an SSL-compliant Web server (which means that any information sent to or from it is encrypted for privacy); the ability to process orders online and verify credit card transactions as they happen. My philosophy on Web design—"keep it simple"—means that the pages themselves aren't all that special, but with CGI (Common Gateway Interface, a way to make Web pages dynamic, changing in real time to respond to user needs), and SQL database availability (for mail order, real estate, and information-search applications), I can pretty much do anything I want. As can my Web site customers—and my dialup users.

How to do you get people to come to your site?

Mostly people come to my site because they are my dialup users, and new information is always posted there first. I get people to come to my Web users' sites by posting them to search engines and appropriate resource pages, advising them on useful marketing concepts on design, and integrating their Web site with other promotional media, site updates, and product ideas. (I have one site, for example, that was selling a take-at-home HIV test, *www.test4hiv.com.* I suggested that she also sell some related nutritional products for fertility, birth control, and general health, and we are presently redesigning her site for her new product line, which I think will outperform her old one by at least threefold from incidental sales alone.)

How do you get people to return to your site?

I get them to return by frequently updating my site with useful tidbits of information aimed specifically at my users. On my Web users' sites I suggest new (related) products, frequent format and informational updates, special promotional announcements, subscriptions, guestbook e-mail, and low- or no-cost subscription products (anyone who checks a site weekly to win a contest or read the latest AIDS research information is likely to become a repeat customer of products promoted by that site).

How do you move people from being window-shoppers to paying customers?

To close a sale you have to take the customers' money. To that end, I offer online payment methods for credit card and bank checking draft transactions.

What is the most important thing you learned in the past year about marketing on the Internet?

KEEP IT SIMPLE!!! Nobody buys what they don't understand. Web pages that take too long to download get passed by. If customers have to get out of the chair or pick up the phone to buy your product, you'll lose three out of four of them. And suggestive selling works! Would you like fries, or a beverage, with your soda? How about a Web page for your business with your dialup account? Perhaps a voice-mailbox so that you can get messages while you are online? That's two things, but they are both really good.

What is the most effective way to get people to come to your site?

Advertising in market-targeted media will develop initial interest in a site, relatively cheaply; I advertise my site in the yellow pages in the geographic area that I am able to serve. Others for whom I host pages, such as realtors, advertise in realty sales publications locally and in realty trade publications nationally and internationally. Also, offering information on related topics for free, with a link to your commercial site, is a very effective way to bring in new business. I have a mobile home dealer who offers information on great places to go camping and on the current availability of campsites, with a link to a great place to go find a new or used RV. He is even able to sell ad space on his site to a local supplier of fish bait and tackle, camping gear, and supplies.

What is the most effective way to get people to return to your site?

Update the format and information on the site frequently. Drawings and contests help too, but people who are truly interested will be looking for useful information. Keep it up to date, attractive, and informative.

What is the most effective way to get people to buy products or services?

Close the deal. Too many sites force the user to call or write before they can buy. Most dialup users are on after business hours and may be in other time zones. They can't effectively call for your product or service, and they simply WON'T write. Even e-mail is not an effective approach—you'll still lose three out of four, typically, unless you have a particularly riveting product. Take their order! If you don't stand to make enough money from the site to justify the cost and trouble of getting a merchant ID, and taking online transactions, maybe you are choosing the wrong product or advertising medium.

How much money have you made?

I have almost made back my initial investment of $23,000, and I've only been a dialup provider for a little under a year. I was profitable three months after I went into the dialup business, and I've been gaining ground since. My target revenue level requires that I have two hundred dialup customers; I had projected that I would reach that level by my one-year anniversary. It will probably occur about three months later, based on current figures. When I exceed that number of users (in about five months) I will either have to start hiring employees (something I don't really want to do—it's a tax nightmare and a management headache) or curtail my advertising sharply. In fact, I may have to turn away referrals, that I get from my own customers to be able to stop at two hundred. And I'd hate to have to do that.

DIGITAL MALL LANDLORD

Overview

Digital malls are analogous to shopping malls. The mall operator creates a Web site that houses dozens of businesses wanting to sell products and services on the Internet. By colocating on a mall, businesses benefit from traffic to other people's stores.

Qualifications

Excellent programming skills, people management, financial abilities. Digital mall landlords must attract businesses, sell space, provide customer support, hire programmers and designers to create mall stores, take orders and process credit card information, market the site to consumers, and provide security against online thieves.

Rewards

Recurring income from leasing space on your T-1 line. Extra income opportunities from sales of programming, marketing, artistic services.

Risks

Heavy start-up costs. Lots of competition.

Case Study: The Internet Mall

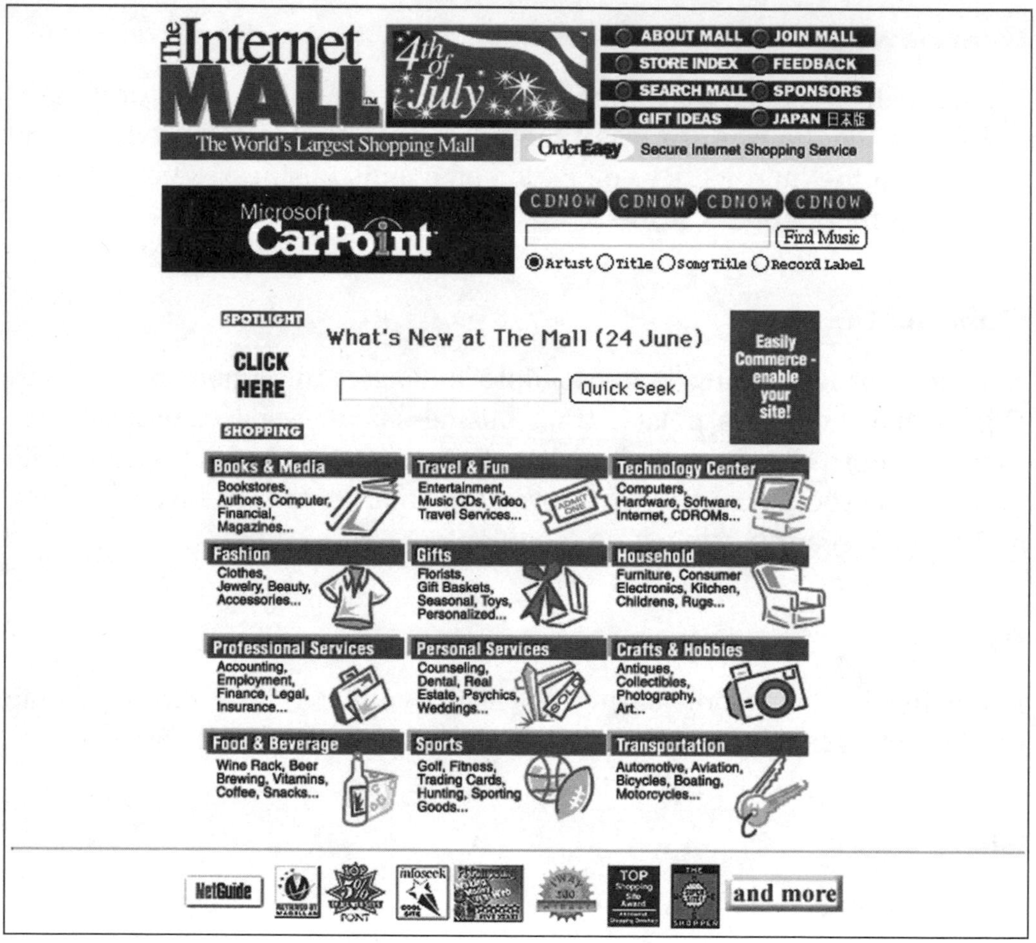

Figure 17–2. The Internet Mall started as a part-time business. Now it has hundreds of merchants and an entire staff. Copyright 1997, Intuitive Systems.

The Internet Mall, Inc.

Dave Taylor

1340 E. DeAnza Blvd., Suite 208

San Jose, CA 95129

(original interview 1995; update January 1997)

taylor@internet-mall.com

www.internetmall.com

What does your company do?

We seek to offer a central spot for consumers to find fun and interesting places to shop on the Internet. With over 2,500 stores listed, we're a lot more fun to visit than even the biggest cybermall, yet we include all the shops in all those malls too!

How does your product or service differ from others?

The Internet Mall is the only online mall that offers free listings for all, and at a growth rate of about 75+ new stores each week, it's also the fastest-growing spot for shopping on the Internet. Also, because we focus on just legitimate shops and services, we allow users to focus on their own interests without worrying about whether the listings they're finding are shopping-related or not.

Finally, the Internet Mall is also a lot more encompassing than those sites that naively believe that the World Wide Web is the beginning and the end of the Internet. We list shops with Gopher addresses, e-mail addresses only, and even those with representatives on AOL, CompuServe, and other Internet-accessible systems. The Internet Mall information is also quite widely available, with versions accessible on Gopher, via e-mail, on Usenet through bimonthly postings, and even uploaded in ASCII format to all of the major commercial services.

Does this business exist only on the Internet?

Essentially, the Internet Mall only exists on the Internet. The purpose of the Internet Mall was philanthropic: Commercialism is colliding with the Internet, like it or not, so I thought that something like the Mall could offer a central spot where people would be less compelled to spam the network [flood the mailing lists and newsgroups with notices] to build a presence, yet still not have to spend hundreds or thousands to succeed.

What is your background and training?

Bachelor's degree, computer science. Master's degree, education. I've worked at HP Labs, edited the Reviews section of *SunWorld* magazine, and written a variety of books and hundreds of articles.

When did you start your business?

I started consulting in 1988. The Internet Mall began in 1994.

How much has your company made?

The Internet Mall has paid out about $7,500 in direct billings and much more indirectly (e.g., speaking gigs, interviews, credibility for consulting jobs, etc.).

Getting Started

Did you create a business plan before going online?

Nope.

How much did time did it take to get up and running?

I had a first version of the Internet Mall up and cruisin' within a few days, because I started out with a non-Web version and gradually expanded to include other Internet services.

Did you create the pages yourself?

I did the pages myself. Indeed, the pages are all automatically generated through some custom C programs I've written that take the output of my actual database (tab-separated fields) and build the over two hundred HTML pages that comprise the Internet Mall you see today. This includes automatically generating all floor and department indices and building the index of companies by company name too. It's about 1,200 lines of C code.

How much did it cost to get started?

Nothing: My account with Netcom was free for some consulting work I did earlier in their corporate history, and I signed a cooperative agreement with Mecklermedia so that they'd pay for the necessary space on the IBM Advantis system where the Internet Mall currently resides (MecklerWeb) in return for a percentage of the gross revenues on the Mall project itself.

Did you need to go to an outside source for start-up capital?

I did not.

What mistakes did you make that you wish you hadn't made?

Best not to comment in print on this one. :-)

What advice would you give someone starting a business?

Scope out the competition, assume it'll take you twice as long to get going as you think, and make double, no, triple, sure that you have a unique slant that will help produce a fun and unusual Internet site.

What skills would a person need?

Excellent writing and presentation skills.

What special qualities are needed to run your site?

An understanding of the legalities of promoting a business that you know nothing about, and a sufficient level of professional decorum to be able to enjoy the adults and ignore the juvenile folk on the Internet that send hostile e-mail.

How did you promote your site?

Listings, articles in magazines, personal correspondence with book and magazine authors, pamphlets and brochures at trade conferences.

How much did it cost to promote your site?

About $200 total, probably.

How long did it take until you got your first sale?

Almost immediately.

How did the start-up phase affect your personal life?

What personal life? :-) Seriously, not too much at all; as a freelance consultant I just integrated the project into the daily workload.

My Day

What does your average day look like?

I work from about 8:30 P.M. to 5 P.M., with lots of breaks to play with my dogs, hang out with my SO (significant other), etc.

What does your job entail?

Varies dramatically—lots of travel, lots of talks at conferences, and lots of on-site client visits.

How many hours a week do you spend working on your site?

I spend no more than fifty hours each week working and answering mail, though frankly I spend too MUCH time answering e-mail: I'm hiring someone to start filtering Internet Mall–related e-mail so that I see only the more obscure requests.

What percentages of time are spent on each task?

N/A

What was the hardest aspect of the work in the beginning?

Keeping up with e-mail.

How long did it take to get established?

N/A

What do you like most about your work?

Freedom, independence, publicity, travel.

What do you like the least?

Varied time constraints.

What was your greatest moment?

Getting e-mail from you to invite me to be in this book. :-)

Seriously, it's all been great fun.

How much time do you spend upgrading your site?

Probably one hour per day or more.

Are there any hazards to running your site?

Legal: I am concerned that I will inadvertently help promote a scam.

How much money do you expect to make?

$25,000.

General

Are you glad you are on the Web for personal and business reasons?

Absolutely. It's 95 percent hype, but 100 percent fun.

Given what you know now, would you do it again?

Definitely.

The Future

What is your next venture?

Who knows?

1997 Update

What is the most important thing you learned in the past year about marketing on the Internet?

For everyone who does it right there are a dozen who do it wrong for various reasons, and of those dozen there are two that are totally unrepentant. It's the easy-money dilemma. There's a perception in the entrepreneurial community that the Internet is the next great frontier so it's totally fine to misrepresent, lie, or otherwise be in-your-face about business or products. The amount of spam e-mail, for example, has increased geometrically and I now receive over a dozen junk messages daily on each of my various e-mail accounts.

At the same time, it's clear that we're moving to a dynamic online business and commerce environment where millions of people will be shopping, buying, and living their lives on the Internet. It's very exciting!

What is the most effective way to get people to come to your site?

Design the site with their needs in mind; we have eschewed fancy Java, huge graphics, incompatible plug-ins, and other technologies that detract from the speed of the user experience. Instead, our goal is to focus on delivering a snappy and coherent Web site that isn't a demonstration of our programming or design capabilities.

Always start your design with the content you seek to deliver, then consider how users will navigate through to find what they seek—then you can begin creating the site.

What is the most effective way to get people to return to your site?

Keep it up to date and offer valuable information in a clean and entertaining fashion.

What is the most effective way to get people to buy products or services?

Remember that it's a selling medium and design the online promotion using standard marketing and sales ideas. For example, start by showing the product and explaining its unique characteristics and capabilities. Sell the product, then show the customer the price and ordering information. Offer a rock-solid secure online transaction capability and offer offline alternatives for those souls who think that a telephone is more secure than an encrypted data transmission.

How much money have you made?

Well, a year ago when we spoke, I was running the Internet Mall as a side project. It's now a full-blown Silicon Valley start-up with its own offices and six employees (to date), very high-profile partners like Cybercash and CardServices International, and we're anticipating a monthly revenue stream in the six or seven digits within six months.

WEBMASTER

The Webmaster is the person who runs the day-to-day administrative and technical operations of a Web site. Depending on the company, her job description could include handling mail from the public, training employees and revising the pages, updating the pages with content, and advising others. The Webmaster is part administrator, part artist and designer, part taskmaster, and part magician.

Case Study: Phase Two Strategies, Inc.

Phase Two Strategies, Inc.   *colemanjolley@p2pr.com*

Coleman Jolley, Webmaster   415-772-8400

170 Columbus Avenue, #300

San Francisco, CA 94133-5148

(original interview 1995; update January 1997)

Coleman Jolley is Webmaster for Phase Two Strategies, Inc., a public relations and marketing firm based in San Francisco.

What kind of person makes a good Webmaster?

You are essentially the art director and chief programmer of the Web site. You might be assigning these out, but you are in charge of the lay of the land.

What skills are needed to be Webmaster?

I would want to see someone with a background in desktop publishing so they have familiarity with conversion of files, because the Web is a different environment. You have to take into account that graphics are optimized for screen and not print. There should be an appreciation for Quicktime and MPEG and video formats. You are asking for people who know a little bit about everything.

It is something you research on your own. There are books on how to learn HTML and there are a lot of resources on the Web. I'm not aware of any school that teaches these subjects. Some of the art colleges are just adding it on now.

What kind of salaries can Webmasters make?

Right now it is a fairly new and exciting field. You can make $35–$50 an hour or up to $100 an hour if you have a hefty portfolio. Webmasters can expect to earn $28,000–$35,000 annually. Heavy commercial sites with UNIX implementation might pay $40,000–$50,000. Wages will drop as these skills become more common.

What skills will Webmasters need to develop?

Commerce servers are the new thing. Webmasters will need to program the CGI (Common Gateway Interface) scripts, which allow you to implement forms and download information into databases and interact with Visa or MasterCard in real time so people can purchase with their credit cards.

What makes a home page good from an artistic point of view?

You have to think of interaction and showtime. It is a little bit different than graphic designers are used to. For example, designing tables is different on the Internet.

To me it is kind of the renaissance of computer use because before the Web you had artists who didn't know how to use computers and computer users who didn't know how to be graphic designers. You have to have a little of both skills. People have mutated into that—a new breed of people who are not quite programmers and not quite graphic designers has evolved. I think that is what Webmasters are in their heart of hearts.

1997 Update

What is the most important thing you learned in the past year about marketing on the Internet?

Availability. Searching for Web pages is a Darwinian experience where only the available survive.

What is the most effective way to get people to come to your site?

Listings in search engines, partnerships through cross-links, and merchandising information to the desired audience.

What is the most effective way to get people to return to your site?

Offer value. Software demo copies for download. List memberships. Links to special promotions. Creativity is the most effective inducement to return.

What is the most effective way to get people to buy products or services?

Again, it's all about offering something of value to the visitor.

Is your site profitable?

Traffic to our site grows on average every month. This is a reflection of our attempts to reach our target market of journalists looking for information about our clients.

WEB SITE CREATOR

Overview

All sorts of people and companies are selling Web site creation services— from fourteen-year-olds in high school to art directors on Madison Avenue. Although off-the-shelf software will help many people gain initial entrées online, there is a need for high-end design and development work that incorporates databases and full functionality.

Qualifications

This type of business is not a one-man shop. Many technical and sales skills are needed. Virtual companies can use this model as well.

Rewards

Large sites yield large profits and updating services.

Risks

Normal business risks and competition.

Figure 17–3. Fine.Com has a powerful client list. Copyright 1997, Fine.Com Interactive.

Fine.Com Interactive	*dan@fine.com*
Dan Fine	*www.fine.com*
1118 Post Avenue	206-292-2888
Seattle, WA	
(oiriginal interview 1997)	

What does your company do?

We build high-end Internet, Intranet, and Extranet sites for companies, organizations, and associations.

What expertise/background do you draw on to operate your business?

We are one of the oldest Web development businesses in the world. Our background in relationship marketing, design, and computer programming, makes us the ideal company to assist businesses with their Internet efforts.

What was your company's goal for going online?

To help other companies go online.

How do you know you have reached that goal?

Because we have built over one hundred Web sites for other companies.

How much did it cost to get started?

We started with $30,000. We have now spent over $200,000 on just our own site.

What makes your site special?

It is heavily database driven. It has incredible 3D graphics and streaming audio. It is very state-of-the art.

How do you get people to come to your site?

Advertising with banners, being listed in all the search engines, and promoting by word of mouth.

How do you get people to return to your site?

That is not really important to us.

How do you move people from being window-shoppers to paying customers?

We ask them to register for more information, then we follow up with a phone call.

What is the most important thing you learned in the past year about marketing on the Internet?

It is not to be taken lightly. You need to go full out and do the job right, from the planning all the way through execution.

What is the most effective way to get people to come to your site?

Build a good site that provides valuable information to the consumer.

What is the most effective way to get people to return to your site?

Keep it fresh and e-mail them offering them incentives for coming back.

What is the most effective way to get people to buy products or services?

Give them a reason to buy through the Web site (faster, better, or cheaper).

How does your site generate revenue?

It provides leads, and the quality establishes us as a leader in the industry.

How much money have you made? Is your site profitable?

Our site continues to provide us value. We do not conduct electronic commerce with our site, but every customer we deal with has checked out our Web site to make sure we are qualified.

DEMOGRAPHICS AND DATABASE MARKETING ANALYST

Overview

Demographics and database marketing analysts are high-level marketers who have adapted their craft to the Internet. They specialize in creating one-to-one relationships with consumers. They are adept at finding every household, for example, with a Volvo and an ice-cream maker.

Qualifications

Number crunchers on steroids.

Rewards

People who are in this field have backgrounds in direct marketing (junk mail) and live by numbers. They can make $75–$150 an hour and up if they have a proven track record.

Risks

Increased competition.

INTERNET SOFTWARE TOOLS DEVELOPER

Overview

The Internet is an immature technology in search of solutions and applications for millions of people around the world. It is the beneficiary and victim of hype that raises expectations of people who think they can do things as easily as in the offline world. What a tragic surprise awaits those pioneers! The Internet needs software tools to make it easier and more reliable to use.

Rewards

There is a bright future for entrepreneurs who start a business writing software tools for the Internet. Netscape Communications, which makes browser software for the Web, went public after only sixteen months and has a valuation higher than Maytag and Broderbund! Smaller success stories abound, but many companies and individuals are getting rich by running businesses that make the Internet begin to live up to its promise.

A benefit to writing software that helps the Internet is that you have the ability to use the Internet as a printing press and distribution mechanism. These two steps are so costly in the offline world that many software publishers with dynamite programs have failed because they couldn't raise enough money to make it in the marketplace.

Your software might be a tool that works immediately to help users, such as Yahoo!, InfoSeek, or WebCrawler, the directory search tools. In these cases, let people use the software for free and charge advertisers for the right to post a small ad or link to their site. In this manner you'll make money by attracting large numbers of readers instead of making money by selling the software.

Another business plan is to let people use the software for free online for a given time and then charge them for the complete edition.

Risks

There are no new ideas. You will face competition—perhaps intense challenges—from people who are just as smart as you are. The software industry is full of products that won because they were first to market, not the best on the market.

Special Marketing Considerations for the Home Page

Sit down, software developers, you aren't going to like this advice one bit. Give your software away—at least for a limited time. That is the best way for people to try it and recommend it to their companies and friends. Netscape Communications retained a 70–75 percent market share for its browser by giving a version away for a limited time period and asking for donations thereafter. In a matter of months it succeeded in positioning product as a standard.

The home page needs to explain how the software helps people. It should then describe the system requirements, how to download and install the software, and how to pay for it.

Reviews from magazines, and testimonials from users will help convince consumers to try the product. Screen shots of the program in action help consumers understand what the product does and looks like.

Case Study: Shelby Group

Figure 17–4. The Shelby Group leads viewers easily to menu selections on its home page. Courtesy of the Shelby Group Ltd.

Shelby Group

John Buckman

174 Santa Clara Avenue,

Oakland, CA 94610

jbuckman@shelby.com

www.shelby.com

www.lyris.com

http://tile.net

(original interview 1995; update February 1997)

Who is your primary audience?

People publishing on the Internet who have databases to publish in Lotus Notes or other formats.

How will they benefit from your product or service?

Most times, when people publish a database on the Web they reinvent the wheel by writing their own HTML exporting program. TILE allows you to easily create Web sites from databases and manages the indices, reports, and forms your site needs to make it easy for your users to find the data they need.

How does your product or service differ from others?

There is no other product out there that creates browseable Web sites from databases. Everything else takes a search approach: Fill out a search form and I'll display what I've found. We let users browse the database along any number of categories. For a telephone book, for instance, you could browse by telephone prefix, by last name, by first name, by city, as well as free-text search.

Is this business an offshoot of your existing business or does it exist only on the Internet?

Internet only.

Where is your office located?

Home converted to office.

What is your background and training?

Master's in philosophy. I've been programming for profit since I was fourteen, working for Yale University.

When did you start your business?

1987 for the business, 1991 for the Internet business portion.

How did you promote your site?

Web directories, lists, but mainly by putting up public-service Web sites that people want to go to.

How much did it cost to promote your site?

Only time. Others are eager to offer services for free in exchange for publicity.

How long did it take until you got your first sale?

We had sales ready when the software product came out of beta testing.

How much money has your company made?

N/A

Getting Started

Did you create a business plan before going online?

No.

How much did time did it take to get up and running?

Four months.

Did you create the pages yourself or did you get help?

Ourselves.

How much did it cost to get started?

Free. Once again, trading services.

Did you need to go to an outside source for start-up capital?

I had previously worked as a Lotus Notes and database programming consultant, which is lucrative, and worked one hundred weeks to pay my (then) three employees minimal wages.

What mistakes did you make that you wish you hadn't made?

Signing up with a provider I could not depend on. This has been a very, very hard mistake to fix.

What advice would you give someone starting a business?

Find people who return your telephone calls and work with them. Responsibility and professionalism seem to be absent from almost all companies working on the Internet. This is especially true for the bigger companies.

What skills would a person need to conduct business?

The ability to teach yourself and, most importantly, thoroughness. Eighty percent of our current business is repeat business or directly obtained by reference from current customers. Every single customer has to be happy, and you have to always have time to talk to them.

My Day

What does your average day look like?

I work from 9 A.M. to 11 P.M., with one to two hours of breaks. I do this six and a half days a week.

What does your job entail?

Everything from tech support to sales and programming.

How many hours a week do you spend working on your site?

Ten hours a week for e-mail. I have someone else who answers most of it, and she takes about two hours a day. About ten hours a week working on our sites.

How much time do you spend conducting business, marketing, selling, and upgrading your site?

About ten to twenty hours a week.

What was the hardest aspect of the work in the beginning?

Learning to do everything, too much to learn.

What do you like most about your work?

The potential for success.

What do you like the least?

The risk.

What was your greatest moment?

That's a hard one. Getting *anything* written about you in the major press (be it *USA Today* or *PC Magazine*) is always a great victory.

How did the start-up phase affect your personal life?

I had/have none. :)

Are you glad you are on the Web for personal and business reasons?

Yes.

Given what you know now, would you do it again?

Yes.

Where can people find advice about running a site like yours?

At the site itself (*http://tile.net/*), as that's the purpose of the site. People are supposed to be impressed by the site and want to do it themselves.

The Future

What is your next venture?

Concentrating on this for the time being. Have found that doing too many things is what kills the business.

1997 Update

What is the most important thing you learned in the past year about marketing on the Internet?

People notice quality work. If the work isn't up to snuff, don't bother putting it on the Internet.

What is the most effective way to get people to come to your site?

Offer something people want. Our *http://tile.net* site offers comprehensive indices to mailing lists, FTP sites, Usenet groups, and computer vendors.

We get twenty-five thousand different IP addresses coming to *http://tile.net* every day. We also arrange cooperative advertising exchanges with like-minded sites.

What is the most effective way to get people to return to your site?

Offer something that has depth, so they don't exhaust your Web site in the first visit.

What is the most effective way to get people to buy products or services?

We offer free working copies of our list server program, with decreased capacity. That way, people can use the program, see if they like it, and purchase it if they do.

Is your site profitable?

We are profitable. Because our marketing effort is completely Intenet-based, it is not possible to say that our sales grew x percent because of the Web. However, the majority of our sales originated from our Web sites.

MULTIMEDIA CONFERENCE COORDINATOR

Overview

The teleconferencing business, which allows people in different locations to see live broadcasts and interact with people in different locations, is booming, but it is expensive. The Internet can cut the costs by using such software programs as VocalTel (or WebChat for text and files only).

Rewards

This can become a very lucrative business for a person who understands how to use and install the technology and knows how to market services.

Risks

Normal business risks.

Special Marketing Considerations for the Home Page

Prepare a demo of a conference that can be viewed online or sent via videotape to potential customers.

Links to Home Pages

This is a new business I created. Run with it. There are no examples—yet!

18 Internet Sales, Advertising, and Publicity

Nothing happens without sales, as the old saying goes. The same is true for Internet-related business. There is a tremendous need for salespeople who can transmit the benefits of the Internet to a wide range of potential audiences, from consumers to merchants. The first wave of Internet entrepreneurs is full of people from technical and engineering backgrounds who not only don't have sales abilities, they have a disdain for sales in general!

This chapter explores the sales job opportunities on the Internet—qualifications, duties, locations, and incomes. Then we'll look at the marketing service providers who advertise, publicize, and promote companies on the Web.

ADVERTISING SALES

Overview

As the Internet becomes more and more commercial, companies with Web sites will need salespeople to sell advertising space and manage other salespeople.

Qualifications

Salespeople should have a firm footing in both sales strategies and netiquette. They must thoroughly understand the mind-set of people who operate businesses on the Internet. One group might be very savvy and understand the economic dynamics of advertising links in this new medium. Others, from traditional businesses, must be educated on the technology and new marketing paradigms of marketing on the Internet (see chapter 2).

The number of new home pages grows at a phenomenal rate every month and the size of the Internet audience grows exponentially as well. Demographers are just beginning to create reliable tools that track numbers of visitors. This step is essential as the basic model for advertising is based on the cost per thousand of consumers who see the advertisement or, in this case, the home page that displays the ad or the link to the advertiser's site. Different rates are charged for each level of service.

Duties

Sell advertisements and links to potential advertisers.

Where the Jobs Are

Traditional advertising agencies, online advertising agencies, traditional mailing list brokers (including Worldata Corporation, a leader based in Pompano Beach, Florida). This is the kind of business you can start yourself by making arrangements with both advertisers and Web site managers.

Rewards

Our survey showed a variety of income opportunities ranging from straight salary to a combination of salary and commission. The potential for income is unlimited because commission work doesn't have a ceiling—earnings can be directly related to the effort, skill, and energy of each salesperson. Advertising rep firms generally take 50 percent of all the revenue they collect from ad sales. However, they also must pay all expenses related to making the sale.

CONSUMER AND BUSINESS NETWORK SALES

Overview

As the battle for signing up consumers to online services grows, customer sales representatives will be needed to sell Internet access services to two groups of customers: businesses and consumers. Businesses will be sold on the idea of using Internet service providers (ISPs) to house and maintain their Web sites. Consumers will be sold subscriptions to local and national ISPs.

Qualifications

Sales, presentation, and speaking skills; understanding of the Internet and the numerous services and home pages that can benefit different audiences; technical knowledge of the Internet.

Duties

Demonstrate the service to large groups of people; sell products.

Where the Jobs Are

Internet access providers targeting business and consumer use on both national and local levels, (e.g., U.S. West, Pacific Bell, AT&T, and MCI) and commercial online services (e.g., CompuServe, America Online, Prodigy, and Microsoft Network).

Rewards

Commission or salary base plus commission. Unlimited potential for income.

CONTENT SALES

Overview

Content is king on the Internet. As more companies go online, the need for editorial matter to attract readers and make pages informative will grow, and with it the need for people to create the content (like a writer or marketing company) and for agents to find useful articles and pictures that can add value to a home page.

Qualifications

Ability to understand a client's needs, act as acquisition editor to purchase or license material, and work with home page marketers in understanding their market mission; ingenuity in finding or commissioning material. Talk to a lawyer about copyright issues, fair use, and first rights.

Duties

Find out what client's needs are and find the material.

Rewards

You can be paid by project, by hour, or by word (usually for writing).

ONLINE ADVERTISING AGENCY

Overview

Online advertising agencies create ads, research Web sites that match target audiences, buy advertising, and track results. This is a tremendous growth industry.

Qualifications

Outstanding marketing acumen; ability to transmit ideas and concepts to HTML programmers and artists'; sales skills to land new accounts; financial abilities to run a profitable company and charge what the job is worth in a market that is increasingly price-competitive; management skills.

Rewards

Madison Avenue advertising agencies that are getting into the Web business are charging $25,000 and up for a home page.

There are two opposing goals for both the online advertising agency and the online public relations agency: Sell services and projects or sell out! Modem Media, an online advertising agency and research firm, was bought for $29 million in stock by True North Communications, Inc., of Chicago.

Risks

Prices are falling, competition is increasing. To succeed, base your sales pitch on quality, not price.

ONLINE PR AGENCY

Overview

An online public relations agency helps companies promote their Web sites using the Web media, search engines, and other techniques, as well as using traditional print and electronic media.

Qualifications

Outstanding writing and people skills; Internet-savvy communications skills; understanding of netiquette; traditional PR skills.

Rewards

Companies charge for their time or on a project basis.

Risks

Everyone and his brother thinks PR is an easy business, so they enter it. Qualified firms will have to compete against inexperienced companies.

PROMOTION SERVICES

Overview

Search engines are one of the best ways of finding Web sites. Although it is easy to register companies on search engines, some people prefer to hire others to do the job. Two types of companies have sprung up to handle this need. One type registers pages manually for a fee. A list of these companies is available through Yahoo!

The other type creates tools that allow people to register their home pages on hundreds of search engines by filling out one standard form. Two of these latter companies are Submit It, www.submit-it.com, and Register-it, *www.register-it.com*. WWW.Site.Promoter is a software program sold at retail outlets.

Qualifications

Marketing skills; ability to think creatively; client skills.

Rewards

Fee for service.

Risks

Competition.

PRESS RELEASE DISTRIBUTION SERVICE

Overview

PR Newswire and Business Wire both send company press releases to reporters. However, these services are general in nature. They target only a few vertical markets, such as computers and automobiles. Entrepreneurs can create their own news service for their own industry. They will make money by charging companies to print and distribute their news release over the Internet or any other e-mail, fax, or mail service the company selects.

GINA, *www.gina.com*, and Newstips, *www.newstips.com/newstips*, both distribute press releases to reporters in the high-tech and online industries. They make money by charging clients (companies) a fee. Reporters are asked if they want to subscribe to the free list of press releases, which is sent once a day or week and deposited in their e-mail boxes. Reporters do not pay a fee for this service.

You could use this model to send press releases to a different industry. The key is for a majority of reporters in that field to have e-mail accounts.

Rewards

There is no upward limit on how much money you could make, as you can print and distribute an unlimited number of press releases. PR Newswire charges about $400 to send a press release to its entire nationwide network of reporters. Additional fees can be obtained by writing press releases or performing other publicity services for companies.

Risks

Normal business risks.

Special Marketing Considerations for the Home Page

The features and benefits must be spelled out clearly, along with the costs. Press release services generally offer many different layers of service and service options, so pricing can become confusing. Be explicit.

Links to Home Pages

Marty Winston's Newstips is an institution in the computer industry. Despite competition from PR Newswire and BusinessWire, Newstips has an active following among companies and reporters who eagerly await each issue. To learn all about this fascinating source of information, go to *www.newstips.com/newstips.* Marty says the home page "more than paid for itself" just a few weeks after going online.

CONTEST CREATORS

Overview

Contests are a great marketing tool to attract people to Web sites. More than a thousand contests are conducted on the Web at any given time. In some cases, in-house company personnel create these contests, but a market exists for imaginative people to create, design, and operate contests and to provide database support and product fulfillment requests.

Qualifications

Marketing abilities and a penchant for creativity.

Rewards

Fee for service. You might be able to negotiate a percentage of sales.

BANNER ADVERTISING BROKER

The Internet Link Exchange, (ILE), *www.linkexchange.com*, has relationships with 85,000 Web sites that exchange banners with each other. ILE acts as the broker between the sites. It gives each site in the network a line of code that pulls in a new banner ad each time the site is viewed. For every two banner views that appear on the client's Web site, ILE places a banner ad for that company on another client's Web site. ILE keeps the other banner placement in its inventory and sells it to a paying customer.

19 Internet Creative Marketing Services

Creative people—musicians, writers, and artists—can find work selling their services to Web site managers who need original content that appeals to the needs of their target audiences, enhances their sites, or leads people to them. Good creative material has been shown to attract prospects to Web sites and keep them coming back. Interactive fiction, soap operas, music, and other creative media will become an integral asset to commercial Web sites as they add more value and pizzazz to what would otherwise be a dull catalog. As multimedia standards are raised on the Web and companies need more jazz to rise above the noise level, creative artists will be able to profit. This chapter explores several business opportunities and interviews leading pioneers and practitioners.

WEB PAGE DESIGNER

Overview

When the World Wide Web first offered commercial sites, the page design was spartan at best. Most sites offered a gray background and links to additional pages. IBM's Web site looked the same as a start-up company's. Professional designers have entered the market and the results are obvious to even an untrained eye. Professionally designed sites have raised the barrier to entry.

An HTML designer creates the HTML coding for a home page. This process unites the home page, subpages, art, and marketing materials, and transforms the result into a format the World Wide Web can understand and display to consumers.

Qualifications

Persons who want to do this should understand HTML programming and have a good flair for design.

Rewards

HTML designers/programmers can earn $50–$75 a hour, but prices are falling as more people learn these skills.

Risks

Programmers also face competition from software programs that automatically convert text files into HTML. While these programs might not be perfect, they certainly reduce the amount of time needed for human intervention. I predict that most desktop publishers will develop the skills needed for HTML programming within the next eighteen months.

Case Study: John Eberle

Figure 19–1. A Web page designer's page will reflect the quality and style of the artist. Copyright 1997, Lowenhart Internet Productions.

Loewenhart Internet Productions   *john@loewenhart.com*

John H. Eberle, President   *www.loewenhart.com*

19915 Scanmar Lane

Cornelius, NC 28031

(original interview January 1997)

What does your company do?

We design interactive Web sites for small-to medium-sized businesses and individual professionals.

What expertise/background do you bring to your business?

Self-taught, but was responsible for the MIS function for a small regional bank. Been working with computers and programming since 1982. I also have a background in marketing and advertising. Loewenhart Internet was founded in 1995.

What was your company's goal for going online?

Our goal was to help other small businesses learn how to EFFECTIVELY use the new technology of the Internet to reach a broader market and more effectively target their best customers.

How do you know you have reached that goal?

We know we've reached that goal because we have begun receiving second-generation referrals—in essence, a referral from a referral. This is a great compliment to our own Internet marketing plans. Further, a site we designed, www.dogperfect.com, was voted a Yahoo! Cool Site. Quite an honor.

How much did it cost to get started?

We try to help most companies get on the Web for between $500 and $1,000 dollars.

What makes your site special?

Our sites are special because we design them using our three cardinal rules:

1. Load fast.

2. Be fun and interesting—remember the customer's needs first!

3. SELL SOMETHING!!!

How to do you get people to come to your site?

We've had excellent success in analyzing how search engines spider a site and design in key features to the sites that facilitate a high ranking. Most importantly, though, we choose keywords based on what the customer thinks is important—not necessarily the business.

How do you get people to return to your site?

Virtual couponing, message boards, free offers, and cooperative links. Nothing drives customers back to a site better than updating it and giving them something in return for the privilege of having them visit.

How do you move people from being window-shoppers to paying customers?

The key to moving customers from lookers to buyers is to ask them to buy!! The terminal decision location of any site we design should be obvious on the entry page, and no more than one or two jumps away. A site that doesn't sell on the entry page is a waste of the browser's time and your money.

What is the most important thing you learned in the past year about marketing on the Internet?

Don't hide your light under a bushel. If you aren't aggressively cross-marketing your site and using coupons, direct mail, direct e-mail, or other means you will not receive maximum marketing value. It is amazing to me how many people will visit if only you tell them how via good search engine registration and some cross-marketing.

What is the most effective way to get people to come to your site?

Tell them where it is and make them glad they came.

What is the most effective way to get people to buy products or services?

Offer them value and ease of purchase. SELL SOMETHING ON THE ENTRY PAGE!!

How much money have you made? Is your site profitable?

The sites we design are very successful because our customers believe in what we believe in. Realtors are often seeing a five-fold return on their investments. Retailers are seeing coupon response well ahead of expectation—often better than direct mail at a fraction of the cost. Business-to-business sites are having excellent response to online catalogs at a fraction of the cost per piece mailed. How do I really know we've succeeded? Our customers come back to upgrade and enhance their sites, and are enthusiastic referrers.

ILLUSTRATOR

Overview

Illustrators who want to design for the Web must understand the need for creating interesting, interactive artwork that makes few demands on a computer system's overhead. This is an active field, as 75 percent of Web sites will undergo a major revamp within twelve months of their launch, according to the Gartner Group.

Because pictures need to be a small file size, illustrators must understand the need to limit colors and other intricacies of the new art form.

Qualifications

Artistic ability and the knowledge of how to translate it to a computer screen.

Rewards

Established artists can make $35–$100 an hour on their own.

Risks

Because many artists want to break into this field, it is not unheard of to find artists working for $10 an hour.

WEB PAGE MUSIC AND SCORING

Overview

Sounds and music are basic components of TV and radio ads because they grab attention and create moods, yet few home pages use music. That will change.

Qualifications

Musical background; understanding of audio formats and conversion techniques for computers and Web; client skills.

Rewards

Charge fees for services and royalties.

Case Study: Joel Fisher

Figure 19–2. Music emanates from this home page to set a mood for all who enter. Copyright 1997, Joel Fisher Music Services.

Joel Fisher Music Service

2349 Walnut Boulevard

Walnut, Creek, CA 94596

(original interview January 1997)

score@ccnet.com

www.ccnet.com/~score

510-933-8636

What does your company do?

Compose and record original music for film, television, Internet, videos, CD-ROM.

What expertise/background do you have?

Over seventeen years of musical training. Experience composing music for clients such as Wells Fargo Bank, Pacific Bell, Sybase, Novell, United Way, Sunmaid Raisins.

What were your company's goals for going online?

1. Expand client base outside of San Francisco area.

2 Directly illustrate how music can enhance a Web site.

How do you know you have reached that goal?

1. By getting clients outside the San Francisco area.

2. By getting more Internet-based projects (i.e., creating music for Web sites).

How much did it cost to get started?

There was no cost to get started. Because I was using an exciting technology (Real Audio streaming) to play music clips, I found an Internet designer, Newhoff Consulting, newhoff@ccnet.com, who agreed to do my page free of charge to get experience with Real Audio.

What makes your site special?

Music automatically starts playing with animation as the page is downloading. Very few sites on the Web currently offer this feature.

How do you get people to come to your site?

I always make sure to give my Web address to prospective clients. People also get excited when I tell them that something special will happen when they visit my site. That special something is music automatically playing with animation while the page is downloading.

How do you move people from being window-shoppers to paying customers?

Because music samples are included on my page, customers do not have to wait to receive a demo reel in the mail. They can decide right away if they want to hire me. They can then contact me via e-mail or telephone.

What is the most important thing you learned in the past year about marketing on the Internet?

Your site should contain enough information or examples of work for the customer to make a decision about using your services. It is not enough to just provide a list of services.

What is the most effective way to get people to buy your services?

Include as much detail and direct examples as you can about your products or services.

How much money have you made?

I have had a tremendous response to the Real Audio streaming capabilities. The site has allowed me to demonstrate my services quickly to anyone in the world.

EDITORIAL CONTENT WRITER

Overview

Content providers will be in great demand to generate factual material as well as fiction.

Qualifications

Creativity; understanding clients' marketing goals; ability to create content that achieves those goals, ability to meet deadlines; client skills.

Rewards

Fee for service and/or royalties.

Case Study: Steve Schaffer

Sign up (FREE) to receive the weekly Solve-it by email

Solve-it
Solve the weekly mystery
5 min on Wednesday

Twist
Start the week with
a little mystery
5 min every Monday

Mysterious Photo
Write or read
a short mystery
2 min every Friday

Sign-up- FREE
Receive the Solve-it
by email

More About
The Case

Bookmark this page or add it to your Favorite Places:
http://www.TheCase.com/thecase/

MysteryNet.com TheCase.com is a product of MysteryNet.com:
"The online network for everything mystery"

Figure 19–3. Mystery writer Steve Schaffer features great stories on The Case. His professional Web site is at Newfront Communications. Copyright, 1997, Newfront Communications.

Newfront Communications

Steve Schaffer

2350 Greenwich Street

San Francisco, CA 94123

steve@newfront.com

www.newfront.com

www.the case.com

What does your company do?

Produces and publishes online mysteries and mystery Web sites.

What expertise do you have?

I have over ten years' experience in software marketing, development, sales, and business development.

What was your company's goal for going online?

To prove we could get visitors to sign up and return to the site.

How do you know you have reached that goal?

We have consistent traffic and over thirty thousand registered members.

How much did it cost to get started?

N/A

What makes your site special?

MysteryNet.com includes a series of online mysteries and mystery Web sites.

How do you get people to come to your site?

Good design and high quality. TheCase.com offers three free mysteries every week. TheCase.com Solve-it is sent via e-mail every week.

How do you move people from being window-shoppers to paying customers?

It is all free for now.

What is the most important thing you learned in the past year about marketing on the Internet?

It is hard sell improved or upgraded. The Internet and the Web is about what is new.

What is the most effective way to get people to come to your site?

Promotion to our installed base of registered users. Good online press.

What is the most effective way to get people to return to your site?

Weekly e-mail reminder.

How does your site generate revenue?

Advertising and sponsorship.

How much money have you made?

We have over ten paying advertisers. We have produced four mysteries for other companies. We have over thirty thousand registered users.

ADVERTISING COPYWRITER

Overview

As companies realize that Web sites are all about marketing, the need for good copywriting and editorial content will grow.

If Web sites aren't making money it might be because the sales material is not written properly. The first wave of marketing materials on the Web simply presented the company and product. Sites that really work use tried-and-true methods of direct marketing. Professional writers and marketers know the words that sell and the techniques that convince prospects to buy. If you can write marketing materials, the Web is a blank page on which to write your own future profits.

Qualifications

If you can write advertising copy or advertorials (editorial copy), you can sell your services an ever-growing number of businesses on the Web.

Rewards

Fee for service.

Case Study: Ivan Levison

Ivan Levison – *Direct Mail & Advertising Copywriting*

Welcome to my Web site!

I'm a freelance copywriter who builds profits for high tech companies.

In fact, I've spent over 20 years writing money-making advertising, direct mail, product packages, and more, for industry leaders like Hewlett-Packard, Adobe, Apple, cc:Mail, Claris, Intuit, Netscape, Sybase, and The Santa Cruz Operation.

Want to find out more about how my writing services can do wonders for *your* bottom line?

Just click here and I'll be happy to show you.

Thanks for visiting!

Figure 19–4. The graphics resembling coupons on Ivan Levison's page show you he is a direct mail copywriter. Copyright, 1997 Ivan Levison & Associates.

Ivan Levison & Associates

Direct Mail & Advertising Copywriting

14 Los Cerros Drive

Greenbrae, CA 94904

(original interview March 1997)

ivan@levison.com

www.levison.com

415-461-0672

What does your company do?

I'm a freelance direct mail and advertising copywriter for high-technology companies.

What is your background?

I have over twenty years of experience writing for companies like Adobe, Claris, Intuit, Netscape, Sybase, and many others. I also publish a newsletter: *The Levison Letter, Action Ideas For Better Direct Mail and Advertising.*

What was your company's goal for going online?

I wanted potential clients to be able to check me out, quickly and easily, without my having to send an expensive information pack. People reading my advertising and newsletter could also get more information about my services.

Another point. I do big projects but also highly focused consulting by the hour by fax and phone. The Web generates these profitable smaller consulting projects. I find it very useful for that.

How do you know you have reached that goal?

People have a lot of kind things to say about my site and I know it's making a good impression. I'd hate to be in business without it!

How much did it cost to get started?

I swapped out the HTML coding with a programmer friend and of course, I did the writing. It didn't cost me a penny—aside from nominal ISP costs.

What makes your site special?

I like to think it's the breezy, informal, personal tone. I want my site to reflect my personality.

How to do you get people to come to your site?

Through advertising and my newsletter that goes out to 1,400 people.

How do you get people to return to your site?

I really don't care if people return or not. I'm using it as a one-shot reference. This has real value too!

How do you move people from being window-shoppers to paying customers?

They call me. I talk with them and hopefully show them I can be of real service. My conversion rate is very high.

What is the most important thing you learned in the past year about marketing on the Internet?

If you want your Web site to be successful, it has to have personality and LIFE. Pasting up a data sheet or brochure just doesn't do it!

What is the most effective way to get people to come to your site?

You can't count on one method. As always, you need an integrated marketing plan that covers all the bases.

What is the most effective way to get people to buy products or services?

Use the Web as a lead generator and don't expect to necessarily see people there. You can gather names, create interest and leads, and then CONVERT them by other methods.

How much money have you made? Is your site profitable?

I'd say revenues are up by 20 percent, thanks to my Web site.

Case Study: Al Bredenberg

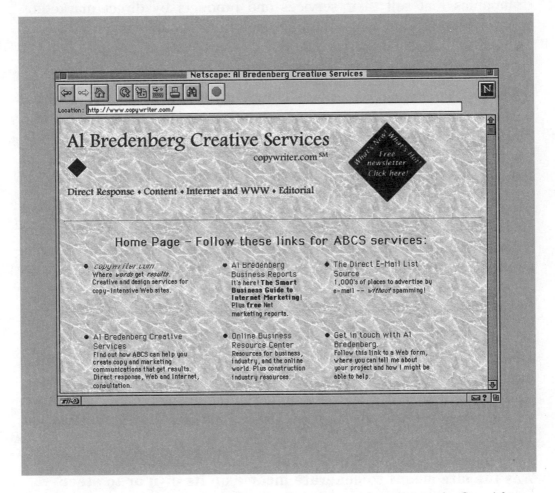

Figure 19–5. Writers have virtual portfolios of unlimited size to show their works. Copyright 1997, Alfred R. Bredenberg.

Al Bredenberg Creative Services   *ab@copywriter.com*

Al Bredenberg   *www.copywriter.com*

256 Kent Road   860-672-0382

Cornwall, CT 06753-0151

(original interview 1995; update January 1997)

Who is your primary audience?

Companies that sell their services and products by direct marketing. Businesses that want to use the Internet as a marketing vehicle.

How will they benefit from your service?

I deliver no-nonsense direct marketing copy that sells. I offer a strong business background and firsthand selling experience. I publish material that helps businesses market more effectively.

How does your service differ from others?

I cut my teeth as a businessperson and manager rather than at an ad agency. I have in-depth understanding of business, industry, and many technical subjects. Rather than creating image advertising, I am committed to direct marketing.

Is this business an offshoot of your existing business or does it exist only on the Internet?

This is my regular business. However, since I started working on the Internet I have begun offering my services doing creative work for companies' World Wide Web sites and online marketing materials. Also, I have written an electronic book, *The Small Business Guide to Internet Marketing*, which I am selling over the Internet.

Was the site meant to generate income on its own or to steer people to your offline business?

In the beginning I meant to use my Internet presence to generate leads that I would follow up in the conventional way. Now it is starting to generate some revenue on its own.

Where is your office located?

I operate out of a home office in my apartment.

What is your background and training?

I have been a published writer since 1972. 1 have been in business and management for over twenty years. I have a master's degree in management from Antioch University. I've been working as a commercial copywriter since 1989.

Getting Started

When did you start your business?

I started working as a copywriter in 1989 and have been at it full-time since 1991.

Did you create a business plan before going online?

Yes.

How much time did it take to get up and running?

Really, I was able to start almost as soon as I had an Internet access account. There's much that a businessperson can do online using e-mail and participating in electronic forums. I've been on the Internet since 1993, using an account provided by a university I was writing for. In December 1994 1 got my own commercial account. I set up my own Web site in May 1995.

Did you create the pages yourself or did you get help?

I did most of the HTML myself, but I had help from my provider, who knows the codes much better.

How much did it cost to get started?

Costs for Internet access and phone charges: $50–$100/month. Software: about $200. 1 worked out a partnership with a provider who lets my Web site live on his server rent-free.

How did you promote your site?

So far the site is what I would call unannounced. I still have more material to put up before I have it listed in databases and search engines. The site has been mentioned in a magazine article and on some electronic forums. I include the URL with my discussion list postings and e-mail messages. I refer people to my site if I think it might be of interest. I now include the URL on my office stationery.

How much did it cost to promote your site?

So far this hasn't really cost anything. I may have NetPost register the site for me. It charges about $200.

How long did it take until you got your first sale?

About six months. This was from one of the contacts that I made in my first month online. This is par for the course in my business. There's often a long cultivation period when I'm developing a new client.

What mistakes did you make that you wish you hadn't made?

All of them! <g> Relying in the beginning on an older and slower PC. It was fine for word processing, but when it crashed I was out of touch with Internet correspondents for a number of days. Now I have a reliable 486 and it's quite a relief.

To be truthful, I'm not aware of having made many mistakes. I've checked things out carefully and worked according to a plan.

Ask me again in five years!

What advice would you give someone trying to start a similar business or any business on the Internet?

Get Internet access and do some exploring and participating. I find many businesspeople are eager to start marketing over the Internet before they've even gotten access.

- Take time to work out a plan. Don't jump into it without a clear idea of the options.

- Don't buy into get-rich-quick schemes.

- Do lots of reading about the Internet. I recommend my *Small Business Guide to Internet Marketing*. Really! I think it's good.

- Remember: Marketing is marketing. You still have to have something worthwhile to sell.

- Don't neglect conventional offline business and marketing strategies.

- Maybe your product or service isn't suited to the Internet!

What skills would a person need to conduct business?

- Ability to write hard-sell direct marketing copy.

- Creative problem-solving skills.

- Ability to listen and communicate clearly.

- Basic business and office skills.

What special qualities are needed to run your site?

- A willingness to learn new skills.

- Recognition that being in business means providing good service for the customer.

My Day

What does your average day look like?

I spend four to eight hours per day working on writing projects, one to two hours on marketing my own business. I check e-mail at least twice a day and respond as quickly as possible to inquiries. I often spend time in the evening following electronic discussion groups or working on special projects.

What does your job entail?

Much reading and research.

Intensive creative work coming up with concepts, ideas, words, turns of phrase, sentences, the best way to say things.

Writing, rewriting, checking, rechecking.

Delivering the best copy I can and delivering it on time.

How many hours a week do you spend working on your site?

Eight to ten hours. Reading and answering mail, 25 percent; reading and participating in discussion groups, 25 percent; special projects, creating Web and marketing copy, other tasks, 50 percent.

What was the hardest aspect of the work in the beginning?

Acting and sounding like a newbie and maybe a complete idiot for a number of weeks before I started to feel like I halfway knew what I was doing.

What do you like most about your work?

Every day I get up and I can't wait to get to work!

What do you like the least?

Filling out any kind of form for any purpose.

What was your greatest moment?

Having several Internet experts tell me how much they liked my new Internet marketing book.

How did the start-up phase affect your personal life?

A lot of late nights hunched over the keyboard!

Are you glad you are on the Web for personal and business reasons?

Yes. More for business reasons. As far as my personal life, I would much rather spend time with my family, go for walks outdoors, and develop spiritually than surf the Web.

Given what you know now, would you do it again?

Yes.

What is your next venture?

Fully roll out the marketing plan for *The Small Business Guide to Internet Marketing*. Evaluate the plan's effectiveness and consider other publishing ventures if things look good.

1997 Update

What is the most important thing you learned in the past year about marketing on the Internet?

I've learned that businesspeople still have a great need for assistance in such basic areas as how to use a computer effectively, how to use e-mail, how to find things on the Web, how to create effective advertising, the basics of online marketing, how to draw traffic to a Web site, and similar issues. This is true of people from both large and small businesses.

Companies are still wasting money unnecessarily by using ineffective marketing methods on the Internet.

What is the most effective way to get people to come to your site?

Most people come to my site via search engines and links from other sites. However, I find it is also worthwhile to participate in online discussion groups as well as various publicity efforts. In the past year I started up a free e-mail newsletter, the *NETResults News Service*, which has also helped build traffic to my site.

What is the most effective way to get people to return to your site?

I make an effort to provide valuable content at my Web site: free how-to articles on Internet marketing, links to useful Web resources, automated sign-up for my free newsletter and other resources. I try to update the site and add new content as frequently as possible. The newsletter is an effective vehicle to let people know about new resources at the site.

What is the most effective way to get people to buy products or services?

Most Web sites benefit from application of sound direct marketing principles. Some Web sites are set up to provide branding or image advertising, but many are set up to achieve direct response results, whether direct sales or leads. So a compelling offer, hardworking copy and design, easy-to-navigate pages, a call-to-action, straightforward online forms, and other direct marketing methods are essential for success.

How much money have you made?

In 1995 and 1996, my first two years of intensive Internet marketing, my business volume grew by 50 percent each year. In eighteen months operating the Al Bredenberg Business Reports area of my site, I grossed about $7,200 in direct sales of self-published reports. This is not a tremendous volume. However, because of the low marketing costs of selling on the Web, the profit margin was almost 75 percent!

20 Bulk Mail Services

Some people think of sales as a numbers game. The more contacts you have, the more sales you will make. While this model might work in the real world, its online implementation falls far short—and annoys many people in the process.

These people seem to think the way to riches is to buy a large mailing list and send everyone a note with misleading subject lines. I've received dozens of these messages on my America Online e-mail account. Because I never give this address out, I know these mass mailers have not qualified my name in any manner, except to say that I have an account on AOL. These irritants have sent such misleading and annoying headlines as:

- Get rich quick with 900 numbers!

- Make money while you sleep!

- Make money for having sex!

The text tends to promise the moon—make tons of money with little time or investment. As we all know, anything that sounds too good to be true is too good to be true. Mass mailers who use this practice waste their own time, energy, and money as well as that of the recipients. In the real world, we'd call this junk mail. If you want to read the mail, you do. If you don't, you toss it out and no one gets upset. That isn't the case in the online world. People don't like getting unsolicited e-mail from advertisers because it takes time to read and delete the messages. If people are on the road and retrieve e-mail from hotel room phones, they are actually paying toll charges to download e-mail. You can imagine how maddening this is. Sending unsolicited e-mail is a breach of netiquette (see chapter 2), which is not a good thing —unless you *like* getting hate mail in return. I've never heard of one case of a mass mailer claiming to have made a fortune by sending out these unwanted advertisements. Don't waste your time or money either.

Companies that violate netiquette and sell mass mail to untested consumers are a scourge in the industry. Don't even think of starting a business that performs this "service." One large bulk mailer has been sued repeatedly by America Online to halt this annoying practice. The latest court rulings have sided with AOL, although the plaintiff is contesting the verdict.

This chapter looks at how mail list vendors can operate productively on the Internet. Much of the material comes from an interview with a netiquette-wise business run by George Thibault, president of Revolution Software, Inc., 19722 East Country Club Drive, Aventura, FL 33180-2527; 888-738-5478, 305-682-8154.

LIST OWNER/GATHERER

There's gold in mailing lists. A company can sell names on a mailing list for 10–15 cents a name in lots of five thousand names with a five-thousand-record minimum. Companies in the real world can make significant incomes by renting their lists. So can cyberbusinesses.

Due to netiquette, you can't simply read newsgroups and copy names of people. As these people didn't ask to be on your list, they might react negatively to your sending them advertisements via e-mail. This approach can exist on the Internet and provide value to customers if customers are asked for permission before names are placed on the list. If permission is denied, *don't* use the name. Period.

You can gather names legitimately simply by being straightforward about asking for them and for permission to use them. As people read your home page, let them know they can receive information about new products or services from companies that they might find interesting if they submit their names, addresses, or e-mail addresses. If they submit the information, you are on your way to creating a mailing list. If they don't, so be it. At least you haven't annoyed a potential customer by deluging him with e-mail from an unwanted source.

As you record each name, try to capture job title, phone and fax numbers, e-mail addresses, business size, business type, number of items purchased, date of purchase, date of last mailing to the record, industry code, household income, and gender. The more information you collect, the more valuable the list is.

This business can make money as it attracts a highly targeted audience whose members have given permission to be contacted and delivers them directly to advertisers. The model for this type of business is to offer high-quality content in exchange for the right to send e-mail. If people don't want to receive the e-mail, they should not join the list.

Several companies have devised ways to collect names in a proper fashion.

Newslinx, *www.newslinx.com/lists*, collects names by asking people to join any of their forty-plus free e-mail lists, which cover such topics as Web software, Internet business, and Web publishing. Potential subscribers are told that by joining the list—and getting the valuable information contained on the lists for free—they will be sent e-mail from advertisers who are targeting it.

Other companies in this segment ask subscribers to fill out lengthy forms asking them to identify their consumer preferences, like their taste in movies, music, books, vacations, hobbies, and activities. List owners attract people by offering content, like information, contests, or even trial subscriptions to magazines or sample products. These techniques for self-identification are also used by companies that want to sell advertisements on their Web sites.

Hot Sites

- Goldmail   *www.goldmail.com*
- Cyber Gold   *www.cybergold.com*
- Newslinx   *www.newslinx.com*

MAILING LIST MANAGER

A mailing list manager represents a list owner in the marketing and fulfillment of the list orders by list brokers. For example, Your Company, a software publisher, might own a list of 100,000 software buyers. Because Your Company is busy producing software, you hire Global Lists to manage your file. For this, Global Lists collects a fee equal to 10–15 percent of the rental fee. If a company rents $45,000 worth of names, the mailing list manager pockets $4,500–$6,750.

For this fee, the list manager advertises and markets the list, seeks approval from the list owner for each and every potential renter to make sure competitors don't have access, and fills list orders. Some list managers do not keep the file on site but instead engage their own service bureau to fill orders, typically on the 9-track tapes used in the IBM-compatible mainframe world.

MAILING LIST BROKER

A mailing list broker is a specialized advertising agency that has mailers as its clients. For example, a list broker might rent 20–25 lists of 10,000 records each to conduct a 200,000-piece mailing. These lists are ordered from list managers. The extra names are ordered to guarantee that 200,000 records remain after the merge/purge process is conducted by a service bureau. Typically, the list broker will engage the services of a service bureau in the name of the mailer. List brokers typically collect a fee of 20 percent of the rental fee of any list.

Mailers plan well in advance of any mailing, typically 90–120 days. Therefore, list brokers usually place orders with list managers about 60 days prior to the mail date. Under industry standard terms, mailers must pay 30–60 days after the mail date. Therefore, it is generally 120 days after a list is ordered by a broker before the list owner gets its check from the list manager. If the revenue generated is $10,000, the owner's slice is typically 65–70 percent, the broker's slice 20 percent, and the list manager's slice 10–15 percent.

MAILING SERVICE BUREAU

A mailing service bureau maintains a list so that it is free of errors like out-of-date names and addresses. The bureau adds new names, removes duplicates, and purges names of people who want to get off the list.

For example, a large magazine company on the Web has tens of thousands of properly obtained e-mail addresses of people who have requested placement on mailing lists. The mailing service bureau contracts with the magazine to provide the following services: Maintain the database, merge text files with names and data, and distribute the completed messages. Additional services could include sending out follow-up material as requested by the recipient and creating reports for the client.

To conduct this business you should have an excellent understanding of databases, e-mail systems, sales, and operations, or have the ability to hire, train, and manage people who do.

SOFTWARE SERVICE FOR BULK MAILERS

If you collect names from your Web site using appropriate methods and want to send e-mail to them, you can use software programs to create individualized e-mail messages. These programs can take thousands of names and insert variables, like name and address, to create seemingly personalized messages. Most important, each message contains the e-mail address of the particular recipient only instead of a cc:list that shows dozens or hundreds of e-mail addresses to individual recipients! Nothing turns off a prospect faster than knowing she is being treated like one of the crowd.

Alpha Mailer, *www.alphasoft.com*, lets you create form letters. Arial Software, *www.arialsoftware.com*, adds the benefit of selecting names from a database on any number of factors, like date purchased or product bought. Both products need to improve their user interfaces and ease of use. Check their Web sites for trial demo versions and updates.

21 Network Marketing

Network marketing companies can enjoy a profitable venue on the Internet if they understand and respect online culture and the proper way to conduct business.

The Internet can help network marketers in several ways:

- Cut overhead and administrative costs.
- Improve communication and training.
- Find prospects.
- Sell products.

Beth Parker, bethpark@juno.com, an independent affiliate of The Peoples Network, uses e-mail to tell her organization about meetings, compensation plans, new products, and motivation. Because her organization includes people from all around the United States, she saves a fortune on phone calls—even her e-mail account is free at Juno, which offers free e-mail service to anyone (800-654-JUNO). Because e-mail can be forwarded, she can pass along messages from group members to others in seconds so everyone can benefit from each other's experiences.

Network marketers can also create their own e-mail newsletters and special reports that contain interesting information about their products. The content impresses people only if it is useful information, not an advertisement. To comply with netiquette, the newsletter should be sent only to people who have requested it. See Chapter 4 for more information about this strategy.

Web sites can be used to recruit new network members and sell products. Oxyfresh, *www.oxyfresh.com*, is a good example. It contains information about:

- products that can be ordered online

- how to become a distributor, including links to several distributors (who have paid a fee to post their bios and contact information) and a description of the compensation plan

- a contest used to qualify potential distributors

- information about the company

Hot Site

Candlelight Press, *http://swswsw.com*, offers free advice and books for sale to the multilevel marketing audience.

Interview: Jim Clements

Jim Clements   *thm@xmission.com*

1929 East 9400 South   801-553-8716

Sandy, UT 84903

(original interview 1995; update January 1997)

Jim Clements is an independent distributor with a network marketing company whose parent office won't give distributors permission to speak for the company. That's not unusual for any business. His comments are quite valid and should be valued by network marketing professionals who want to use the Internet as a marketing tool.

What was your purpose in putting a home page on the Web?

We use our Web pages primarily to direct people to learn more about the company and its product line. We also use the Web to help keep our down-line informed of changes that may affect them. These products are new to our culture.

How has the home page helped your business?

In the past, sharing information was primarily done by mailing audiotapes, videotapes, and brochures to people who requested more information. The Internet provides a way for us to direct people to our home page; the information there will answer most questions about the company, product, and business opportunity. This is a great savings of time and money.

What advice would you give to a person starting a business on the Web?

Do not become disillusioned if the orders do not start pouring in.

In my opinion, business will eventually boom on the Internet for the retailer as well. That day is probably still a year or so in the future. Hopefully

Win95 and other programs will make gaining access to the Web easy to use by the real buyers, women with credit cards.

Until that day, put up a Web site and advertise its existence whenever and wherever possible. When the buyers do come and if they are looking for a widget, they can do a search on the Web and you want your widget to be referenced everywhere they look.

Internet users have been wary of multilevel marketing (MLM) companies posting unsolicited notices to get rich quick in news-groups. What is your opinion on this matter?

I do subscribe to several newsgroups that may attract people who may benefit from the products that we offer. I listen, learn, and contribute to the conversation when I can. The extent of my advertising in these groups is a four-line signature line that identifies me as an independent distributor and provides URL information on our site.

It is upsetting to see some of the newsgroups trashed by spam and the kinds of posts that you mention. MLM is nothing more than a means of product distribution. It is not a get-rich-quick business. One of the reasons that MLM has developed a bad reputation is that too many people incorrectly promote it as such. It has the potential to generate a good income, as with any other business, if you work at building the business.

Actually, the services provided by the Internet greatly support the MLM business. There is no better way for the parent company to disseminate information to the large number of distributors in the field.

I think that growth in the Internet will assist in the growth of network marketing companies as well.

Case Study: MLM Woman Newsletter

Welcome to MLM Woman Online!!

You are the 26834th MLM Woman (or MLM Guy) to read this page

The Challenge

Let others lead small lives, but not you.
Let others argue over small things, but not you.
Let others cry over small hurts, but not you.
Let others leave their future in someone else's hands, but not you.
–Jim Rohn

What's MLM Woman Newsletter All About?

Figure 21–1. Segmenting a market is a great way to stand out from the crowd on the Internet. Copyright 1997, Regent Press.

Regent Press   *regent@west.net*

Linda Locke   *www.west.net/~regent/mlmwoman*

MLM Woman Newsletter   *www.regentpress.com*

Insider's Bookshelf

2073 N. Oxnard Blvd., #251

Oxnard, CA 93030

(original interview 1995)

What does your company do?

I am a newsletter publisher and also sell business books and audiotapes through my company, Regent Press. My newsletter, *MLM Woman*, is a bimonthly publication that focuses on issues of interest to women in MLM (multilevel marketing) also known as network marketing, which I started publishing in April 1995. Since then, *MLM Woman* has been named as one of the Top Ten MLM publications by industry experts and my Web site on the Internet provides articles, business tips, resources and Web links to help women in network marketing run a successful business. I also have a companion Web site, The Insider's Bookshelf, which is an electronic bookstore, where I sell business books and tapes and offer free articles and information of interest to aspiring entrepreneurs.

What expertise/background do you have to operate your business?

I have been in business for six years and have operated a variety of small businesses in that time including newsletter publishing, network marketing, desktop publishing, and teaching through continuing education at my local community colleges. I have a B.A. degree in comparative literature from the University of California at Santa Barbara and have used my writing and computer skills in such diverse jobs as engineering technical editor/writer, lifestyle reporter for the *Las Vegas Review Journal*, software documentation writer, and multimedia/Web page developer for a small, employee-owned computer consulting firm.

What was your company's goal for going online?

1. Reach a national and international audience for a very low cost.

2. Study Internet marketing firsthand, find out what works and what doesn't, and convert that knowledge into profit.

How do you know you have reached that goal?

The amount of sales generated and the feedback we receive from our customers and other online marketers about our products and Web sites.

How much did it cost to get started?

I do all the design and maintenance of my sites myself as well as the marketing and promotion (my husband helps a lot too). Our total out-of-pocket start-up cost for my first Web site plus sweat equity was about $150 and an ongoing monthly cost of about $80.

What makes your site special?

My MLM Woman Web site provides articles, resources, and business tips for women in MLM that are very difficult to find anywhere else, on the Internet or off. As the ONLY publication for women in MLM I have carved out a niche for my publication that is not covered in any of the other MLM publications available. My Insider's Bookshelf site offers business books and tapes that are also unique to the entrepreneur and personal development market.

How do you get people to come to your site?

I use all the standard methods of Internet marketing: classified ads, free reports, e-zines, uploading articles and posting in forums on AOL and CompuServe, autoresponders, links on and to lots of other Web sites, search engines, offline publicity in MLM industry publications, frequent guest spots on AOL chat sessions, networking with other MLM industry publishers, and word of mouth.

How do you get people to return to your site?

By constantly adding new content to our site via free reports, new articles, business tips, and new Internet links and resources.

How do you move people from being window-shoppers to paying customers?

What seems to be working best right now is satisfied customers, which results in good word-of-mouth PR about our newsletter and unique products. Also, regular follow-up via e-mail works well as a reminder of what we have available.

What is the most important thing you learned in the past year about marketing on the Internet?

How to effectively use autoresponders to generate leads and direct people to our Web sites or to our other informational autoresponders, which eventually results in sales or requests for additional information.

What is the most effective way to get people to buy products or services?

Providing enough information on your Web site and/or autoresponder to help customers make a buying decision. It also helps if you can get your customers to relate to you as a real person and not just a bunch of electrons.

How does your site generate revenue?

Sales of newsletter subscriptions to the printed version of *MLM Woman* and sales of books and tapes. We will also be adding banner ads to the newsletter site in the near future.

How much money have you made?

We have reached the point now where both of our sites are profitable in that they pay for all their expenses and make a small profit monthly. We are at a point now that to increase profits we must increase the number of visitors to our sites and pursue more aggressive marketing on and off the Internet to achieve this.

Tradespeople

This chapter was originally called "Businesses You'd Never Expect to See on the Internet." You'd wonder what a plumber would be doing on the Internet.

Making friends and influencing people is the answer.

In many ways, the same business models that work for professionals work for tradespeople as well. Neither can perform their jobs online, but both can use the Internet to find new clients. They can use Web sites to build credibility by showing pictures of their successful projects, printing testimonials from satisfied customers, and displaying their credentials, licenses, and association memberships. The good sites have an "answer man" feature in which the craftsman answers questions from Web visitors.

PLUMBER, ELECTRICIAN, PAINTER

Overview

I wouldn't have suggested that a plumber create a home page, but after seeing Hill's Plumbing home page, *www.theplumber.com/hillsplb*, I've changed my mind. Hill's prides itself on being the plumber of choice on Vashon Island. The company is staking out a position in a specific market and it is using the

Internet to reach out to people who live there and have a computer account. Using this strategy, it will dominate its market.

Rewards

You can reach your techno-literate audience—especially in a place like Seattle—and probably be assured of being the only plumber (or electrician, painter, gardener, handyman) in your neighborhood to be on the Internet. You'll build instant rapport with your clientele because you speak the same language of the Internet.

Risks

Visitors to your site might not be from your service area and could waste your time with questions. On the other hand, you could refer them to tradespeople in their location, and receive a finder's fee.

Special Marketing Considerations for the Home Page

Consider asking people to submit questions. That way you can capture names and begin building relationships. When you answer a question, you've begun a dialog that will be essential in building trust, credibility, and a phone call when the washer leaks!

Hot Site

The Plumber, *www.theplumber.com*, is a mix of facts and fun. The Plumber answers plumbing questions, shows pictures from the appliance man's fall fashion show, hosts the Thomas Crapper Memorial Poll (it's a hoot!), and has links to Simon the Plumber in Brighton, U.K., and Tom the Furnaceman. Professional links to plumbing tool companies and associations make the site a model for other tradespeople. You can also read about the history of plumbing from ancient days to present. This is an enjoyable site!

23

Speakers, Agents, and Seminars

Distance learning is becoming a viable commercial medium online as major universities, such as the University of California at Berkeley, offer courses via modem. Professional associations, such as the PR and Marketing Forum on CompuServe, also sponsor ad hoc seminars. The Internet offers rich opportunities for seminar companies to advertise or offer courses online. Speaker and trainers also are using the Internet to showcase their services. Bureaus and agents are online to act as a one-stop shopping center for meeting planners who need keynote presenters and seminar leaders.

PROFESSIONAL SPEAKER AND TRAINER

Overview

Speakers inform and entertain people at conventions, conferences, and dinners. Often, the highlight of a meeting is the address given by the keynote speaker. Topics can range from inspiration, business advice, and practical information to humor. Speakers also provide consulting services for corporations that seek outside experts and a fresh way of thinking.

Rewards

Speakers can promote their services to meeting planners and sell their books and tapes to their audiences.

Risks

Competition for these lucrative positions is intense. Many speakers have Web sites or list their services with an online speakers bureau.

Special Marketing Considerations for the Home Page

Credibility is a key factor in selecting a speaker, so your Web site should reflect your expertise by containing articles you've written and overviews of books, tapes, and instructional videos you've produced. Include your speaking schedule, testimonials, mission statement, and topic list. Audio files will be crucial for success, as will videos.

Hot Sites

- Diana Fairechild, *www.flyana.com*. Diana Fairechild promotes her public seminars and sales of her book on her home page. See the case study that follows for a business plan from a model citizen of the Internet. Her home page and interview radiate with warmth and sound advice.

- Daniel Janal, *www.janal.com*. Most speakers take the approach of showing their one-sheet (a condensed bio and topic list). I wanted to stand out. I set up my Web site as *Dan Janal's Online Marketing Magazine* and it has the look and feel of a newspaper or newsletter. My goal was to present so much free marketing information that when the prospect sees the site his initial impression is, "This guy knows his stuff. He is credible." After that, he can read my bio, testimonials, topics, and speaking schedule. I also ask people to subscribe to the e-mail version of the marketing magazine for free. Hundreds of people have taken advantage of the free offer. I've received numerous speaking requests from all over the United States as well as Canada, Mexico, Brazil, and India. This page was cited in the *New York Times*.

Case Study: Diana Fairechild

HEALTHY FLYING
With Diana Fairechild

Travelers all over the world are discovering they don't have to be victims of **jetlag, insensitive policies,** or **fear of flying.**

This web site is the complete source for healthy, safe, and efficient travel information, your guide through air travel mazes and pitfalls -- **recycled air, lost luggage,** unwholesome **airline food, pesticide showers** in flight, and **blocked ears.** This site is also the forefront for a networking and lobbying campaign to **improve conditions** for airline passengers.

Diana Fairechild will help you to minimize the emotionally draining, irritability-causing, and even life-threatening effects of flying. "Diana Fairechild is an aviation health and safety analyst."-CNN

The Yahoo Internet Life
June 9, 1997

You will want to check out a Web site called Healthy Flying

"Visit her site, if only to learn a little compassion for the people who serve you in the unfriendly skies."

"Fairechild is one of the plaintiffs in the secondhand smoke lawsuit, but she says that there are many other indignities that she and other flight attendants, not to mention passengers, have had to endure. On her site, there's a fascinating page about pesticide spraying. Fairechild claims that some countries still spray passengers with pesticide before they can disembark."

Figure 23–1. Books and speaking services are sold on this Web site, which dispenses the author's advice on air travel and safety. Copyright 1997, Flyana Rhyme.

Flyana Rhyme   *diana@flyana.com*

Diana Fairechild   *www.flyana.com*

PO Box 1177

Kilauea, HI 96754

(original interview 1995; update January 1997)

Who is your primary audience?

My audience is anyone who travels by air or who knows an air traveler. My seminars are for everyone who wants to enjoy air travel, arrive feeling refreshed, and get the most out of life. They can travel once or as a frequent flyer—all will benefit. My book, *Jet Smart*, is for everyone who wants to feel good and look good when they travel by air. All travelers of any age, type of work, and region benefit by knowing how to travel easier, sleep soundly, and eliminate jet lag. The column "Healthy Flying with Diana Fairechild" is published on the Internet and is moving toward international syndication in print.

How will they benefit from your product or service?

I provide travel wellness information for healthy people who want to stay that way and for the less than healthy who want to travel for business or personal reasons. Airline passengers deserve to arrive at their destinations with vigor, stamina, and vitality.

How does your product or service differ from others?

I personally flew ten million miles as an international flight attendant over twenty-one years. I know the hidden secrets of how to stay healthy when you travel. I believe I am the only person worldwide providing the service on how jet travel can be easier and enjoyable.

Is this business an offshoot of your existing business or does it exist only on the Internet?

Offshoot. I am the author of *Jet Smart*, an informative guide to air travel that has sold over fifty thousand copies worldwide.

If it is an offshoot, was it meant to generate income on its own or to steer people to your other outlets?

"Healthy Flying with Diana Fairechild" is offered on the Internet as a free service to airline passengers so they can travel more safely, more comfortably, and especially more healthfully. This Internet site provides a sampler of the information in *Jet Smart*, which is for sale on the Internet, in bookstores worldwide, and through an 800 number.

Where is your office located?

I have a laptop and sometimes I log on in my office, sometimes at the dining room table, and sometimes I sit outside in the garden.

What is your background and training?

I have a B.A. in French literature and speak several foreign languages. During my two decades as an international flight attendant, while I was circling the earth—literally more than a hundred times—I studied esoteric yoga and other healing techniques with acknowledged teachers in Europe, India, Asia, and the South Pacific. I have been subscribing to daily meditation, hatha yoga, and a vegetarian diet for twenty five years.

When did you start your business?

1992.

How did you promote your site?

I started with a Lycos search and sent press releases to people who were involved in travel. I was very quickly annotated by a number of travel agents, an aeronautical university, Yahoo!, the rec.travel library, and GNN's travel page; I was also offered the position of guest editor on Galaxy.

How much did it cost to promote your site?

Nothing.

How long did it take until you got your first sale?

A week or so.

Getting Started

Did you create a business plan before going online?

No.

How much time did it take to get up and running?

I got my account in February 1995. My site was online in March in an adequate but, I now realize, a preliminary form. Six months later the pages represent a state of clarity and organization where I think I can stop fiddling with them—that is, except for regularly updating information and adding new columns.

Did you create the pages yourself or did you get help?

I started writing the pages myself because I enjoy writing. HTML was easy to learn, thanks to the Source and View buttons in Netscape. I also asked for and received assistance from many people.

What advice would you give someone starting a business?

Think about what you want to give to the Internet community. Think about what you would like to contribute. Offer something of value and people of like mind will find your site. People appreciate the content and sincerity of my column.

What skills would a person need to conduct a Web business?

They need to be passionate about their field of expertise and believe that others will benefit from their service.

My Day

What does your average day look like?

The first thing I do at about 4:30 A.M. is check my e-mail. 4:30 A.M. in Hawaii is 7:30 A.M. on the West Coast and 10:30 A.M. on the East Coast. I find that many people write me late at night and I am always excited at the prospect of connecting with others of like mind first thing in my day.

What does your job entail?

I write columns in response to the e-mail I get from readers. I see myself as an experienced resource for travelers—like their own flight attendant friend. The people I serve travel on all the airlines, and I offer them something that enhances the coffee, tea, or milk.

How many hours a week do you spend working on your site?

I don't keep track because I love what I do. It is part of my day—even the surfing, where I get ideas for enhancing my site. And I often e-mail other sites that I think would like to link me, and they usually do.

This is where the "inter" part of "Internet" comes into play. We see how our work links up to commercial prospects, and also to life situations and to people of like mind.

What was the hardest aspect of the work in the beginning?

Mastering Windows and all the various needed programs of communications and graphics software. Although I had been word processing for many years, this required a tremendous amount of studying up on my part to arrive at the point that I am so comfortable with all the software that it enhances my thinking and I can easily take off on creative trajectories.

What do you like most about your work?

I love helping people. I do not have children of my own, so it is especially rewarding for me that people worldwide are benefiting from my experiences.

What do you like the least?

There is nothing about this I don't like. When I was a flight attendant I met people from all over the world—this was my lifestyle. When I stopped flying, I found I missed ethnic diversity. But now my site is visited by people from forty countries—places as diverse as China, Korea, and Iceland. This excites me.

What was your greatest moment?

At the beginning of every month my Webmaster sends me the last month's statistics of reader requests (hits). My fourth month online, reader requests had increased incrementally to over twenty thousand. This thrilled me!

How did the start-up phase affect your personal life?

It literally became my focus. Most of the people I feel like interacting with now are involved in Internet.

Are you glad you are on the Web for personal and business reasons?

Absolutely. I am glad that I am on the Web because I can live and work remote from civilization where I am not forced to breathe the industrial wastes of our world and the perfumes and other irritants that affect those who are chemically sensitive. It is my wish that the world will come to its senses soon and allow those who react adversely to such pollutants to be able to mix normally in the workplace, among others in public, and when traveling in jets. The present profusion of chemicals in society is a sad and severe problem that seems to be diluting the consciousness of humanity. This is the subject of my next book.

Given what you know now, would you do it again?

Yes.

What is your next venture?

MaMa Online, www.maui.net/~mama, an Internet service. I have a partner in this venture, another woman whom I met on Internet; we offer seminars in Hawaii and e-mail/phone consultations to assist others as they create their home pages, then broadcast them out to the global community.

What else would you like to say?

Thank you for finding me and interviewing me via the Internet. It is a perfect example of the linking available to all of us, which I am very interested in.

1997 Update

What is the most important thing you learned in the past year about marketing on the Internet?

Helping people is the charm of the World Wide Web. The direct access of communication is a joy.

What is the most effective way to get people to come to your site?

1. content

2. beauty

3. kindness

What is the most effective way to get people to return to your site?

Like-minded people automatically return. The site has become a networking and lobbying vortex to improve conditions for airline passengers. We uncover newsworthy information.

The site has several survey areas that help me to know how people feel and what people want.

What is the most effective way to get people to buy products or services?

My book and a couple of products are available. The book sells consistently. There is also a noticeable sales increase in stores.

Please give me an idea of your success.

I consistently receive awards. The most prestigious was the *New York Times* (both CyberTimes and print edition) choosing "Healthy Flying with Diana Fairechild," as one of the "twelve most creative Web sites of 1996." That day I had seven thousand hits.

SPEAKERS AGENT AND BUREAU

This model also applies to talent agencies (models, actors, singers, performers, etc.).

Overview

Speakers bureaus help match the sponsor of the event with a talented speaker who could fill the bill. The Internet lets meeting planners search a bureau's database to find appropriate speakers and trainers.

Rewards

Agents can make as much as 25 percent of the fee, which can range from $1,000 to $25,000 and even higher for celebrities like ex-president Bush, sports figures, and news reporters. Bureaus can also charge speakers for space on their pages.

Risks

None beyond time, effort, and start-up capital.

Special Marketing Considerations for the Home Page

Because agents represent many speakers, the Web site should have an easy search mechanism for finding speakers in various categories, geographic regions, and price ranges. Expertspace includes value-added articles on how to hire a speaker.

Hot Sites

- ExpertiseCenter   *www.expertcenter.com*
- National Speakers Association   *www.nsaspeaker.org*

Case Study: KPI Lecture Agency

Figure 23–2. Helpful articles add value to the KPI Lecture Agency site. Copyright 1997, KPI Lecture Agency.

KPI Lecture Agency

Phillip Knowlton

Studio 236

10 Libertyship Way

Sausalito, CA 94966

lectureagent@expertspace.com

www.expertspace.com

What does your company do?

Get connected with the right keynote speakers. The site helps meeting planners find the business speaker or celebrity speaker that's right for their group.

What expertise/background do you draw on to operate your business?

Eight years as a technical recruiter in Silicon Valley and almost seven years now as a lecture agent just north of the Golden Gate Bridge in the San Francisco Bay Area. A master's in educational psychology and four years as a counselor and therapist with private and agency practices in the southwest.

What was your company's goal for going online?

The growth of the Web has made professional speaker information more accessible than ever. Take a tour through the virtual LectureAgent site to find some places to start your hunt for information and to receive guidance online.

How do you know you have reached that goal?

Bottom line profit reached using the above. New products and services to market extend beyond projected growth rates.

How much did it cost to get started?

Including the first year of costly mistakes,under $10,000.

What makes your site special?

LectureAgent at Expertspace is a highly focused online service that provides solutions to specific needs in the convention and tradeshow industry. As part of its core business, it has formed a team approach with other networked event providers and suppliers to make client success easy.

How to do you get people to come to your site?

- organized e-mail posts to related news groups
- links to industry sites
- highly targeted event promotion

How do you get people to return to your site?

Provide timely and relevant content.

How do you move people from being window-shoppers to paying customers?

- Provide an 800 telephone number for customer service and sales process.
- Offer an easy-to-use and helpful online product/service order form.

What is the most important thing you learned in the past year about marketing on the Internet?

Keep listening to what other experts, like you, are saying [absolutely true] and don't be afraid to take risks and make mistakes.

What is the most effective way to get people to come to your site?

E-mail targeted promotion.

What is the most effective way to get people to return to your site?

Provide a caring, skillful. and helpful service that reflects customer buying needs.

What is the most effective way to get people to buy products or services?

Stay with the proccess of benefits and features.

How does your site generate revenue?

Revenue streams are from consulting and agent booking work. These are commissions and finder's fees.

How do you know your site is a success?

I am looking for an associate and am developing closely related business ventures with other companies.

Expertspace has been given positive reviews and exposure in *The Journal of the Chronicle of Higher Education* and the *New York Times*.

My ISP Web stats show the site has been receiving six to eight thousand hits per month during the last six months. Yes, I know it's deceptive, but I get pretty decent targeted traffic including representatives of IBM, Lucent, EDS, Motorola, Pfizer, Corning, Thompson Financial, Hill and Knowlton, Burson-Marsteller, American Society of Landscape Architects, Harvard, the World Bank, and the CIA. [Go figure.]

People and companies that actually buy from me are also interesting: law firms, community civic groups, state governor's office, Fortune 500 companies, and trade associations.

Speakers that were booked include former senators, comedic personalities, motivational speakers, technical experts, and authors like you.

INTERNET-BASED SEMINAR BUSINESS

Overview

In the offline world, seminars are very expensive yet potentially lucrative ventures. The main cost is to print and mail thousands of brochures to people in the hope that 1 percent of them will actually pay to attend. Costs also are incurred for the meeting room, refreshments, and the trainer's fee.

An online venture can cut out almost all these expensive marketing costs. You must, of course, pay the trainer to produce the materials and answer students' questions.

Courses can be held with one person who interacts directly with the teacher or with a whole number of students who interact with the teacher and each other. You will need to promote the seminars with online marketing techniques, which, as discussed in chapter 3, involve more time than money.

Material can be accessed in several ways:

- *E-mail account*—Send course material directly to the student, who reads the material, completes assignments and sends material on to the instructor. Each week a new section of the course materials is sent. For a real-time discussion, the class can be scheduled to meet in a chat room.

- *Mailing list*—Send course material to students via a mailing list, which is an electronic bulletin board. They can send assignments and questions directly to the instructor. They can also interact with the instructor and other students by sending letters to the list in response to questions posed by the instructor and other class members. Students can be required to post answers by certain dates to maintain the flow of dialog. Your ISP can create the mailing list.

One advantage of online seminars over traditional ones is that the students can turn pages at their convenience and link to other documents and resources that the instructor has set up or that other students share.

Rewards

The beauty of running an online seminar business is that you create the course work once and sell it many, many times. Unlike with books, there aren't any incremental costs for creating or duplicating materials. You can have a class with one student or a hundred students and make a profit in either case. Also, unlike the offline world that demands that everyone attend a meeting in a certain room at a specified time with the same beginning and end dates for everyone, the online seminar can involve people who begin when they want to and read the material and complete the assignments when they have the time. In this manner, the online seminar leader is freed from the bonds of time and space that minimize the rewards of the offline seminar.

Risks

What if they gave a seminar and no one came? You would be out the costs for marketing the seminar and creating the material. Also, your material can be copied and distributed without your being paid.

Special Marketing Considerations for the Home Page

Creating credibility and interest are the key missions of the Web site. You also can't give away the store. Therefore, your Web site should contain the course overview, objectives, benefits, and deliverables, as well as a session-by-session outline of material covered. The instructor's biography also should be available. To increase exposure, link to related sites.

Hot Sites

See references in Chapter 13 (cooking schools) and Chapter 11 (photography seminars).

24 Wacky and Wonderful

Some businesses defy description. That's why I created this chapter! You'll find the most oddball businesses on the Internet right here.

ASTROLOGY CHART BUSINESS

Overview

If astrology can predict the future from stars in space, chart readers should be able to sell prognostications from virtual space on the Internet.

Rewards

You can make money by selling charts on a customized, pay-for-service basis.

Risks

Check with your lawyer regarding risks and liabilities.

Special Marketing Considerations for Home Pages

Your home page could look real cool with artwork. Be prepared to include files that explain what astrology is and isn't. Educate your new public.

Case Study: Astrogram

Figure 24–1. Astrogram presents its wares on its entry page. Copyright 1997, Astrogram.

Astrogram

Moira Collins

3920 North Lake Shore Drive, 9

North Chicago, IL 60613

astrogram@astrogram.com

www.astrogram.com

www.kiddygram.com

(original interview 1995; update January 1997)

What is your goal for being on the Internet?

Birthdays are our business. We provide astrological chart reports based on a customer's precise birth data (date, year, exact time and place of birth). Since 1986 we've provided an unusual service that lends itself to being featured on the World Wide Web. Our goal is to be marketing in cyberspace as we move into our second decade. However, our first reason to be on the Web is to position our reports as an upscale, elegant, and affordable introduction to the ancient art of astrology and a great source for beautiful birthday gifts! Our second goal was to print fewer glossy brochures and save a few trees. Our ultimate goal will be to provide our reports online when we can design them in a graceful and intriguing fashion.

How has being on the Web helped your business?

Our presence has been acknowledged and two of our reports have been written up (one featured) in Jaclyn Easton's book *Shopping on the Internet.*

What advice do you have for people starting businesses on the Internet?

Be prepared to invest time and energy in a world that has not yet come into being! Check other Web pages and find a talented and dedicated cadre of young designers.

Be prepared to know nothing. Be prepared to jump and then say, "Oh! I wonder where I've landed!"

Be prepared to say, like Miranda, "Oh brave new world that hath such people in it."

Be prepared to say, like Prospero, "Gentle breath your sails must fill or else our project fail which was to please."

1997 Update

What is the most important thing you learned in the past year about marketing on the Internet?

We have learned that the response to a Web page is global. Our dedicated fax line can deliver orders from Spain to be shipped to Denmark. Although we have reports available in other languages, we hadn't thought to market them on the Internet.

What is the most effective way to get people to come to your site?

Our site has been a point-of-presence site. However, we know the best way to get people to come to a site is to provide information. We have recently set up an account with Amazon.com to provide information on books that we recommend on astrology. This bookstore in cyberspace will allow us to feature authors who we feel have written worthwhile books as well as authors whose appeal to the mainstream has introduced many a serious student of astrology to the fun and excitement of studying the charts of their friends and family.

What is the most effective way to get people to return to your site?

To provide information that is current and is changing and can be down-loaded quickly. In our case, we are moving from our initial "brochure in space" to providing interactive opportunities such as clicking on sample celebrity chart reports that can change and be added to as current events warrant. This also enables us to build a library that can become a point of interest to curious Web seekers.

What is the most effective way to get people to buy products or services?

Get back to e-mail and fax queries promptly. Provide, through an 800 number or e-mail, printed information such as brochures and flyers underlining the fact that we do business off the Web as well! In our case, we have stickers that announce we are celebrating our eleventh birthday this year that go out on our snail mail. We want people to know that Birthdays have Been our Business for over a decade.

How much money have you made?

Our personal site has made modest gains this year. We're always pleased with orders that come online as they are easier to process and to track. We haven't begun to promote it except by listing it in the various search engines. It certainly does not make as much money as one of the companies on the Web that sells our products. Personal Creations, a personalized product firm, has sold our basic Astrogram through its seven stores and catalog for over a year and just recently featured our lovers' report online in its Valentine's Day promotion (as well as in its catalog). Being featured on AOL's Marketplace with big-league companies such as Starbucks and Sharper Image and Spiegel automatically provides a company with audiences in the millions. However, they feature our products in a beautiful way and are careful to present Astrograms in an upscale and, elegant fashion. We have become more successful by being online; however, we don't know if it's the synergy of having the product featured on a larger site or the fact that we did indeed hire another person and that our registered trademark was renewed after ten years of use. Our trademark lawyer was amused that in the refiling we provided sample reports for Michael Jeffrey Jordan, but then, we are a Chicago-based company.

FAN CLUB

Hundreds of fan clubs for rock stars, actors, and even Barbie dolls populate the Internet. While some of the Webmasters are doing the page as a hobby that they love, others are creating businesses. They attract people by putting up content of value—biographies, concert schedules—and create interaction by hosting chats among members (and sometimes with the stars themselves). They make money any number of ways: selling advertising to companies that want to reach a target audience, selling classified ads to hobbyists who want to exchange or sell memorabilia, even arranging an auction of products.

DATING SERVICE, MATCHMAKER

Overview

If you've been finding love in all the wrong places, consider starting a matchmaking service. Since the dawn of online services, software has existed to help bring people of all ages and sexes together. Yahoo! lists almost 150 dating services. These services charge about $25 to list your classified ad and may charge additional fees to show your picture. Some businesses try to get viewers to call their 900-number telephone lines, which can charge several dollars per minute.

Entrepreneurs can start similar services but differentiate themselves by specializing in a geographic area, a sexual orientation, an age group—or have them all!

Rewards

You can make an unlimited amount of money in this type of business if you target the right audience and charge appropriately, as there are millions of eligible singles. As many Internet users are college age and have free accounts, there is a large audience out there. However, they might decide they'd rather spend the $25 enrollment fee on beer and videos instead of a chance for a date.

Risk

Check with your lawyer on privacy and security issues. Remember, we are talking about a legal dating service, not an illicit escort service.

Special Marketing Considerations for the Home Page

This enterprise involves a lot of data entry and financial controls. You need to create forms and software that collect biographies and store them in a format that can be sorted and searched. Next you need to collect money from the people placing ads. You might decide to charge visitors as well, but that probably would hurt your ability to attract people. If you want to go this route, consider allowing visitors to search the database but not letting them have access to the contact information, such as name, phone, or e-mail, until they pay.

Case Study: Christian Singles

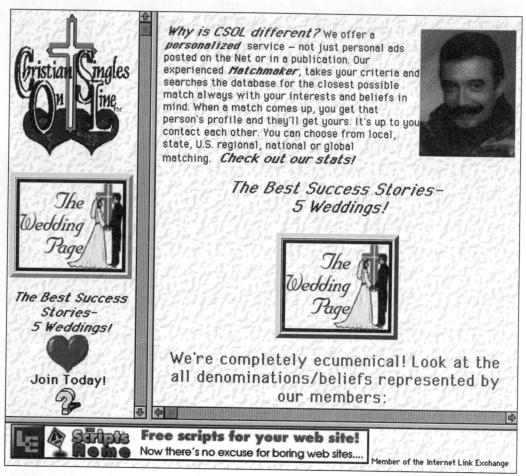

Figure 24–2. Christian Singles Online reaches out to the lovelorn. Copyright 1997, Christian Singles Online.

Christian Singles Online

Giselle Aguiar

PO Box 610543

North Miami, FL 33261

gigi@christsingles.com

www.christsingles.com/singles

What does your company do?

Christian Singles On Line is the first Christian computerized global referral service on the Internet connecting members with potential mates who closely match their beliefs, interests, and specifications. Over 650 members globally! Five weddings already!

What was your company's goal for going online?

Being able to reach Christian singles all over the United States and worldwide to bring them together.

How do you know you have reached that goal?

We have over 650 members globally and five weddings already! Our first international wedding is this August.

What is your primary audience?

Christian Singles On Line is a computerized matchmaking service for Christian singles of all ages.

How will they benefit from your service?

It caters strictly to Christians. It's more than personal ad listings, and we provide a newsletter, live chats, and browsing of the profiles.

Is this business an offshoot of your existing business or does it exist only on the Internet?

It was created based on the Internet but you don't have to have Internet access to join. Seventy percent of the members have access to e-mail at least. Most have Web access.

Where is your office?

Home.

What is your background and training?

I have a B.S. in business administration and experience in advertising, marketing, public relations. I am a self-taught Webmaster. I was president of our local singles ministry.

How much money has your company made online?

$1,910 in 2.5 months.

Getting Started

Did you create a business plan before going online?

Yes.

How much time did it take to get up and running?

About three weeks.

Did you create the pages yourself?

I did them myself. In fact, my other business is creating Web pages.

How much did it cost to get started?

Online setup $150, $75 per month. About $50 in postage.

How did you obtain your start-up capital?

Was able to start without borrowing.

What mistakes did you make that you wish you hadn't made?

Not setting up an accounting program from the beginning. I've had to reenter all transactions since day one.

What advice would you offer someone starting a business?

Do your research. Find out about other similar businesses, check out their pages, find out how they get payment, how easy it is to place an order, etc. Make your site better.

Once the site is up, publicize, publicize, publicize. Register with all the online directories and search engines. Send press releases to all online publications, send URL announcements to appropriate newsgroups, send releases to offline press, especially those related to your business, and of course to your local daily newspaper. I got great press in the *Miami Herald* and got most of my local members from it.

What skills would a person need to conduct business?

You have to be a people person. Know your way around databases, sorting, etc. Know how to keep members happy. Be very creative.

What education is needed to run your site?

I wouldn't be where I am today without my B.S. in business administration and marketing.

What special qualities are needed to run your site?

Creativity, good organizational skills, diligence, endless energy, patience.

How did you promote your home page?

I'm listed in almost every directory. There are new ones popping up all the time, so I have to keep up with them. I will be advertising in online and offline publications.

How much did it cost to promote your site?

So far, zero $.

How long did it take until you made your first sale?

A few days.

How did the start-up phase affect your personal life?

What personal life? I'm single, no kids, work at home, put in about fifteen hours a day on this and the other business.

My Day

What does your average day look like?

First thing I do is pick up e-mail and print out any profiles that have come in. Then I go to the post office to pick up checks, which I then take to the bank. I send confirmation messages to those whose payment I've gotten. Once a week I enter the matches in the system, update the browser, and run matches. This is basically a part-time business. Once a month I write a newsletter and I'm starting once-a-week chats on AOL.

How many hours a week do you spend working on your site?

About twenty-two hours a week. I spend 60 percent of that time entering and doing matches. I also spend two hours a day on picking up e-mail and checks and making deposits.

How much time do you spend conducting business?

Another eighteen hours spent this way:

- 86 percent—marketing

- 2 percent—selling (it sells itself)

- 12 percent—upgrading the site

What was the hardest part of the job in the beginning?

Finding the time.

How long did it take to get established?

Three weeks.

What do you like most about your work?

I work at home, I may be changing people's lives for the better, it's fun!

What do you like least?

Data entry.

What was your greatest moment?

Hasn't happened yet. The first wedding will be the greatest.

Are there any hazards to running your site?

I try to cover myself with my disclaimer. There may be personal burnout.

How much money do you hope to make?

$25,000 per year.

General

Are customers concerned about security for their credit cards?

No; we don't take them yet.

Are you glad you are on the Web?

Yes. It's new, exciting, everyone wants to know more about it. Everyone wants to be on it.

1997 Update

What makes your site special?

We now have a Christian Singles chat room. We offer a unique service.

How do you get people to come to your site?

The chat room is our new draw. We are also listed in every major and secondary search engine and directory plus many Christian sites and directories. We're also posted in America Online's Christianity Online message boards. We've gotten many members from AOL.

How do you get people to return to your site?

No need. Once they join, there is a special members-only site with a monthly newsletter; from there they can browse the profiles.

How do you move people from being window-shoppers to paying customers?

We have an extensive FAQ (frequency asked questions) page that answers their questions. Customers fill out the form and can easily pay by credit card or send in a check.

What is the most important thing you learned in the past year about marketing on the Internet?

You must accept credit cards online. If you let them think about it while they send a check in, you'll lose them. You need to get them when their interest is hot.

What is the most effective way to get people to buy products or services?

Offer a unique product or service. Make it interesting. Offer a newsletter if applicable.

How does your site generate revenue?

Membership sales. Advertising in the members-only section.

How much money have you made?

With very little overhead (I work out of my home) zero start-up costs, let's say it's kept me fed and a roof over my head. If I had had a few thousand to put into advertising from the beginning, I'd have over two thousand members by now.

Index